THE BATTLE

OF THE PRESS

**As Told in the Story of the Life of Richard Carlile
By His Daughter,
Theophila Carlile Campbell**

By Theophila Carlile Campbell

For your free PDF copy of our latest catalog,

or to order a full color print version of our latest catalog,

please visit our website at

WWW.THEOPHANIA.CA.

Address all correspondence regarding editorial matters,
advertising, commercial wholesale ordering, and all
publishing queries to:

Theophania Publishing

1040-8th Ave SW, Calgary, AB

T2P 1J2, Canada.

Follow us on Twitter at:

@TheophaniaBooks

ELIZA SHARPLES CARLILE ("ISIS").

From a Crayon Copy of an Oil Painting.

3

PREFACE.

In presenting to the present generation of England and America the comprehensive though necessarily condensed history of the life and work of the great pioneer in the cause of mental freedom, I am actuated by two principal motives, the foremost of which is the desirable duty of presenting to the people of to-day a faithful account of the work done by Carlile and the enormous sacrifices he made, as well as the terrible imprisonments he endured in the accomplishment of the task he set himself to do, namely, to establish for his countrymen a really Free Press, and the right of free oral discussion, as, up to his time, neither right had ever been accorded to any of the peoples of Europe by either Church or State.

In the prosecution of his self-appointed task he was assailed by the reigning powers with all the malignity and religious fury that characterised the days of the Inquisition. No lie was too black to be hurled at him, no motive too low to be imputed to him, the minds of his countrymen were purposely influenced against him in order that they might not understand his real object—that of benefiting them— and to divert attention from his enemies' misdoing. So he was given the horns, hoofs, and tail of Satan himself, and invested with all the attributes of this fallen angel. It is not to be wondered at that the majority of the people at that time were so influenced, when we consider the very limited resources of the times in regard to information. Almost all of this was carried and given by word of mouth, and it was naturally colored by the views or feelings of those who gave it out.

To rescue the name of a true friend of the people from the undeserved obloquy or silence under which it has been so

5

long obscured, and to place his memory and name where it truly belongs in the list of the honored dead of his country, and in the hearts of his countrymen, there to dwell as long as English history lasts, is the second motive. In doing this we may turn upon all the evidences, both public and private, the modern searchlight of critical investigation, and I am satisfied that when the clouds of malignant abuse and the mass of unsubstantiated charges that were heaped upon his name and fame by those who were interested in doing so are cleared away, his name and the record of his life will stand out from the past as a star of the first magnitude stands out from the darkened sky of night—bright, clear, and pure.

I therefore, with confidence, commit the record of Carlile, as a man with the highest aims, unselfish purpose, and finest motives, who gave the efforts of a noble life and high moral purpose for the advancement of truth and the benefit of his fellow-men, to an enlightened and unbiassed generation, not doubting that it will recognise the true merit of the man and appreciate the value of his accomplishments for the benefit not only of his countrymen but of the world at large.

THEOPHILA CARLILE CAMPBELL.

PART I.

THE BATTLE OF THE PRESS, AS TOLD IN THE LIFE OF RICHARD CARLILE

CHAPTER I.

INTRODUCTORY

We who rejoice in a Free Press to-day can hardly realise the condition of the Press in Europe at the opening of the nineteenth century. In England, eighty years ago, he who dared to express opinions in opposition to the Established Church, or in any way offensive to the government of the day, rendered himself liable to heavy fines and severe imprisonment. The following extract will show better, perhaps, than anything else what a deplorable state the Press was in when Richard Carlile entered upon his great fight, and the obstacles he had to encounter:—

"It is difficult to imagine a more degraded and dangerous position than that in which every political writer was placed in the year 1817. In the first place, he was subject by a

Secretary of State's warrant to be imprisoned upon suspicion under the suspension of the Habeas Corpus Act. Secondly he was open to an *ex-officio* information under which he would be compelled to find bail or be imprisoned. The power of *ex-officio* information had been extended so as to compel bail by an Act of 1808; but from 1808 to 1811, during which three years forty such informations were laid, only one person was held to bail."*

This was the time and this the state of affairs which greeted Carlile when he first entered into public life. He did not then see a man who had the courage to stand up boldly against such formidable odds. He, therefore, resolved to raise the standard of an absolutely Free Press, and be himself the bearer of the colors. This he knew involved possibilities of imprisonment, of exile, losses and suffering. He believed that his example would rally the weak and scattered forces of the writers of the day, and rouse the people to a sense of their degradation and dangerous condition, and to a recognition of the oppressive character of the rulers then in power.

In gathering materials for the life of Richard Carlile, I have drawn freely from his own publications, and also from a mass of correspondence extending over many years of his life. These letters were in most cases strictly private, yet every one of them would bear publication as far as Carlile is concerned. He, however, was the recipient of many confidences on the part of his friends—their sorrows were always his by sympathy. The claims of friendship, long since past, still hold good, though he would profit and not lose by the publication of the whole correspondence.

Chief amongst his publications were the fourteen volumes of the *Republican*, a weekly paper of thirty-two pages, ten or more volumes of which were edited in Dorchester Gaol.

The very name of Republican in those days was a challenge to combat. This publication was the direct outcome of the Manchester massacre. The name had once before been adopted, but was withdrawn by Mr. Sherwin, the proprietor, as too dangerous.

After the rash and brutal conduct of the Government at Peter's Fields—or "Peterloo", as it came to be called—Carlile took up the paper, restored the name *Republican*, and, raising the war-cry of "a Free Press", kept it up through five of his six years of imprisonment in Dorchester Gaol and for one year after.

The horrors of the French Revolution, and the declaration of independence of the Colonial States of America, were yet too fresh in memory for the authorities of the time to see without alarm what seemed to be the flag of Republicanism flaunted in their very faces, and they sought to put it down at all hazards. The story of the battle between the authorities and Carlile will be found in the story of his life. It lasted for many years, but Carlile lived to come off a victor. The Government finally declared themselves defeated by him in his mode of moral warfare in the struggle for the freedom of the Press, pronouncing him invincible in the course he had taken.

It was said of the *Republican* that the only section of the British Press which could be said to be free at that time, was that which was issued from Dorchester Prison!

Before his six years of imprisonment had expired, Carlile was informed that it was Lord Castlereagh, the then Prime Minister, who was so determined to crush him, and also that it was his publication of the horrors of the Manchester massacre and his open letters to the King and Lord Sidmouth that gave the offence—Castlereagh himself having given the order for the massacre, and being solely responsible for it.

The charge of blasphemous libel was decided upon, after much consultation, as the strongest that could be brought to bear upon Carlile, as in that case the help and strength of the Church could be had, and the minds of the people could be turned from the contemplation of that bloody affair at Manchester. So our hero was marked for slaughter. The fiat had gone forth! Judge, Attorney-General, and all the prosecutors were whipped into line and made to try this case and find this verdict, however reluctant they might have been, and *were*, to do so.

With this view of the case, which I believe to be the correct one, the reader will more readily comprehend how those stingingly sarcastic letters to Gifford must have stung and rankled in the wounds.

Carlile may be said to have travelled his native isle like the champion of old—always mounted on his charger of fearlessness, and armed cap-a-pie for the encounter of his enemies. They always knew where to find him, and he was always ready to do battle for the right and against wrong. He never skulked nor concealed himself, nor took ship to avoid his enemies. He wore his colors in his helmet in plain sight of all, with proud defiance, and if, as sometimes happened, he was for the time worsted in an encounter, he neither cringed nor fawned, nor asked for quarter. He nursed his wounds as best he might, and never wavered in his determination to fight for the right while life endured.

The names of the various publications brought out by Carlile indicated in a measure the attitude he assumed. They were the *Republican*, the *Deist*, the *Moralist*, the

Lion, the *Prompter*, the *Gauntlet*, the *Christian Warrior*, the *Phoenix*, the *Scourge*, and the *Church*.

Carlile never changed the character of a paper to suit the times, but always stopped the old paper and started a new one whenever he felt that the old one had accomplished the purpose for which he had started it.

In the matter of praise and blame Carlile ran the whole gamut, from the highest *crescendo* of approval to the *basso profundi* of malediction. He was called "the intellectual Saviour" and the "moral regenerator of mankind" by his friends, and "the great Satan of the day" by his enemies; and he was equally unmoved by the extravagance of either. During the whole course of his public life he did not turn aside for one instant nor stray one foot from the path he had marked out for himself. Fines, confiscations, or imprisonments could not crush him, and we find him saying, on entering into the tenth year of imprisonment, that "he was now well seasoned for the fight"!

He was warned by a faithful friend, previous to his sentence of imprisonment in 1830, that a measure had been discussed in the private councils of the Government, that the old law of flogging should be revived for his suppression, fines, confiscations, and imprisonments having failed to accomplish it. On hearing that the measure had been abandoned and a further imprisonment agreed upon, he "confessed to having drawn a long breath ". He never despaired, however, but was always confident of success, and never had any misgiving as to the future outcome of the fight.

And now I come to the close of this introductory chapter, and ask the readers of the present day to turn over the pages of the life of this much misrepresented man.

If to map out a plan of duty in youth and to follow it out till death through good and evil report, unspoiled by praise, unmoved by assaults the most ferocious; if to endure losses and the sacrifice of all domestic comforts and apparently unending imprisonment, and never to lose courage or be cast down in spirit; if to bear every evil unshaken and to keep his eyes steadily fixed on the object to be attained, though that object be no selfish one, but for the benefit of down-trodden humanity; if to stand at the helm through storm and fire, through adverse winds and tides, and at last to pilot the barque of a noble purpose to a sure haven—if this be evidence of greatness of mind, then he was great, for this he *did!*

He was great, too, in his ability to lead the people. He was a great educator of the people; he taught them to think for themselves. He started hundreds of young men, taught them to read, to think, to compare. No man ever did more of this work than Carlile. He taught the working men to be cleanly in their habits, to shun liquor and tobacco, and to dress well.

All his followers, at least all the young men he acknowledged as such, were models of intelligence and upright conduct, and all who survived him did credit to his teaching, and lent valuable aid in the struggle for a Free Press. And so he kept on till death came, all too soon; but not till he had seen above him the bow of promise on the clouds of ignorance, which promised for all a brighter and more beautiful day—the day of mental freedom.

CHAPTER II.

HIS BIRTH, YOUTH, AND EARLY MANHOOD

R. C. to E. S. C.*

"Enfield Highway,

"*December 7th*, 1842.

"Love,—This is calculated to reach you at Ashburton on my birthday. In the year 1790, fifty-two years ago, I first drew breath at three in the morning of the eighth day, in an upper room of a large barrack-like house, the lower corner of Steave-ahead Lane. The manger of Bethlehem was not more humble. I was born into much the same conditions I now find my children. With a father much too talented to apply himself to any of the ordinary business of life, my subsistence depended on the industry of a mother, and the kindness of relatives. I was in this condition till five years of age, when a shop at the corner of Lawrence Lane, given up to my mother by an old uncle, for ten years furnished moderate supplies for subsistence. In this respect I was brought up, like yourself, on the side of a mother, save that you had a better father as a family man. I lost my father at four and a half years old, but I cannot see that he ever ministered to my subsistence, though he was a man of much talent; at last he profligately enlisted for a soldier, under which discipline he soon died at the age of thirty-four. In the chapel of Lawrence Lane, where, from nine to twelve years of age, I got some Latin, you will probably find my name cut in the boards, if it be worth looking for. At 'Lads-Well, at the bottom of that lane, you will see the

13

scene of some early exploits of mine, one of which was, 'Julian like',* with a new suit of clothes on, trying to jump over this well.

I jumped in! and on a Sunday, too! The stile of the first meadow was a leaping bar, and in the church-yard you cannot see a tomb or headstone, forty years old, but I have jumped over it. Should you see the centre of the town flooded in its drains, you may see my picture as a boy (Julian like, again) beating through it. I have bathed and fished in every brook, and stolen apples from every tree within a mile of the town. Julian is not near as excitable over his paper cap, embellished on and before the 5th of November, than I was then in scouring the hedges for miles around, from daylight till dark, to gather a faggot wherewith to burn the effigy of 'old Tom Paine', my now venerated political father! I have played at hoop through every crick and corner of the shambles and market-place, have well pelted both towers with tennis-balls, and the flagstones of the street with peg-tops, and have often formed one of the troops of rag-a-muffins of old 'Stoaf Jeffery'. I have hooted Bob Nicholls because he was a little man; and have 'dabbed' at, instead of eating, cakes and treacle on Brim Park. As a boy I had neither father nor master, nor can I bear anything of the kind as a man. With me the rights of the boys and the rights of men are one and the same thing, and you know how much I advocate the rights of woman. [At another time he tells of his early efforts at school, which we will let him do in his own way, and shall prefer this method throughout the entire history wherever it is practicable.] My first schoolmistress was old 'Cherry Chalk', who taught me the alphabet on a horn book, and performed all sorts of cures without medicine by the potent power of charms. She was a witch, but much respected as one who performed wonderful cures. There was another old woman who had the title of 'Witch', and one in a town is enough on whom Christian ignorance might vent its spleen. It happened that I escaped all injury from the witch, as I was a favorite boy with her until I grew old enough to be mischievous to her. Whether old 'Cherry Chalk' perfected me in the alphabet I cannot now say, but I perfectly well remember that I was taught about Christ, Cross, or Criss-Cross; now, I dare say that this emblem of the Christian religion was at the bottom of all her charms and spells. I had two other school mistresses of a more respectable stamp than old 'Cherry Chalk'. I believe the first taught for three half-pence a week and the other for twopence. When I got to a five-penny school it was considered an extravagant affair, too expensive to be borne, and a successful effort was made to put me upon the list of free scholars. From the age of six to nine I was at writing and arithmetic; from nine to twelve at Latin. But the sum of all this narrative is that though at twelve years of age I left school, with a knowledge of writing, arithmetic, and the Latin language, and a pretty good knowledge of words and the tact of spelling them, I was wholly ignorant of grammar. I remember well when my severe old writing and ciphering master was told that I was about to leave him to learn Latin, he said, 'Hi, hi! you had better learn English first'. This old man never gave me a chastisement without saying, 'There, you larned rascal, take that! You will thank me for it by the time you are twenty years old.' For my part, I had no more idea of school education than that it was a pastime for boys, and I sought an exchange from old Hanaford's to the Latin school with no idea but that of more play and less punishment, and because all the better dressed boys *were* there; but I found after that this smattering of Latin gave me everywhere an air of superiority, and among such company as I was able to keep I passed for a scholar. The very vanity and flattery attached to this state of mind, I believe, induced me to seek further knowledge. It is a singular circumstance, but I can trace both the *Quarterly*

Review and the *Republican* to the free schools of Ashburton. Wm. Gifford* and Dr. Ireland, the Dean of Westminster, both received the rudiments of their education at these free schools, and I came after them to undo, I hope, all the mischief that they as politicians have done. These free schools of Ashburton were not so free for the poor as for the rich; one of them was a school for Latin and Greek wholly, free by endowment, and here only the children of the richer people were admitted. Here, also, I followed Dr. Ireland and Wm. Gifford.

Having a knowledge of Latin, Carlile was placed with a chemist and druggist, a Mr. Lee, of Exeter, but stayed there only four months owing to the actions of a young man, a brother of Mrs. Lee, who assumed a mastership over him, and dominated him in a manner that young Carlile could not endure. The next four months were spent in his mother's shop, where he occupied himself in drawing and coloring pictures—which were sold to his mother's customers. Subsequently, to please his mother, of whom he was very fond, and very much against his own inclinations, he consented to be apprenticed to a tin-smith for seven years. Of this apprenticeship he spoke very bitterly in after life. The work was hard and the hours very long—fifteen or sixteen hours a day—the food was neither good nor plentiful, nor was his master an agreeable one in any respect. Carlile however, kept to it until he mastered the trade, and near the close of the term fought himself free of his home and table. He succeeded in earning the respect of his master, and later this same man put himself to considerable trouble, unasked, to go to London from Exeter, and testify to the excellent moral and personal character of his former apprentice, at which Carlile was pleasantly surprised. He often asserted that after such an apprenticeship as he had experienced for seven years, imprisonment was no punishment. In Exeter, while still in his apprenticeship, he became acquainted with several young men who were bookbinders. This led to conversations about books, and in turn to book reading. Young as these companions were, they avowed themselves *Deists*; but he received no impression as to the word, and was wholly ignorant as to what a Deist signified. These young men were Painites, but they failed entirely in making any impression upon him as to their principles of religion or politics. He says of himself:—

"My first attraction to politics was in 1816, in consequence of the general distress then prevalent and the noise made at public meetings. Then for the first time I began to read the *Examiner, News*, and independent 'Whig' papers. I was pleased with their general tone, but thought they did not go far enough with it. I had the same notion of Mr. Cobbett's papers, his 'twopenny sheets' and of *Hone's Register*, and indeed of all that were published in 1816. In the manufactories where I was employed, nothing was talked of but revolution, and I soon became so far fired as to begin to build castles in the air. My first ambition was to write something for the papers that should be printed. I tried several, but from one only could I get a notice. I remember I felt highly honored with a couple of 'notices to correspondents'—'"A Half-employed Mechanic" is too violent'; and an answer to 'Cincinnatus' about the propriety and existence of political tract societies. I wrote something for Mr. Hone's *Register* with the motto, 'Gold and silver have I none, but such as I have I give unto thee'. These were my first steps toward fame. I was an enthusiast, but with the best intentions, and with an anxiety to do more good than I saw being done. As soon as the Habeas Corpus Act was suspended in 1817, I saw nearly all the political tractsellers of 1816 shrink from the sale of even *Cobbet's Register*, This was a matter of great astonishment to me, as I looked upon it as a mere milk-and-water paper compared

17

to the *Black Dwarf* and some of the other newspapers. Mr. Cobbett's own writings even exhibited evident alarm, and this made me indignant. I then resolved to get into the front of the battle and to set the best possible example. These were the reasonings of my individual mind, then unconnected with and unknown to every public man. Of imprisonment I made quite sure, but felt inclined to court it rather than to shrink from it. Amidst these thoughts I was delighted to see Mr. William Sherwin start a weekly paper under the title of the *Republican*. Here, surely, thought I, I can find a congenial mind, and I at once sought his acquaintance. I was particularly shy about personal intrusion, though bold enough to run every risk and kind of danger, and the way I sought an acquaintance was by offering to carry the publications round to the shops for sale. I did not put it as a matter of trust, but purchased them for that purpose. I soon found myself a most welcome hand to Mr. Sherwin and to Mr. Wooler's publishers, and here I can give a proof of my singular spirit on this occasion. Though I knew that *Cobbet's Register* outdid the other publications beyond all comparison.

I refused to carry it, or did not apply for it, because it was not strong enough and did not come up to my notions of right. 'Why don't you bring us *Cobbett's Register?'* the dealers asked; 'you will make much more by that than any of the others.' No, I said, I will not touch it; nor did I till I had a shop of my own. Mr. Sherwin, though a much younger man than myself, being only eighteen years old, had a better education, and though unpractised as a public writer, was a fair grammarian, having aspired to authorship for some two or three years. He had read Paine's works, avowed his admiration of them, and got turned out of his situation. Nothing daunted, he wrote a pamphlet and came to London to find a publisher; but all were afraid of it. Disappointed, but not discouraged, and having some money, he resolved to get a shop and print and publish it himself. Thus originated Mr. Sherwin's, who was most certainly my coadjutor in getting myself fairly before the public. After Mr. Sherwin had made himself fully acquainted with my temper and disposition, he came to the manufactory where I spent part of my time, there not being work enough to occupy it fully, and offered to give up his shop to me and make me his publisher. This I felt was a great point gained, and I embraced the offer without hesitation, and henceforth I saw my way quite clearly. Fairly before the public as a publisher, I cared less about writing myself, seeing that I was in a fair way to improvement and ultimate success. During 1817 and 1818 I wrote nothing but a few papers and placards, and a few articles for Mr. Sherwin's *Register*. I had not an idea of becoming a regular public writer before my imprisonment, for publishing the "Age of Reason" and the "Principles of Nature"; the starting of the *Republican* was the work of a moment. Mr. Sherwin, seeing me likely to go to prison, and himself being likely to be more exposed, and having just been married, was induced to give up all the most dangerous part of his business to me, and when matters began to look serious after the Manchester massacre, he came to me to say that he should give up his *Register*, and I might take it up with the same title or any other that I might think best. I did not hesitate a moment, but gave it the title of the *Republican*, I may look upon myself as the author of all of Mr. Sherwin's bold writings, for it was always the work of my responsibility, and he was always encouraged by me to go his full length, under a pledge that I would never give him up as the author unless he wished it. This fearless responsibility on my part brought out the 'Gorgons' and led to many other spirited publications; and I may, I think, without vanity, consider myself the author of all the excitement of 1819, and verily think that but for my coming forward as I did in the spring of 1817, none of the

19

previous publishers would have stood out against Lord Sidmouth's circular letter and suspension of the Habeas Corpus Act. All would have become as quiet as Castlereagh, Eldon, and Sidmouth wished. Cobbett had fled to America. Hone had flinched, and it was a question as to the propriety of strangling the *Black Dwarf* at birth."

This brings us to the commencement of the Republican, and also to Carlile's entrance into the public arena.

One of those fatal mistakes which so many men make in their youth, i.e., an unfortunate marriage, was made by Carlile. At the early age of twenty-three he united himself to a woman of thirty. He had been staying at the little town of Gosport for a short time, and there became acquainted with this very good-looking woman, who was capable, well connected, and possessed of a considerable talent for business. After a courtship of only two months' duration, they joined the ranks of those who "marry in haste and repent at leisure". It is an ungrateful task to criticise adversely the character of a woman who did good service (however unwillingly) on behalf of intellectual freedom; but in the cause of truth individuals must suffer, and Truth and Justice should ever go hand in hand.

Carlile had not been married a week before he realised the great mistake he had made, and years after he told of it in this way:—

"I was in a dilemma the very first week of my marriage. I had but two responsibilities in life. The first was to assist my mother, who had now become infirm and poor, the other was to finish the apprenticeship of a son of a real friend. Neither of these engagements could be ignored or set aside. My wife knew of these before marriage and tacitly approved them, but set herself directly against both of them immediately after. I can truly say that as far as mental peace makes happiness I had never one day's happiness during the honeymoon or any other moon during the entire continuation of that marriage. I cannot pronounce her a bad woman, or of being the possessor of any particular vice. She was as variable as the atmosphere, and was in herself a complete 'System of Nature' both as a microcosm and macrocosm. The social as well as the moral evil was that her temper could never be relied on, and was often both terrible and dangerous. I have known her to exhibit for days together such appearances than which none could be more amiable or agreeable, more generous or more affable, and then on the most frivolous grounds—for merely *imagined* wrongs—become tempestuous to delirium and hysterics. It was her physical rather than her moral properties that were the seat of the disorder. Her violence generally fell on my immediate friends, man or woman, and a mere act of kindness shown to my mother or sisters has endangered my life as far as threats and preparations were appearances of danger. I never considered my life safe, and lived for years in almost daily apprehension of some terrible domestic tragedy. The wonder is that I ever accomplished anything under such a state of feeling, and I confess, what I have often told her, that to me imprisonment was a great relief; and this is part of the secret why I bore it so well. During the whole of my married life I felt the annoying condition of being without a home to which I could proceed in peace, and introduce a friend with the ordinary rites of hospitality and required civility from the mistress of the house. This necessarily drove me from home and caused me to form associations that I otherwise would not have done. As early as-1819, a separation took place (as was always the conversation through every year of our association) and was continued for some time, and during our united imprisonment in Dorchester Gaol—it was a matter of constant and sober conversation and future prospect—it was mutually understood that it was to be whenever I should be in a condition to make a sufficient settlement upon her. It was carried out at precisely that time, the moment at which the annuity of £50 a year, left me by Mr. Morrison, of Chelsea, was cleared of legacy duty. It was not till the month of May, 1832, that the first clear quarterly payment became due, but I anticipated it by the advance of a quarter's money in the February of that year, Mrs. Carlile was allowed to take everything in the way of furniture that she desired, and £100 ($500) worth of books from the stock which was at her mercy when she left. She did take every article of furniture, every bed, table, and chair in the house, even the chairs which had been purchased for the lecture room. She left me nothing but the business, its stock and debts, and she took the nearest shop she could wherein to oppose and injure me. At that time I had not seen her for a year, though I was in prison; nor would she send me so much as a Sunday dinner. We had separated from all pretences of being man and wife for nearly two years before that. She was only fit for what she now possesses, viz., single retirement with a competency to secure her from the cares and turmoils of life."

So much for the unpleasant details which are necessary to the understanding and justification of later events. It is more pleasant to record the manner in which this wife helped in the business, and how well she withstood the assaults of their common enemy. On the whole, and considering that she had absolutely no sympathy with Carlile's aims and ideas, and that her sole idea of a cause was the profits to be made by it, remembering also that she suffered a two years' imprisonment and bore two children to him in prison, that she fought for him as well as at him, also bearing in mind that to be the wife of a reformer one must suffer toil and privation, loss and sorrow of every kind, then we must feel she did her part in the good cause and bore her trials well. Whatever may have been her faults she is entitled to her share of the gratitude and remembrance of those who now enjoy the blessings of a Free Press.

She bore her husband five children in all, only three of whom reached maturity. These were Richard, Alfred, and Thomas Paine Carlile. It cannot be said that any of these sons followed in their father's footsteps. Though they were associated with him, by turns, in the practical part of the publishing business, they seemed not to have inherited either their mother's thrift or their father's talents, and were the source of much uneasiness to him. It would appear as if the uncongeniality of the parents had affected their children unfavorably. Carlile set them up in business several times, but always with unpleasant results; the unpopularity of the name.

Carlile at that time may have had much to do with their non-success, but not all. Carlile was at all times a most patient and kind parent. Always a great lover of little children, he contrived to have one or more of them with him as much as possible during his imprisonment. Again and again did he try them in business as they grew to manhood, and made many sacrifices for them. In a letter addressed to Mr. Thomas Turton, March 6th, 1838, after relating his anxiety and efforts for their welfare, he said:

"I begin to feel that there can never be any advantageous union whatever between me and any portion of that family. I can see no other purpose in them than the aim to get from me whatever they can, without regard to doing themselves or me any good. In this they have been trained by their mother from their infancy, and that training remains in them. Alfred is the best of them, but even he has exhibited

23

too much of that feeling. The whole family has dealt with me as though they had a secret interest to provide for distinct from mine; and I must meet them accordingly, for their own benefit as well as mine."

In another letter to the same gentleman, condoling with him on the loss of a very bright and intellectual son, he writes:

"Be assured of my sympathy and condolence, for indeed 'I mourn with you'. Neither of my own boys promising to be anything, I had pictured yours as being one of my future aids. I had formed high hopes of him, he was one of the brightest youths I had ever met. I had often wished that my boys were like him."

At another date, after some more unpleasant experiences with his own boys, he writes again to Mr.

Turton, who for more than twenty years was his bosom friend and shared all his secrets, if he had any. "The only idea that my boys entertain of a father is that he is a person to be fleeced. They sell my goods and make no return of the money." And then in a burst of feeling he concludes: "Such a family as I have neither God nor devil could manage." But enough of these unpleasant matters, which would not be given but that it is necessary to do so to serve their purpose in the cause of truth. Carlile's patience and forbearance with the unfortunate peculiarities of this wife earned for him the sobriquet of a noted sage. The Rev. Robert Taylor complimented him many a time and oft, and said, "that it was a Xantippe alone who could have made him into such a perfect resemblance in manner and character to Socrates".

Richard, the eldest son, emigrated to America soon after his father's death, and settled in Wisconsin, near Milwaukee;

and was elected to the House of Assembly from that State. He died of ship fever on his return to America after paying a visit to London in 1855.

CHAPTER III.

THE MANCHESTER MASSACRE

The following account of the memorable and terrible Manchester massacre is given by Carlile himself. It was his escape from this, and his subsequent publishing of the particulars concerning it, that drew down upon him the vengeful malice of the then Prime Minister, Lord Castlereagh, who was thereafter bent on Carlile's undoing.

"Early in the month of August, 1819, I was invited by John Knight, in the name of the committee, to attend an open-air meeting in Manchester, to take place on August 16th, 1819, at St. Peter's Field, the object being to meet and discuss their grievances publicly, and to unite upon a plan to be submitted to the House of Commons for the purpose of seeking and demanding the restoration of those political rights of which they had recently been unlawfully deprived by the passage of the Six Acts Bill, and the suspension of the Habeas Corpus Act; and to take action with a view or endeavor to procure other reforms from a notably corrupt Parliament. There had been rumors of the military being called out if the meeting should be held as proposed. I wrote the Chairman of the committee saying that as the advocates of reform were threatened with military execution at that meeting, I felt it my duty to be there, as a matter of example, at the post of danger. It was announced in the *New Times* before I left London that General Byng had reviewed the troops on St. Peter's Plain, and that they were in fine condition for coping with the Radicals, at the coming meeting, on the 16th August. I travelled from Birmingham to Manchester. There was a general expectation of an attack from the military, and some of the leaders were anxious to arm themselves, and there was a proposition afoot that fifteen thousand men should be there armed with pikes as a precautionary measure, but it was vetoed by some one of the leaders. About eleven o'clock in the morning the people began to assemble at the cottage where Mr. Henry Hunt had taken up his residence. At twelve Mr. Hunt, myself, and others entered the barouche that was to convey us to the place of meeting. We had not proceeded far when we were met by a committee of women from the Women's Reform Committee, one of whom bore a standard with the figure of a woman holding a flag in her hand, surmounted by a cap of liberty. She was requested to take a seat on the box of the carriage, which she did, and sat waving her flag and her handkerchief till we arrived at the hustings, when she took her stand at the corner of the hustings in front. Bodies of men were seen everywhere marching in military order with music, and colors flying, and carrying mottoes inscribed on them such as 'No Corn Laws', 'Liberty or Death' 'Taxation without Representation is Tyranny', 'We will have Liberty', etc., etc. Such cheering was never before heard! Women from the age of 16 to 80 years were seen with their caps in their hands waving and cheering, and their hair consequently dishevelled, the whole scene exceeding the powers of description. In passing through the streets the crowds were very great, and word was brought to Mr. Hunt that there were 300,000 people at and about the place of meeting. As the carriage moved along and reached the shops and warehouses of Mr. Johnson, of Smedley, three times three were given, also at the Police Court and at the Exchange. We arrived at the place of destination about one o'clock. Mr. Hunt expressed his disapprobation of the hustings as arranged, and feared that there would be some accident happen, they not appearing to be very secure. After some hesitation he ascended, and the proposition being made that he should be chairman, he was made so by acclamation. There were five women upon the hustings; four of them took a stand in the

27

bottom of the waggons that formed the hustings, the other, who was Mary Fildes, I believe, was elevated on one corner of the front with her banner in her hand and resting on a large chain. A most singular and interesting situation for a woman at such a meeting; Joan of Arc could not have been more interesting. Mr. Hunt had just begun his speech by thanking the people for the favor conferred on him, and made some ironical remarks on the conduct of the magistrates, when a cart or waggon, which evidently took its start from that part of the field where the police and magistrates were assembled in a house, was driven through the middle of the field, to the great annoyance and danger of the people assembled, who quietly made way for it to pass. The waggon had no sooner made its way through, when the Yeoman Cavalry made its appearance from the side on which the waggon had gone out. The meeting at the entrance of the cavalry and from the commencement was most orderly. The appearance of the women on the platform made the occasion particularly interesting, and everyone present wore bright and happy faces; but as the waggon drove out the cavalry made their appearance, and charged upon the defenceless people with the utmost fury, riding down everyone who could not get out of the way, and cutting down men, women, and children, commencing their premeditated attack with the most insatiable thirst for blood and destruction! The police, too, were as expert in applying their clubs to the heads and shoulders of the people as the cavalry their sabres. The brutality of the police equalled in ferocity the blood-thirstiness of the soldiers. On the first appearance of the cavalry I was standing by Mary Fildes, but I found her above everything like fear. I turned to cheer the other four women, and found them too in good spirits. Many people were rushing on the hustings, and many others getting off, and an opening between the two waggons enabled them to pass down through. After many others had done so, and just as Mr.

Hunt was arrested, I passed down through the aperture and had a very narrow escape of my life in so doing, for the pressure of the crowd was so great that, just as I jumped down, the two waggons came together with a crash; and I lost my hat by its being jammed off my head, between the two waggons, in such a manner that I could not extricate it. I was no sooner under the hustings than I found the horses' feet up close to me; but the hustings being cleared, they moved around and followed the crowd who were driven from the hustings, and I then walked out without a hat and was seized by the police. Their first question was, 'Who are you? What business have you here?' I told them that if they thought proper to take me in charge I would soon let them know who I was and how I came there. 'Damn you!' says one; 'let him go about his business'; and I lost no time in doing so. And I found no further interruption except a few blows from their truncheons. I, being a perfect stranger in that city, made to the nearest houses, which I believe were called Hall's Buildings, Windmill Row. Here I found a number of people sheltered. The place formed a little inlet from St. Peter's Plain, but no thoroughfare. All houses were close shut, and on no account would people open them, until there was one woman who looked out of window, and seeing me, a well-dressed man without a hat, supporting a woman who had received a severe contusion on the breast, she was moved with sympathy, and under the idea that I was a doctor and could assist her, she came down and let us in, when there was a rush of about a dozen persons, mostly young people of both sexes. I could not move from the house till six in the evening, when the husband came home from his work. On his arrival I commissioned him to purchase me a hat, which he had great difficulty in doing, as all shops were closed. He at last succeeded, and then I got him to pilot me through the town to the 'Star' Inn, where I had slept the night before, and left my portmanteau. On coming to the inn and finding it surrounded by the cavalry

29

who had done all the mischief in the morning, I thought it prudent not to enter. I then made my way to Mr. Wroe's house, as he was the only man I knew in Manchester, and on consulting with him I concluded that I could do no good in Manchester, but might do much good in London by an early publication of what I had witnessed. I resolved to leave by the first mail, but my portmanteau was still in the enemies' quarters. A person in Mr. Wroe's house undertook to bring me to a coach stand, and having got into a coach, I ordered the man to drive me to the 'Star' Inn, to the door of which we had great difficulty in getting owing to the pressure of so many mounted yeomanry. I got out boldly, and told the coachman to wait, and went into the travellers' room. I made sure of being known, as we had driven past the inn in the morning in the open barouche, and were seen by all the servants, who did not fail to hiss a little as their house was the rendezvous for the enemy, a circumstance I did not know when I went there. On calling the waiter he was quite sullen, saying they had kept me a bed at a great inconvenience to other customers. I pacified him by telling him to charge for it, but I had to ring again and again before the bill and the portmanteau were brought, and all the time I thought there was something brewing for me. At last a different waiter came, and then my things were soon brought and bill settled. Having pleased the waiter beyond his expectations, I slipped on a great coat and a pair of white gaiters, and he ushered me to the coach with a great deal of ceremony, and the yeomanry in front were requested to make way for one whom they had been sent to kill in the morning. While I had been waiting so long for my bill, etc., my coach had to move on to make way for another, and so I was shown to the wrong coach and drove off to the 'Bridgewater Arms', from whence the mail coach started. I had just got out and paid the man when there was a hue and cry after me by the first coachman I had hired, and unknowingly left behind at the 'Star' door. My first impression was that the police had scent of me, but I soon found my mistake, paid the man, and all was right. At three in the morning the coach left, and great was the terror of the coachman, guard, and passengers that it would be stopped by the Reformers before it got to Stockport. I had nothing to fear on this head, but was not free of apprehension that one of my fellow-travellers was a police officer in disguise set to watch me, or to keep at my heels at any rate. He was despatched from Manchester as an express agent to London, either to the Government or to some mercantile house. There were four of us in the mail, two were friends of the master of the 'Bridgewater Arms', and had been there on a visit, and appeared to be coach-masters themselves living somewhere between Macclesfield and Derby. Those two worthies were well filled with wine, but a bottle was brought to the coach door by the master to have a parting glass, when to every glass was the toast, 'Down with Hunt!' One of them would insist on my taking a glass as a fellow-traveller to join in the sentiment of 'Down with Hunt!' To pacify the fools and disarm suspicion as far as possible, I drank the glass of wine with 'Down with Hunt!' which was considered the proof of my being a good fellow and a fit companion for them. The panic which prevailed in all the towns from Manchester to Northampton can scarcely be conceived, and it fell to my lot to detail the particulars of the massacre at each town we passed through, as nothing but post-horse expresses had passed through till the arrival of our mail coach."

Mr. Hunt received a sentence of two years' imprisonment in Dorchester Gaol for his part in this affair. The reader is spared the details of the bloody onslaught. The instances which came under Carlile's immediate observation were sickening in the extreme, and drew from him immediately on his arriving in London a spirited letter to Lord Sidmouth, describing the whole affair, and calling on him to call the Manchester authorities to account for their dastardly conduct. The letter itself gave great umbrage, and a council of three, consisting of Lord Sidmouth, Sir John Silvester, Recorder, and John Atkins, Mayor of London, studied over it for several days to see if it could not be made out to be itself a treasonable affair. In the meantime, the Prince Regent had directed Lord Sidmouth to return the magistrates of Manchester, and all the officers and privates concerned in the attack, "Their thanks to them for having so promptly preserved the peace and tranquillity of the country."

This drew from Carlile two more letters of the same kind as the first, but stronger, one to the Prince Regent, George, afterwards George IV, and another to Lord Sidmouth. The boldness of this proceeding was something very unusual and not to be tolerated; but Carlile never knew what fear was when he had a pen in his hand, or indeed at any other time. Moreover, he could not believe that the Prince Regent could have been properly informed, or he would not have done this, and he was boiling with indignation at the treatment of peaceable citizens.

This letter of Sir Francis Burdett on the Manchester massacre was adjudged libellous, and procured for Sir Francis a fine of £1,500 or a year's imprisonment, in the usual manner of those days. (Sir Francis preferred paying the fine.) It ran as follows:—

"To the Electors of Westminster,

"Aug. 18th, 1819.

"Gentlemen,

"This, then, is the answer of the boroughmongers to the petitioning people—this is the proof of our standing in no need of reform—these the practical blessings of our glorious boroughmongers' domination—this the use of a standing army in time of peace. It seems our fathers were not such fools as some would make believe in opposing the establishment of a standing army and sending King William's Dutch guards out of the country! Yet would to heaven they had been Dutchmen or Switzers, or Hessians, or Hanoverians, or anything rather than Englishmen who have done such deeds! What? Kill men unarmed and unresisting, and, gracious God, women too, disfigured, maimed, cut down, and trampled on by dragoons? Is this England? Is this a Christian land? A land of freedom? Can such things be and pass us by like a summer's cloud, unheeded? Forbid it; every drop of English blood in every vein that does not proclaim its owner bastard. Will the gentlemen of England support or wink at such proceedings? They have a great stake in their country; they hold great estates, and they are bound in duty and in honor to consider them as retaining fees on the part of their country for upholding its rights and privileges. Surely they will at length awake and find they have duties to perform. They never can stand tamely by as lookers-on whilst bloody Neros rip open their mothers's womb; they must join the general voice, loudly demanding justice and redress, and head public meetings throughout the United Kingdom to put a stop in its commencement to a reign of terror and of blood, to afford consolation as far as it can be afforded and legal redress to the widows and orphans—mutilated victims of this unparalleled and barbarous outrage. For this purpose I propose that a meeting shall be called in Westminster, which the gentlemen of the committee will arrange, and whose summons I would hold myself in readiness to attend. Whether the penalty of our meeting will be death by military execution I know not; but this I know—a man can die but once, and never better than in vindicating the laws and liberties of his country. Excuse this hasty address. I can scarcely tell what I have written; it may be a libel, or the Attorney-General may call it one, just as he pleases. When the seven bishops were tried for libel, for the support of arbitrary power, the army of James II, then encamped on Hounslow Heath, gave three cheers on hearing of their acquittal. The King, startled at the noise, asked, 'What's that?' 'Nothing, sire,' was the answer, 'but the soldiers shouting at the acquittal of the seven bishops.' 'Do you call *that* nothing?' said the misgiving tyrant; and shortly after abdicated the Government. 'Tis true, James could not inflict the tortures on his soldiers—could not tear their living flesh from their shoulders with the cat-o'-ninetails—could not flay them alive! Be this as it may, our duty is to meet, and England expects every man to do his duty.

"I remain, Gentlemen,

"Most truly and faithfully

"Your most obedient servant,

"Francis Burdett."

CHAPTER IV.

RECORD OP PERSECUTION

Under the administration of Lords Liverpool, Castlereagh, Canning, Sidmouth, etc., Richard Carlile, of Fleet Street, London, publisher, was arrested on the 14th of August, 1817, on three warrants granted by Mr. Justice Holroyd on the oath of one Griffin Swanson, a common informer, for publishing a book called "The Parodies",* the sale of which had been suppressed by Mr. William Hone, but for which Mr. Hone was afterwards put on three several trials and as often acquitted, to the great joy of the people, to the great grief of the administration and Sir Samuel Shepherd, Attorney-General, to the acceleration of the death of the then Chief Justice (Ellenborough), and to the mortification of the succeeding Chief Justice, who saw his great prototype defeated as well as himself. On the 15th Carlile was committed to the King's Bench prison by Mr. Justice Holroyd in default of bail to the amount of £800 ($4,000) on three several warrants. On the 13th of November, being called to plead, he was surprised with a fourth information by the aforesaid Attorney-General, founded on the 18th No. of Vol. I of Sherwin's Political Register.

On the 20th of December he was liberated after an imprisonment of eighteen weeks by entering into recognizances of £300 ($1,500) without either of the four informations being submitted to a jury then or ever afterwards. On the 16th day of January, 1819, he was informed that "The Society for the Suppression of Vice" had presented a bill to the Grand Jury, then sitting at the Old Bailey, on a charge of blasphemous libel for the publication of Thomas Paine's theological works. Bail was immediately presented and the arrest prevented. The indictment was removed by a writ of *certiorari* to the Court of King's Bench at the instance of the Society, and further bail required on the first day of Hilary term, when an information was also filed and presented to the court by the Attorney-General (Shepherd) against the same publication. To both the indictment and information the defendant imparled under an order to plead within the first eight days of Easter term. On the 11th day of February a warrant was granted by Chief Justice Abbott against the defendant, on an oath made by George Pritchard and Thomas Fair, that the defendant had continued the sale of Paine's works, and that the said George Pritchard intended to prosecute. The warrant was put in force at 8 o'clock in the evening, and by 10 o'clock defendant was lodged within the walls of Newgate. On the 15th day of February, he was brought from Newgate by a writ of *habeas corpus* to the chambers of Mr. Justice Bailey, and bail was tendered and taken a third time to appear and answer to the charge against the same publication. On the first day of Easter term, Carlile pleaded to an information and indictment, and in addition to these had presented to him *another* information at the instance of the Attorney-General, founded on No. 6, vol. 4, of *Sherwin's Weekly Political Register*, and another indictment at the instance of the Society for the Suppression of Vice founded on that part of the 1st vol. of the *Deist* entitled "Palmer's Principles of Nature". To these last two he again imparled, and on the first day of Trinity term he prayed the court to stay this accumulation of informations and indictments until those to which he had already pleaded and was prepared to defend were disposed of. But the lenient and impartial judges of the Court of King's Bench could see no need of this, and he must stand prepared to defend five or perhaps nine informations and indictments at the same time, should it be the pleasure of the Attorney-General. The sittings after the terms of both Easter and Trinity had been allowed to pass without bringing the question to an issue, whilst the publications had been invariably kept on sale.

On Saturday, the 21st of August, Carlile was arrested on a warrant issued by John Atkins, Lord Mayor of the City of London, and lodged in the Giltspur Street Compter. The warrant set forth that defendant had published a malicious, seditious, and inflammatory libel, tending to create disaffection in the minds of his Majesty's subjects, and breaches of the peace. On the Monday he was conducted to the Mansion House and brought before the Lord Mayor, who, on finding bail ready, said that he should require twenty-four, if not forty-eight hours' notice of bail. This was evidently for the purpose of annoyance and to gratify a malicious caprice, for the names tendered were unexceptionable. On the Tuesday he was again brought before the Lord Mayor, and was *committed for want of sureties*. The person objected to was a Mr. Wooler, who owned several large houses and offices in the City, and who was as wealthy a man as the Lord Mayor himself. A Mr. Lindsay then offered to deposit the amount of bail required at once, when Lord Mayor Atkins refused and committed Carlile *for want of sureties!* On Thursday Carlile was again brought before him, and not being able to carry his caprices any further, he at length accepted the bail, but with the threat that if he continued the sale of the letters (to Sidmouth and the Prince) he would do so at his peril. Thus the reader will see that it was not the articles mentioned in these indictments and informations that were the real cause of these persecutions, but the letters to the Prince Regent and the Home Secretary, which Carlile had so indignantly and fearlessly addressed to them, immediately after he reached London, on his return from the scene of the Manchester massacre. He not only dared to write them such letters in which he appealed to and arraigned them, as man to man, but he published them and they were read. That was the sore that smarted and rankled and would not heal, though they dare not make this the ground of these indictments.

On the 16th of September, 1819, Carlile addressed the following letter to Attorney-General Sir Robert Gifford.

"Sir,—As the adjourned sittings of the Court of King's Bench are near at hand, I beg leave to enquire whether it is your intention as his Majesty's Attorney-General to prosecute in the ensuing sittings in the month of October those informations filed against me by the late Attorney-General, Sir Samuel Shepherd, and should such be your intention, which of them you will be pleased to take up first? Flattering myself that I shall find in you a generous opponent, I would entreat the earliest notice that might possibly be given, as it is my intention to serve with subpoenas several persons of rank and distinction, eminent in the theological, literary and scientific world, for whose convenience and accommodation I am solicitous to obtain the earliest notice, as many of them are resident in distant parts of the country, and would wish at least a week's notice for attendance. "I am, Sir,

"Your obliged and obedient servant,

"Richard Carlile."

To which he received the following reply.

"Sir,—In answer to your enquiry, I have to state that it is certainly my intention that the informations against you, which stand for trial at the adjourned sittings in October, should be tried at those sittings, and that the informations against you for publishing a blasphemous libel which stands prior in order in the list of causes, will first come on for trial.

"I am, Sir,

"Your obedient servant,

"R. Gifford

"Lincoln's Inn, September 7th, 1819."

This made the publication of the theological works of Thomas Paine the first cause to be tried, and one of the first persons to be subpoenaed was the Archbishop of Canterbury, and the following letter was written after receiving one from the Archbishop's lawyers signifying his willingness to be present at the trial.

"Fleet Street, September, 1819.

"My Lord,—I feel it my duty to express to you the warmest approbation I felt on receiving the candid reply from Messrs.

Foster, Cooke, and Frere, where your grace may be found in the month of October, should the presence of your grace be required on my trial. I beg to assure your grace that my motive for serving your grace with a subpoena was neither idle nor frivolous, and shall deem the presence of your grace to be of the highest importance, not only to my own interest, but in the interest of Truth and Justice, and consequently the interest of mankind in general. In conjunction with your grace, it is also my intention to serve with a subpoena those persons in this country most eminent in theology, astronomy, and oriental literature. I beg leave to assure your grace that such questions for such evidence as I may find necessary to elicit shall be put by me with a due impression of the importance and rank of those to whom I shall be addressing myself. I beg leave to subscribe myself,

"Your grace's most obliged and most obedient servant,

"Richard Carlile."

These letters being published in the *Republican* gave the authorities an inkling of the elaborate defence he intended to prepare for his trial. Such presumption and boldness amazed them, and was such as they never had to cope with before Carlile's time. William Cobbett escaped to America when he saw danger of prosecution, and Mr. Hone, though thrice tried and thrice acquitted, yet had given up the publication of the book of contention as a matter of general policy. But in Carlile's case the authorities encountered a man who had no idea of yielding a single point in the cause he felt to be just. He prepared to fight them on their own ground. He knew before he entered the court that the verdict would be against him; no matter how strong a defence he might make, conviction was, in his mind, a foregone conclusion. Those letters to Sidmouth and the Prince were not to be forgotten or forgiven. They must not be allowed to become a precedent for some future occasion.

Carlile resolved to do all that could possibly be done to set the subject of establishing the freedom of the Press fairly and squarely before the thousands that would read the account of the trials. He hoped by this means to reach a large body of thinking people, and arouse them to a sense of the danger of allowing to go unchallenged such actions on the part of the authorities as the last two years had witnessed. The simple reading of the newspaper accounts of his trial and defence would of itself, he argued, educate people and make them cognisant of his ends and aims, therefore he set himself to do what he could do for himself and the cause at this momentous epoch of his life.

The following article appeared in the 7th No., Vol. I, of the *Republican*, October 8th, 1819, written by Carlile.

"To the Public.

"The important moment has arrived when the trials which have attracted so much of the public attention and curiosity have been determined upon, and before another issue of this publication will be entered upon. The general expression of feeling that has been displayed on both sides of the question evinces that these trials are looked forward to with more than usual anxiety. I feel myself but as an insignificant being at this crisis, the mere instrument with which despotism in the back-ground is playing its game. I should not feel anxious for, or value my personal liberty, did I not know that its preservation by an upright and inflexible and discriminating jury is of the utmost importance at the present eventful moment A verdict of *guilty* will be hailed by the ministers as a cloak and sanction of all their late actions. They will triumph and go on in their destructive career; they will assume that an unlimited confidence has been placed in them, and there will be no bounds to their already frightful oppression. A verdict of *not guilty* will stagger and shake them from their holds, will destroy the remains of ignorance and superstition, and establish the liberty of the Press and free discussion with all its valued influence. Every stratagem will be used by my persecutors and by that portion of the Press which adheres to them to excite a feeling of prejudice against me. I was informed nearly a month ago that a loyal declaration would be ready for signatures in the City of London expressive of its abhorrence of seditious and blasphemous publications, about a week or ten days before my trial would take place. This declaration has been made, and however directly it may have been levelled at me, I cannot plead guilty to being its object, but do most heartily concur in its premises, and consequently I attended at the London Coffee House on Ludgate Hill and placed my name and address to it, which I shall expect to see published with the list of signatures. To such sentiments as are there set forth no honest man would hesitate to subscribe, but it becomes a question as to which part of the community they are applicable; I feel no connection with them. Because I have witnessed the existing privations and sufferings of certain classes of my fellow countrymen with the feelings of deepest concern, and because I feel sensible that all the treasonable and turbulent attempts to subvert the wholesome laws and regulations of the country emanate from the Cabinet, these are the reasons for my placing my signature to this declaration, and I would recommend everyone who is prominent for reform to go and do the same. As many persons and perhaps many of the readers of the *Republican* are ignorant of the contents of the 'Age of Reason', and led away by the general clamor of blasphemy against its author, I will give them a specimen of what is the subject of this false and absurd charge.

"'On the Deity.

"'Do we want to contemplate his power? We see it in the immensity of the Creation.

"'Do we want to contemplate his wisdom? We see it in the unchangeable order by which the incomprehensible whole is governed.

"'Do we want to contemplate his munificence? We see it in the abundance with which he fills the earth.

"'Do we want to contemplate his mercy? We see it in his notwithholding that abundance even from the unthankful.'

"Thus by searching has Paine found out God, and I call on all the priests of Europe to produce, in the same space, quotations from all the sermons that ever were published, anything like this grand demonstrative proof of the power, wisdom, goodness and mercy of the great proprietor of nature. Those are the blasphemers of his name and attributes who first inflict on mankind all the miseries that human nature can endure, and then attribute it to an angry, implacable and offended God! The pulpits of this country are resounding with the assertion that all the miseries that have been and are now inflicted on the people arise from their own wickedness. It is a gross falsehood! they arise from the wickedness of the rulers of this country, who, like a dissolute and debauched father, squanders everything that can be converted into money, and leaves his family to starve in misery and wretchednesss. Let us hope that an honest jury can be found to do justice to the writings of Paine, and in so doing they will do justice to their fellowmen."

CHAPTER V.

THE TRIAL

An article in No. 8, Vol. I, of the *Republican*, written by Mr. William Sherwin, the partner and friend of Carlile, gives a very good idea of the status of the case as it appeared to him and his friends. The trial had then been in progress two days:—

"The Trial of Mr. Carlile.

"Before this number of the *Republican* is issued to the world the fate of Mr. Carlile will probably be decided, whether the verdict of the jury who are to decide upon his case shall consign him to a dungeon for the next two or three years, or perhaps for life, or whether it will restore him to his family, his friends, and his business. In either case he will carry with him the greatest satisfaction an honest man can enjoy—the consciousness of having done right in the first instance, and of having bravely defended himself in the hour of trial and difficulty. When Socrates was about to be deprived of his life, one of his friends expressed his regret that he should die innocent of the charge against him. 'What,' said the sage, 'do you wish me to die guilty?' The greatest consolation a man can receive while suffering beneath the iron rod of persecution is the confidence which results from his injustice being undeserved, and should the jury give a verdict against Mr. Carlile, he will receive this consolation in a great degree. The unprecedented interest and sympathy which his case has excited is a proof that public opinion is with him; that the mass of the people are his friends and the enemies of religious persecution, intolerance, bigotry, and tyranny. The question with the public is not whether Mr. Carlile is right or wrong in his opinions, but whether he has acted from purity of motive? whether he is a malicious person, in short, whether he has published the 'Age of Reason' with a view to corrupt the morals of society? If the parties engaged in this prosecution are unable to prove this, their case cannot be made out, for where there is no bad intention there is no crime. It is in vain that a servile tool in the garb of a judge declares in the accustomed jargon of the Bar and the Bench that 'Christianity is part of the law of the land'. Mr. Carlile has proved over and over again that the Act of Parliament, usually called Mr. Smith's Bill, has completely destroyed the protection which the Christian religion received from the laws of the country. That Mr. Justice Abbott should wish to explain away the application of the statute is not surprising when it is considered that the Act authorised any person to deny the existence of the Trinity. The conduct of the judge and of the Attorney-General has been partial and malignant in the extreme during the proceedings. The only mode of defence by which Mr. Carlile could hope to escape the vulture-fangs of the law was by showing that he had no evil intention in publishing the work, and he could not do this better than by showing that it contained nothing immoral, and that the objections which Paine makes to the divine origin of the Bible were well founded. This was his only defence, and the only one he could have which would be likely to justify his conduct to the jury and to the world. He was permitted to read the 'Age of Reason' through, but the moment he began to comment upon the various passages of the Bible he was interrupted by the judge, who declared that he would not suffer any observations to be made that would impugn the divinity of the Christian religion. By means of this sweeping declaration he deprived Carlile of the greater part of his defence, and as the latter very justly observed, showed the determination to confine him in a dungeon without even the privilege of a hearing! One of the most arbitrary practices in a trial of this description is the privilege which the Attorney-General is allowed of interrupting the defendant when the latter happens to make any observation which may be considered by the Attorney-General too harsh for the delicate ear of his opponent. During the first day's proceedings there was no room for the exercise for this tyrannical mode of annoyance, but to-day has afforded several opportunities for the harpies of the law to interpose their malignant objections. Whenever Mr. Carlile was entering upon anything that was likely to show that he had published nothing that had not been published many times before without exposing the authors to the notice of the law officers of the Crown, nay, that several of these authors themselves had actually been pensioners and parasites of the present government; whenever Mr. Carlile was attempting to do this he was immediately interrupted by the Attorney-General, whose appeal was directly answered by a prohibition from the judge. When we consider the powerful array of talent and learning that the defendant has to contend against, when we see three or four of the most dexterous, diligent, and cunning sycophants the Bar can produce selected to oppose him, and to watch for any false and faulty step he may make for the purpose of throwing him into confusion, it is almost impossible that a fair trial can be expected. Is it not enough that a wily hypocrite in the character of a judge should be watching for opportunities to interrupt him and to lead him off his guard, without being exposed to the impertinent intrusion of men who are officially employed to pursue him to destruction? But in the English Government of to-day everything is of a piece, everything tends to despotism. The judge in what should be a Court of Justice explains the law as he pleases, which is always on the side of his employers and if the law is in any case doubtful, instead of allowing a defendant the benefit of the doubt he turns it against him, by giving an opinion which is at once recorded and observed as a solemn legislative decision. In such a state of things it is impossible to look for anything but tyranny from the Bench, and the only chance the defendant has is the probability that an honest jury will set the dictum of a wicked judge at defiance. The folly of this prosecution is equal to its malignity. The proceedings of the trial will make more Deists than Carlile would have done in selling the 'Age of Reason' during the remainder of his life. Every interruption he has received will be considered by the public as a proof that his prosecutors apprehended that he was going to say something that would be unanswerable. Besides which there will be the publicity which will be given to the work by means of the trial, a publicity that will far exceed that of any other work on the same side of the question that ever was written. In the next number there will be room for making some observations on the results of the trial, a result which will be of more consequence than any event which has ever taken place in the history of the criminal jurisprudence of this country."

Carlile had reason to believe that Lord Chief Justice Abbott was very unwilling to have the trial take place in his Court, and had had a correspondence with Lord Castlereagh on the subject. He opposed the whole proceeding from the filing of the first information down to the trials themselves; but he was over-ruled; by what argument or proffered reward does not appear. Then as to the jury. It was a special jury, but Carlile was not allowed to challenge the jurors, although even while in court he received warning that at least five of them had publicly declared that they would hang him if they could, or give him at least five years' imprisonment on bread and water, and they went so far as to say to him in open court "that his defence would not help him". They were allowed to separate and go to their homes, and mingle with everybody and anybody the night before the verdict was rendered, which all goes to show that the case, as Carlile said, was predetermined, and the whole proceeding on the part of Judge and advocates a travesty and mockery of justice.

His defence on the second day was momentarily interrupted, and on the third day was completely suppressed. In this connection may be mentioned the case of a man who had been summoned on this jury, and who had left a sick bed to sit with them at the trial. This man was of the same belief as Carlile, and had said to friends that he had no doubt at all of the sincerity of heart of the defendant, and that he, the juror, knew that Carlile would go to the scaffold if need be in defence of those opinions as *he* would. This man had left a sick bed to do what he could for Carlile on the jury, yet at last, and for some unknown reason, he allowed the verdict to be given without a dissenting word on his part.

At the close of each day's proceedings, Carlile issued a full report and sold it in twopenny sheets. These sheets were headed, "A Full Account of Richard Carlile's *Mock Trials*", and were sold with marvellous rapidity. They were immediately condemned by the authorities as indictable, and Mrs. Carlile was threatened with prosecution for selling them in the shop; but the sale kept on, and the trade at the Fleet Street shop exceeded anything that was so far known in the annals of the bookselling business.* Besides this, Carlile addressed open letters to his judge and jury, arraigning them for the illegality of their conduct, and spread them broadcast. He also continued a series of articles in the *Republican*—called the "Crisis"—of the most daring character. They show the indomitable spirit and fearlessness of Carlile even while under heavy bail and, later, under conviction. Even while in prison he never faltered, no matter what the consequences to himself. Feeling that he was *right* in the position he had taken, he threw caution and diplomacy to the winds, and dared and defied the enemy to do their worst! One parallel only can I recall, and one which comes up in memory often as the daring deeds of this unconquerable spirit are recounted. It occurs in a little book called "The Bridge of the Gods". It is an Indian story, and the epoch is also far distant, in William Penn's time, I think. A scout, a white man, has fallen into the hands of his enemies, the Indians, and they prepare to torture him to death in their extremely horrible fashion, but he laughs at their devices, and even as they heap coals of fire upon his breast, he laughs at and derides them, and taunts his murderers by reminding them of all he has done against them, some of which acts they had seemed to forget, and while the coals of fire are (literally) burning their way to his heart he laughs and jeers them on to fresh horrors, never flinching, but daring and defying them till the last moment. Carlile's case was a civilised counterpart of this Indian story, yet with a happier result. The reader will realise the force of this comparison better as he reads further of Carlile's many encounters with his enemies and the enemies of intellectual freedom.

What would be thought in America of a President, who occupies about the same relative position as a Prime Minister of England, who would instruct a judge on the Bench as to his conduct of a case to be brought before him? The sun would not set before an impeachment committee would be organised for active work. That is, if a judge could be found base enough to be dictated to, and we do not think a judge could be found in either country to-day who would lend himself to such a thing. But in former days in England things were in such a servile state, that place and power were freely, almost openly, given for services, menial and degrading. It was only necessary for an aspiring barrister to relieve himself of his conscience and place it in a hermetically sealed vault, and he was ready for any

49

amount of official climbing (by the backstairs) and the forthcoming reward of promotion.

The second day's proceedings were very interesting, and make excellent reading, even in this busy age. They will be found in the appendix, and are copied verbatim from a leading daily paper of the time. Having copies of all the papers of that date, I choose the *British Press* for its more general fairness in its report, although its editorial at the conclusion of the trial was bitter and severe on the defendant. In those days it was something gained, as even now, when one could get a fair report. The other papers were too palpably influenced by fear or discretion to give anything approaching to an unbiassed report.

Scores, nay hundreds of letters poured in upon Carlile before and after the sentence. The verdict of guilty shocked many of his friends for the moment, and made everyone feel unsafe and uneasy, none knowing what would be the outcome or where these prosecutions might end. But this state of feeling did not last, and the rebound came, and with it such an awakening and mental uprising as was never before known in any country. And though Carlile felt, as he says in his letter to Mr. Morrison, deserted by some who had been officious enough before the sentence, yet he was in no way deserted, it was merely that his friends were suffering from the shock. The circulation soon started, letters and encouragements and money poured in upon him with the highest encomiums upon his bravery and fearlessness, and admiration of his wonderful defence, wonderful indeed when his youth (still in his twenties) and former condition of life are taken into consideration, and the very short time—only two years—he had been before the public. It must have taken an immense amount of nerve and backbone to stand up alone and confront that array of clever but unscrupulous men! He was entirely unassisted except by what Mr. Hone prepared for the third day. He had to defend his own case, for it is doubtful whether any lawyer could have been obtained, or, if obtained, whether he could have been relied upon to be proof against all the temptations that would have been thrown in his way to betray his client. And so great was the amount of prejudice and fear of offending the powers that were, at that time, that it would have had to be a very strong lawyer that would dare to risk doing so, and where was such to be found? The following extract from a letter will show to what an extent prejudice had been created against Carlile, and how it had separated even members of the same family from each other, so that many who had espoused his cause, and were anxious to prove their sympathy, had to do so in secret from their own nearest relatives:—

"Compassion and justice have been refused to you without the precincts of the Royal Tribunal; you cannot therefore expect either within the verge of the modern star chamber, and are no doubt prepared for the worst, for I am sorry to observe that the hue and cry of Atheism, though founded on the most malignant calumny and falsehood, has become so prevalent as to oblige me to write this address to you in stealth from every individual member of my family and fireside, lest one and all might tear me to pieces for heaving one generous sigh on your behalf, or for the ghost of freedom's sake, now vanished from her wonted haunts in your infidel train which has frightened many foolish reformers into fits.

"All the papers of the Empire groaned under the load of his humane Anti-Christian, if not Atheistical principles, at an expense to Mr. Robert Owen of a thousand pounds including profits to this very Government, and the whole identical band of editors who are this season employed in hunting you, a poor plain, upright Deist, to perdition! If this be fair play, I know not what can be stigmatised as foul, base, and infamous from every point of view, and if the notice of it in your pleading does not tend to mollify the oracles of the law into a very lenient sentence for you, the public will estimate their integrity and legitimate equity accordingly. You must excuse this long communication, which as a work of intended mercy has engrossed so completely the Lord's Day that I have been able to think of nothing else. The truth is, since it must be out, I have been dreaming about you and your forlorn wife and children all night, and awoke very early this morning under a species of impulse which forced me from my bed to take pen and ink in this unequal contest against the powers and principalities of the darkest ages, arrayed to annihilate the man with whom they are afraid to argue in the face of the people. Yesterday, the news of the resurrection and transmission of the bones of the persecuted Thomas Paine* to their native soil struck me very forcibly as an extraordinary, almost a miraculous coincidence with the decree that, in the same breath, will probably bury you alive amidst your fellow slaves, for promulgating those same political doctrines for which Paine is on the eve of being canonised by the brave sons of liberty, returning like giants refreshed (after a short sleep) from the shores of America to support radical reform or perish in the attempt. To 'Common Sense' and the 'Crisis', both written by the intelligent Paine, the free Americans are much more indebted for liberation from unrepresented thraldom than to the sword or the genius of Washington, and our posterity may yet owe as precious a debt to Carlile, Hunt, and Cobbett, should you all suffer the martyrdom of captivity, either on the score of political or religious publications, which I think cannot be of long duration, and never will extend so far as death whatever your enemies may intend shall be the result."

One of the most gratifying incidents, if not, indeed, the only one pleasant to dwell upon at this time, is the manner in which Carlile's friends, his bodyguard, so to speak, rallied around him. Mr. W. T. Sherwin and Mr. Julian Augustus St. John assumed the responsibility of the publication of the *Republican*. Mr. William Hone, who had been lately acquitted of a similar charge, assisted Carlile in the construction of the third day's defence, and in this connection the following letter from the *Morning Chronicle*, October 15th, 1819, becomes amusing:—

"Sir,—Perceiving in your paper of this morning that my name is introduced in a manner calculated to lead the public to believe that I was instrumental in preparing the defence of Mr. Carlile, on his trial for publishing 'Paine's Age of Reason', I request that you will afford your readers an opportunity of knowing the true state of the case. Having been present in court as an auditor, I was earnestly solicited at the close of the second day, by several friends to the liberty of the Press, to point out, in conjunction with two literary gentlemen, those authors who had written the most ably in defence of toleration and unrestricted freedom of opinion on religious subjects, and to mark the passages. This I assented to, nor do I apprehend that such a request would have been refused by a liberal-minded man, or that the most scrupulous would have found fault with me for so doing. I accordingly arranged, as well as I could in a few hours the next morning, a connected series of quotations from Archbishop Tillotson, 'Bishop Squire', Doctor Furneaux, Bishop Watson, Professor Limborch, Professor Campbell, Mr. Locke, Doctor Enfield, the Rev. Mr. Wyvil, Rev. Mr. Aspland, 'the Christian Reformer,' and other authorities of equal weight and tendency. This was read by Mr. Carlile on the third day with interpolations of his own, and this with the loan of 'Erasmus ', Miltosermons and pamphlets, constituted the whole of my exertions on this n's

'Areopogetica', De Laume on Non-conformity, a volume of 'Blackstone', a tract by Lord Somers, and a few extraordinary occasion.

"Your obedient servant,

"45, Ludgate Hill.

"William Hone."

One would naturally ask what more he could have done. However, what he did was equally creditable to his heart as to his head. The original documents are in my possession. Most of them are in Mr. Hone's handwriting, the rest are in a beautiful text, evidently that of "the literary gentlemen" who assisted in the hurried task.

At the time of the sentence a threat was conveyed to Carlile that his wife would be informed against, to which he responded:—

"Your threats, my lords, to file a criminal information against Mrs. Carlile, cannot change my course, sorry as I am that I cannot take the responsibility and the consequent pains and penalties on myself. I am satisfied that my wife possesses sufficient virtue and good sense to realise my wishes, and pursue my directions, and these are that she should proceed in the usual manner as I have done, and suppress nothing."

At the conclusion of the trial and previous to the sentence, a bishop (name not given) sent a petition, an open petition to the authorities, to the editor of the *Observer*, a Mr. Clement, accompanied by a hundred pounds. This paper was published in two or three parts on as many Sundays, previous to the sentencing of Carlile, and which no doubt had its effect on the Christian Judge Bailey. One of the recommendations of that petition was the following: "The patient is maddened by a slow poison, is below human nature, and beyond human remedy; his language is raving, and for the common safety of mankind he must be fettered till he dies." One of the Dorchester clerical magistrates was anxious to proceed practically with this recommendation. This petition also recommended the fining of the prisoner £3,000, by way of making the real fine of £1,500 look like a mere trifle.

The Rev. George Somers Clarke, D.D., Vicar of Great Waltham, was confined in the old jail of Essex for contempt of the Ecclesiastical Court, and insisted on remaining there the rest of his life. This gentleman sent Carlile a ten pound note ($50) just before the trial, and volunteered the following evidence, "That having been the tutor at college of the Lord Chief Justice Abbott, would testify that he himself was a Deist; and that as the Bible was now translated and received, Thomas Paine was justified in writing his 'Age of Reason'." This learned reverend came into court with rolls of Hebrew, Arabic, and all sorts of ancient Scriptures, but the wily Chief Justice would not allow him to be examined.

Carlile's knowledge of the fact that the Attorney-General was himself an acknowledged Deist gives point to the sarcasm that Carlile addressed to him which otherwise would be tame; he actually helped to prosecute a man for professing the same doctrines which he himself held.

"Letters from St. Petersburg to the 30th of November state that the Emperor Alexander of Russia, apprehensive that the morals of his people would be injured by their reading the account of Carlile's Trials, had given directions to the police to prevent the introduction of all the English newspapers containing it."—*London Times*, Dec. 29th, 1819.

As a straw shows the way the wind blows, so this little report shows the apprehension of crowned heads that some one or more of their subjects might see something to admire and follow in Carlile's example. Else why such measures?

CHAPTER VI.

TAKEN TO PRISON

Carlile was sentenced to three years' imprisonment and a fine of £1,500. Almost as soon as the sentence was passed, Carlile was handcuffed and taken in the dead of night to Dorchester Gaol, some 130 miles from London. He was not allowed to see his wife or children, nor to communicate with his friends. As soon as they had him safely locked up, the authorities made a descent upon the Fleet Street shop, seized upon the entire stock and furniture, and closed it from business. This seizure was made ostensibly to secure the fines, but really to cripple Carlile so that he could never pay them, and thus they could keep him in perpetual imprisonment. For if he had been allowed to retain his stock and profitable business, he could have paid his fine of £1,500 ($7,500) before his term of imprisonment expired; but the plan was to cripple him past recovery. The goods seized were mostly books and pamphlets, which would have brought him £2,000 ($10,000) in the ordinary way of sale. This confiscation was no part of his sentence, be it remembered, but an afterthought, and was performed by the power of might over right. This stock was thrown into a damp cellar or warehouse, and practically ruined. His wife and children would have been rendered helpless and impoverished had not Carlile cautioned his wife some time before to prepare for the worst, and to reserve a portion of the money resulting from the large sales during the trials for herself and children. They would have been reduced to actual want, for the officers even took the money found in the money-drawer, although not one dollar resulting from this seizure was ever allowed in mitigation of his fines. The most trying part of the sentence to Carlile was that he was only allowed to take exercise in the open air for half an hour each day, or one hour every other day, at the discretion of the jailer; and even for this half-hour he was to be taken out by the jailer as an animal might be led out at a show for outsiders to gaze at. This was too much for the spirit of Carlile to endure; he absolutely refused to leave his room in any such a manner, and as a consequence remained in his room for two years and a half without ever leaving it, rather than submit to such an insult. This will give the reader an idea of the indomitable spirit of the man. After this length of time he succeeded in getting this part of the sentence set aside, and he was allowed to walk out into the prison enclosure at his pleasure and very much to the improvement of his health. About a year after his incarceration, on reading of the treatment of Henry Hunt in Ilchester Gaol, he writes:—

"I have seen enough of gaols to be fully alive to the painful situation of Mr. Hunt, and since I have read of his present restrictions, I begin to feel myself in a palace, instead of a prison, or Bastille, as I occasionally call it. I am the better pleased with my treatment at this moment, as yesterday I was allowed to see a friend in my room for the first time, and I may add that now my sisters and my wife and children are allowed to visit me during the hours of nine to four each day. My room is large, light and airy, and far excels the state rooms of the King's Bench Prison. I have a sink and water-pipe and complete water-closet attached to the room, so that having provided myself with the necessary apparatus for both hot and cold baths, I have the enjoyment, nay, the luxury of these at pleasure; but when I mention my room and my baths, I can go no further, for the way in which I am locked up seems to me to be ridiculous, and I have had the honor to be a prisoner in the King's Bench Prison, in Newgate, in Giltspur Street Compter, and in the houses of the sheriffs officers (not for debt, but for libel). On entering the prison I told the keeper that as far as money would go to make me comfortable I would spend, but I was immediately informed that all money would do for me was to obtain me a good dinner *from*, not *at* the Governor's table. I viewed this as a secondary object, as I was ever careless about my food so that it was wholesome and sufficient. I also learned that all the fear was that of my corrupting the inmates of this most respectable place. I resolved then to economise and to teach temperance by example, and this I have done to their surprise, for I have shown them that a man with a contented mind and no labor, has need of but a small quantity of food to keep fat and in good health. Such has been the solitude of my confinement in this prison, and so little conversation have I had, that, on attempting to speak, I have in a manner found my voice gone, and have been obliged to make a great effort to be heard. I have a couch which forms a sofa-chair, and on which I consider that I lie sleeping, reading or thinking on an average sixteen hours a day, and I walk about the room or sit in a chair as a relief, excepting the few hours I spend at the writing desk. I am sensible that this is a bad habit, but I have no alternative. As my situation is at present I am quite comfortable, and I attribute the closeness of my confinement to the pretended horror which clerical and fanatical magistrates profess to feel at what they call sedition and blasphemy."

To add to the sorrows of this time came the news of the death of his mother. Carlile had always been a most loving and dutiful son, and he was deeply grieved. He realised fully that her death had been hastened if not caused by his present situation, and in the following letter one can trace the deep concern and regret which he felt. "The bravest are the tenderest. The loving are the daring."

"Dorchester Gaol, March 27th, 1820.

"Mr. A. Morrison,

"Dear Sir,—Soon after I received your parcel, and before I had determined how or when I should convey an answer to you, the post brought me the painful intelligence of the death of my mother. I was in a measure prepared for it, as I felt certain her vital energies were quite exhausted. On perceiving the letter sealed with black I threw it aside, and for four hours could not summon resolution enough to open it. But that painful moment has passed, and I shall only look back to express my gratitude to you and to Mrs. Morrison for the well-timed relief and consolation my mother has received at your hands since my confinement. I had hoped that her life might have extended a few years, that she might have witnessed the result of my present career, as I fear that as far as it has gone it has given her nothing but pain. I feel it to be a duty I owe you to thus publicly, as I have the means, to say that it is my firm belief that my mother would not have survived the first shock of my sentence and its consequence had you not poured the balm of consolation into her bosom. She could see no other source of dependence than myself, and I do not think she would have survived the first few hours that were necessary to convince her that all was not lost. Your kindness to me was more than friendship; you were not of the many hundreds who came to me in my prosperity to shake hands, to hold out specious promises, that I might command your services if ever I had need of them. You, of all my professed friends, you alone held out your hand to me when in prison, where our first interview took place. When I fell among thieves you were the good Samaritan. As my prospects began to look more cheerful, I had hoped that my mother would have lived a few years longer, that she might have felt the pleasure of that filial affection I have always felt disposed to extend to her both as my duty and my pride whenever I have had the means. It gives me pleasure to know that she fell calmly asleep, untortured by priests or superstitious notions. I consider it a duty not to look back except for gratitude or experience, and in doing this I feel that I am rivetted in my esteem of your friendship, and while we live I shall consider myself your debtor.

"I am, Sir,

"Yours with respect,

"Richard Carlile."

This gentleman and his wife were the first to send a contribution to Carlile in prison of £10 ($50), and continued their subscription under the name of "Alexander and Jane Littlehelp". These two most generous friends helped almost everyone who was persecuted for opinion's sake in the same bountiful manner. Mr. Morrison and Carlile were still corresponding as late as 1840, when Mr. Morrison died.

Carlile improved the opportunity of his life, i.e., his prison life, by a very thorough study of the origin of religions, more particularly that of the Christian religion. He procured by purchase or loan every known authority, and made himself the master of the subject. He perfected himself in grammar and in handwriting, having a complete system of this sent to him at Dorchester Gaol; and later when he was allowed visitors, had a writing-master come to the prison to instruct him. Some of his letters still extant, and which were written before his final illness, look almost like copperplate engraving. He also studied theology, political economy, history, phrenology, literature, etc. He turned the quiet and solitude of the gaol to good account. He conducted two weekly papers through the greater part of his term, and kept up a large and varied correspondence, besides making a thorough and critical digest and condensation of the old and new Testament in reply to the Rev. Thomas Hartwell Home's pamphlet on "Deism Refuted". This digest is to-day as useful and time-saving as ever to the student and seeker after truth. It was during the early year of this, his memorable imprisonment, that the disgraceful attempt to destroy Queen Caroline was made. This was the blackest of all the many villainies which were allowed to disgrace the reign of the Georges 3rd and 4th. Carlile espoused her cause from the first, not because she was a queen, but because she was a grossly maligned and persecuted woman. There were few who dared to declare themselves openly to be her defenders. Carlile used his pen with fearless vigor in her behalf, and did not hesitate to use the words of forceful truth against her persecutors. Having the confidence of many thousands of his own readers, he could, and did, do much to create the popular feeling and uprising of the people in her defence, to the everlasting dismay of her enemies, and of whom, next to her husband, the notorious Castlereagh was at the head. The story of this unhappy Queen is most pathetic as portrayed from week to week in the *Republican*, and of itself would, and no doubt has, filled the pages of more than one book. Yet the open defeat of her enemies and the complete exoneration of herself from all the villainous charges brought against her, did not ensure her either a peaceful or a long life. There were more ways than one of disposing of a person who stood in the way, however innocently, of designing persons, and she paid the penalty of her position in spite of her popularity.

The events occurring in Spain at that time, and the attempts that were then and there made for a free and representative government, gave subject and opportunity for many lively editorials on Carlile's favorite subject, "Republicanism", and left him, as he said, "neither an idle nor a dull moment, nor one to spare". To add to his duties and anxieties came frequent annoyances to Mrs. Carlile from the authorities in the form of threats of prosecution. She was frequently arrested, but her trials were as frequently postponed from time to time, only making matters more aggravating by their uncertainty. They were finally brought to an issue, and were laconically announced in the *Republican* thus:— "Trial of Mrs. Carlile. Verdict, as usual, Guilty!"

All these publications for which she was sentenced had been on sale for a long time without interference, except the twopenny "Mock Trial" sheets, and thousands were sold without any complaints being heard about them. The trouble was that Carlile's persecutors had fondly and foolishly thought that they had effectually silenced him for ever; and when the place at Fleet Street was reopened, and the business revived and carried on as briskly as ever, they were really at a loss to know what to do at first. It would never do to keep him in prison and allow the business for which he was punished to go on unmolested; so they proceeded against the wife as we have seen, and got judgment against her. Next they proceeded against the shopman, Mr. Davison, and got a judgment against him and sentence of imprisonment. But now comes Carlile's sister, Mary Ann Carlile, who had been quietly at work making herself familiar with the details of the business, so as to be able to take *her* place in the list of persecutions for opinion's sake, and letters began to pour in upon Carlile from scores of young people offering to supply the place of those removed, and in a very short time he had a long list of names of volunteers, ready for business or prosecution, it mattered not which.

CHAPTER VI.

SIR ROBERT GIFFORD AND THE ODIOUS "SIX ACTS"

As briefly set forth in a letter to Sir Robert Gifford, January 14th, 1820, on the new Acts of the Legislature intended to expel even the shade of liberty from this country (England):—

"My Learned Friend,

"I venture to address you by that common epithet so-much in vogue with those who profess to be opposed to each other in courts of law, and I pledge my word to you with just the same feeling. My views are not so confined, nor my mind so narrow, as to imagine that you have inflicted an injury upon me beyond the period of my confinement; on the contrary, I reflect with pleasure on all that is past, and congratulate myself that by your assistance I have sown the seeds of my future prosperity. The prominent part you have taken in bringing forward and supporting the late Acts of Parliament under the auspices of your patron and preceptor, Lord Castlereagh, has induced me to address you on their several bearings, and to show you how far they may be nullified. Let me first premise that, under the present state of public opinion, their nature and character is such as to render them short-lived. I will commence with 'The Traverse Bill', which is admitted on all hands to be the least obnoxious, as one clause of it has enacted a real benefit by taking away from your office that arbitrary and capricious power of suspending prosecutions over the heads of individuals to any length of time. In consequence of this Act, I shall have the satisfaction of making you acknowledge the abandonment of at least four informations that have been suspended over my head ever since the Michaelmas term 1817, or of bringing them immediately to trial. How far I shall succeed in making you give up or proceed with those half-dozen, or dozen others of later date, remains to be seen. I cannot quit this subject without saying that it will give me much pleasure to meet you often in the Court of King's Bench, and hope that your known dissent from the hypocritical professions of the day will further induce you to promulgate those sentiments that *you* privately and I publicly espouse. With respect to the intended effect of the Traverse Bill. As to accelerating trials for misdemeanors, there is some ground for complaint, because equal justice is not given to plaintiff and defendant to hasten on his trial, and for this the Bill has not provided; whilst on the other hand, he is debarred from the benefit of a delay. The excuse set up for this part of the Bill was, that I had protracted the time of my trial for near twelve months. This, Sir Robert, you know to be false, the delay was on your part, and on the part of your predecessor. I am inclined to believe that prior to the 16th of August, my prosecution was in some measure abandoned. Having been present at the Manchester meeting and narrowly escaped the sabres of the yeomanry, and got better through the truncheons of Nadin and his gang than some of the other attendants of that meeting; and lastly, having eluded the vigilance and search of the magistrates of that lawless town, I came to London and told the plain, unvarnished tale of the massacre committed by the yeomanry at the instigation of the magistrates. The necessity for getting rid of me was immediately resolved upon, that I might not in any instance give evidence on that subject. First, the project of bringing a charge of high treason against me was discussed and as soon abandoned, and the trial for the high-sounding charge of 'Blasphemy' agreed on, for the double purpose of getting rid of me as an evidence and of drawing

65

the public attention from the Manchester affair. The Traverse Bill, considered in its proper character, is merely a clause of 'the Blasphemous and seditious Libel Bill' put into a different shape, to hide the severity of the latter. 'The search for Arms Bill' and the 'Drilling and Training Bill' are enactments of the most hideous character, which nothing but the guilty fears of its projectors could have produced. The latter should have been entitled 'An Act for the encouragement of private malice'. 'The Seditious Meeting Bill' is another of those destructive measures that has brought England on a level with Algiers. The Bills relating to the Press are now to be considered. It is with those, Sir Robert, you have given us a specimen of your disposition to annihilate the liberty of the Press altogether, for we must look on those Bills, not as the act of Parliament, but as the act of the Attorney-General. I shall therefore proceed to make my observations on them, and begin with that which is intended to increase the punishment for whatever you may be pleased to call blasphemous or seditious libel."

After giving the first, second, and third clauses of the Bill, he comes to the fourth clause, which empowers the judges or magistrates who shall preside at the second conviction of the individuals for either blasphemous or seditious libel to use their discretion (!) in fining and imprisoning such individuals or of banishing them from the country.

The fifth clause enacts that a person so sentenced to banishment shall leave the country within thirty days, or in default thereof he will be seized and sent to such a place as the Government may propose.

The sixth clause makes liable to transportation to Botany Bay, the Hulks, or to similar penalty the individual who should be found in any part of the British dominions within the term of his banishment. The letter continues:—

"The last and most important Act is now to be considered, which is entitled, 'An act to subject certain publications to the duties of stamps upon newspapers, and to make other regulations for restraining the abuses arising from the publication of blasphemous and seditious libels', but is, in fact, an imposition of a duty on political knowledge and information, for the better preservation of ignorance amongst the laboring classes. There are some very unfair exceptions in this Act; for instance, every pamphlet written in defence of the Christian religion is exempt from the duty imposed by this Act, whilst every answer coming within the quantity of paper and price prescribed, is subject to it. For instance, Dr. Rudge* might address me on the evidences of the Christian religion in the *Christian Champion* for fourpence (8 cents), but I could not answer him in the *Republican* for less than sixpence (12 cents). These, Sir Robert, are your deeds, and they are worthy of you, for apostasy is always desperate and vicious in proportion to its former profession, while consistency at the same time becomes its mirror and object of attack.

What view your former patron had in pushing you forward is not for me to say, whether he was anxious to find an Attorney-General who should outstrip him in infamy whilst filling that office is best known to himself; but certainly, if that was his object, he has succeeded well. Your profession is certainly one that gives native genius an opportunity of displaying itself, and with a corresponding degree of spirit to reach the highest and most important offices of the State. Perhaps there never was an instance before of so young a man as yourself, or one who has been so short a time at the Bar, reaching the office you now fill, and on hearing your name announced for the office of Attorney-General I, with many others, was astonished at the promotion, knowing you by name only, as the man who was horsewhipped by Mr. Gurney, of Stannery Court notoriety, and your bringing a suit against him. In London you certainly were a briefless barrister. It was supposed that some one had discovered some lurking talent in you, and had been generous enough to push you forward. But how great was the surprise to find that you were destitute of talent as a lawyer, of grace as an orator, and of dignity as an officer of State. There are those who have affirmed that noble minds can proceed only from noble birth; as far as you are the object in view, this maxim is certainly verified, but it must be admitted that history affords us many exceptions to this rule. You, Sir Robert, in the absence of talent and of every requisite for your office and profession, have been fortunate enough to make up the deficiency by the assistance of a powerful friend. If Sir Vicary Gibbs had possessed no other personal means of bringing him out of Devonshire, and the western circuit, than Sir Robert Gilford possesses, both would have remained there to this day, the one a worn-out barrister, the other an attorney's clerk. But fortunately for you, your father had the means as a tradesman of assisting Sir Vicary Gibbs when in a state of penury, and a part of the contract was that you should be pinned on to his tail.

"R. Carlile.

"Dorchester Gaol,

"Jan. 10th 1820."

In a later letter to Sir Robert Gifford, Carlile says in a postcript:—

"I begin to fear that you and I shall never meet again in Guildhall. I mean to occupy the whole time of my imprisonment in preparing myself for the next defence of the 'Age of Reason'. If ever we meet again (in Court), I shall certainly detain you a month. I had calculated on at least ten days before, instead of three. But I had not studied my subject in the slightest degree; I kept everything to my natural feelings and a few hours' arrangement of books. I suffered myself, and foolishly, to be brow-beaten by Abbott. But the next time I will either make my defence or drive him out of Court, or he shall remove *me* from Court to finish the case."

Carlile dedicated the second volume of the *Republican* to Sir Robert in the sarcastic style which he always used in addressing him. I will give the dedication complete, as it is short, and so dismiss Sir Robert from our pages:—

"Dedication to Sir Robert Gifford, Knight, His Majesty's Attorney-General.

"Gratitude being one of the noblest traits in the character of animals, both rational and irrational, to whichever you may deem me allied, I feel that I owe it to you. I therefore embrace the earliest opportunity of dedicating a volume to you, in which I have had frequent occasion, most respectfully, to make allusions to your name and office. If I had followed the old and beaten track of troubling you with an adulatory application, begging your permission to accept this dedication, I am certain that it would have excited your ire to such a degree as to have occasioned a foaming at the mouth; equal to that which I lately witnessed in the Court of King's Bench. Therefore, considering that the soil of Devon has nurtured us both; that we sprang up at nearly the same time and under very similar circumstances, and that our relative situations in London has united us in an indissoluble tie, assuming a frank and friendly conduct, I have presumed to inscribe this second volume of the *Republican* to you as a token of my esteem and my sense of the high honor and benefit you have graciously bestowed on me. Should the Attorney-General be angry and think me over presumptuous, I am satisfied that Sir Robert Gifford will be pleased to have a volume dedicated to him which is replete with matter akin to his own feelings. You, Sir Robert, are amongst those who have taught us that a man, in office and out of office, forms two distinct beings, opposite both in nature and in principle; and I should not be surprised if, in the course of the revolutions of all that is natural, this country should adopt a representative system of government, or, in other words, a republican form, to find you filling some office to which your abilities shall be commensurate on the ground of your former boasted principles. It is a fact, daily demonstrated, that men who are eager to fill official situations never make principle a bar to obtaining them. It is but fair to say that when such men have a principle or attachment to a particular form of government, they are calculated to fill such a situation or office under that system with more satisfaction both to themselves and the public, but they are ever ready to sacrifice principle to interest. Since, Sir Robert, you cannot lay claim to eminence in this or any other degree, I am sufficiently charitable to lay aside the weapon of censure, and grateful to confine myself more to acknowledgment of the utility of your tergiversation towards him who prays that you may fill the office of Attorney-General as long as his Majesty or his heirs and successors shall grace the throne of Great Britain."

CHAPTER VIII.

THE VICE SOCIETY

"A letter to the Society for the Suppression of Vice (self-styled, and by no one else) on their prosecution of the editor and his wife, and the object they have gained by it, namely, an exhausted fund.

"Lords, Ladies, Gentlemen, Bishops, Priests, and Deacons, composing the secret society commonly called 'The Society for the Suppression of Vice'.

"It appears that you and I have come off like all other persons who go to law for justice: one with a ragged coat, the other with none at all, only with this difference, that I who am supposed to have been defeated have got the ragged coat, and you who crow on having defeated me have none at all. I did not attempt to notice your first advertisement begging for relief, and the means of proceeding in your warfare, and setting forth your pretensions and claims to public charity in glowing colors. I thought it probable from the nervous debility of poor John Bull that your warfare on what you call blasphemy, and about which you have made so much noise, might have so far terrified him as to fill your empty coffers, particularly as your advertisement was not repeated for the moment; but it now appears that your bait has not taken. To show you that I am really sensible of the benefit you have conferred on me, and the community at large, by the circulation of such an immense number of Deistical volumes and pamphlets, I shall give your advertisement a gratuitous insertion, and then proceed to compliment you a little further on your meritorious conduct towards myself and wife.

"'Advertisement.

"'"Society for the Suppression of Vice," Committee Room, January, 1820.—The Committee beg leave to state that within the last four years they have been compelled, in order to preserve the public morals from further contamination, to institute no less than eighty-five prosecutions against offenders of various descriptions, all of which have led to conviction or to recognizances by the respective parties, and must prevent the repetition of similar crimes. They have checked the sale of toys and snuff-boxes with abominable devices, which were imported from France and other countries, they have caused the whole stock in trade of some of the most shameless and abandoned traffickers in obscene books and prints, amounting to some thousands, to be seized, and have also destroyed no less than fifty extensive copper plates, from which impressions were from time to time supplied. And lastly, they have brought to condign punishment that most audacious offender, Carlile, who, notwithstanding repeated indictments found against him, still persisted in selling works of the foulest sedition and the most horrible blasphemy that ever disgraced a free press, or outraged the feelings and principles of a British public. The necessary expenses attendant on these measures have greatly exhausted the funds of this Society, but the Committee, etc., etc.

"'Subscriptions and donations are thankfully received by the treasurer, Henry Hoare, Esq., 37, Fleet Street, and by the secretary, Mr. George Pritchard, 31, Essex Street, Strand.'

"It appears that your Society, the names of the members of which you once published annually and ostentatiously, is now reduced to a mere cabal whose names you are ashamed to publish, and that all your business is transacted at the office of your secretary, Pritchard, the lawyer, who, next to myself, has gained more by your charges than any other person. It is notorious that all prosecutions emanate from that office at the instigation of that man, who condescends to drop further proceedings whenever the victim of the prosecution will pay him about £30, which is termed *expenses incurred*. It is further known that this accommodation has taken place more than once with the same individual, so that the preservation of the public morals is evidently but a secondary object with this secretary of yours. The first avowed object of your Society was to seek out the persons who were instrumental in disseminating obscene books and pictures. Had you confined yourself to this, no honest or moral man would have complained of or objected to your conduct as a Society. But you studiously endeavor to connect my publications with those which are justly termed obscene, for after enumerating exertions in putting a stop to the sale of those truly objectionable articles, and while I solemnly swear I never sold anything of the description or in any way connected with them, you in the very same sentence add: 'and lastly, they have brought to condign punishment that most audacious offender, Carlile'. Now what does all this argue? Why, that I, notwithstanding the indictments you obtained against me, could put my books fearlessly and openly in my window for sale, and that the most distinguished and the most virtuous women could come into my shop and put down their money for the 'Age of Reason' or Palmer's 'Principles of Nature', and publicly express their approbation of my perseverance. It was no sooner opened by the sheriffs officer to remove the goods six weeks after the seizure than a gentleman stepped in and said, 'I will give you twelve guineas for twelve copies of the "Age of Reason."' Then I ask what part of the British public I have corrupted? or whose feelings I have outraged?

It is your province to war with obscenity, mine with idolatry. I will now endeavor to show you where the advantage and disadvantage of your conduct towards me lies. I calculate that in consequence of the persecution I sold more Deistical volumes and tracts last year than I should have done in seven years in the ordinary course of business. The consequence was that I was prepared to meet all the violence that has been used on my property; and I leave you to judge whether it is not more than probable that, before the end of seven years, I or some other person shall be able to renew the publication of those works which are for the moment suppressed. Where will *you* be then? You will have to fight the same battle over again at a considerable expense on your part and a considerable profit on mine; besides, if once a jury pronounces a verdict of 'not guilty' on this question—and this requires but one honest man free from superstition to do this—the principle will spread like wildfire. But even admitting that none shall venture to publish those two volumes for which I am at present confined, what do we lose whilst the works of Gibbon, Hume, Voltaire, Volney, and fifty other authors of similar opinions are in full and rapid circulation? Your attempt to lay the pruning-hook to those publications will only redouble the vigor of the roots and remaining branches. Your attempt to impede the progress of truth and liberal opinion will have no other tendency than to detract from that merit and applause you would otherwise have obtained if you had confined yourself to the objects for which your Society was instituted. But your efforts to make blasphemy, or what you call blasphemy, a part of your game will only hold you up to public scorn as bigoted persecutors. In taking my leave of you I have to advise you not to remain under the scandal of being a secret society. Why do you not publish your names and the names of those subscribers of high rank and character you mention in your advertisement? You make profession of your own utility and laudable exertions; surely you cannot feel shame in publishing your names? I have been informed that Mr. Hedgher, who kept that celebrated brothel and sink of vice in St. George's Fields, for so many years called the 'Dog and Duck', is endeavoring to expiate his former conduct by becoming one of the most active and leading members of your Society. I have received this information from many different persons who are strangers to me, and who think it strange that such a man should be one of my prosecutors after living with and encouraging everything that was vicious and vile. The slight notice that I took last week of one of your right reverend Presidents must suffice for awhile.

"I remain

"Your grateful protege,

"Dorchester Gaol,

"R. Carlile.

"February 20th, 1820."

CHAPTER IX.

THE CATO STREET PLOT

We gather from the published statements of Carlile—statements which were never denied as far as we have been able to ascertain, and which were published within a few days of the occurrences having taken place—an inside view of this "alarming conspiracy", and interested readers will be able to draw their own conclusions. The story itself would trench upon the ridiculous were it not that the lives of several men were sacrificed to give coloring to its pretended genuineness. The occupation which Carlile found for the spy Edwards was comical when considered in the light of the supposed cause of Carlile's fines and imprisonment, i.e., the publication of Paine's "Age of Reason". The modelling of the statue of Paine was probably the most honorable work Edwards was ever engaged in. But here is the story as told by Carlile himself:

"A verdict has been obtained by the law officers of the Crown against Thistlewood on a charge of high treason arising out of what has been called the 'Cato Street Plot'. In taking notice of the affair at its rupture, I observed that the trials would prove that the ministers were the instigators of the entire business. I think this assertion has been fully borne out by the evidence adduced on the trial. Here are the particulars. Lord Harrowby' asserted that 'he had received an intimation of the projected assassination a month before the time of explosion'. An annunciation of a grand cabinet dinner appeared in the *New Times*, and that paper only. Edwards the modeller, who has been the spy and the agent of the Government, produced this announcement on the day of its publication to Thistlewood and others of the party, and recommended it as a good opportunity for their object.

This Edwards attended all their meetings, and was very active in preparing all the weapons of destruction. Whether Edwards was present in the loft or not at the time of the capture has not appeared, but it appears that he was the only individual who knew the retreat of Thistlewood, as he accompanied him to that retreat, and must have immediately made his communication to the police. In the list of witnesses Edwards was described as a resident of Ranelagh Place, whereas he has resided in Fleet Street for over the twelve months last past, and an apartment there has been taken for no other purpose than to mislead. The wife and children having continued to live on the third floor of the bookseller's at the corner of Johnson's Court,' Fleet Street, where he has resided since midsummer last, while he and some Bow Street officers have gone to Ranelagh Place in the daytime and just boiled a few eggs, etc., by the way of keeping possession of it. However, there is something too black between the ministers and Edwards to have him produced as a witness. The principal accomplice produced was Adams, who, it appeared, in conjunction with Edwards, lodged the weapons and ammunition at the lodgings of Tidd on the morning after the parties were arrested, and who no doubt were acting in conjunction with the police officers, as the latter reached there within a quarter of an hour of them. It appears that Adams had lately been discharged from the army to follow his business as a shoemaker the better to adapt him as a spy, or an instigator. Of Monument I shall say nothing, as it really appears that he was decoyed to Cato Street ignorant of the object about to be pursued. I am assured that if the manner in which this Cato Street conspiracy had been made to burst and to petrify the minds of the people, had not raised such a strong prejudice against the accused, the juries would have rejected the evidence adduced by the Crown with indignation. Thistlewood's counsel himself could not palliate some of his projects, and could give him no hope of escape from death on one of the indictments, but the charge of high treason should have required more respectable evidence of the plans and intentions of the parties. Another circumstance is much to be lamented, and that is that any other man should fall a victim to the insanity of Thistlewood. It may not be amiss to give a sketch of Thistlewood's career, which has been one of folly and madness. In the early part of the French Revolution he held a lieutenancy in the militia; from thence he exchanged into some regular regiment and went to the West Indies. He left the army and went to the United States; from this time can be dated the origin of those principles which have brought him to his present hapless state. From the United States he embarked for France, and remained in Paris during the whole of the career of the Robespierreian party, and has unfortunately shown himself, ever since, to be deeply impregnated with all the principles and the worst passions that disgraced the French Revolution and finally tended to destroy its benefits. From Paris he returned to London, and being quite a stranger to the political characters of that day, his return from France formed a groundwork of an introduction to many of them who were in the habit of assembling at the shop and house of Daniel Isaac Eaton, a bookseller in Newgate Street. I have met many of the old friends of Mr. Eaton, but could never learn anything of the general tenor of Thistlewood's conduct at that time, so that it appears to me that he was never sufficiently countenanced by any of them to form any intimacies. From this time up to the Spa Fields Meeting, I have no knowledge of how he spent his time, further than that he spent a considerable part of it, and considerable property, at the gaming table, and reduced himself to a state of indigence. I now proceed to notice the character of Edwards, and this I feel capable of doing, because I employed him as a modeller for several figures in the course of the last year or so. On my entering the house at

55 Fleet Street, I became the neighbor of Edwards, who previously held the little shop which Mr. Hone had occupied, and which bore the No. 55 1/2, as being part of 56. Edwards had no sooner become aware that I had taken 55 than he strenuously applied himself to become a tenant or lodger of mine, before I had the least idea of letting any part of the house. I had a strong dislike to his appearance, and gave him no hope of my receiving him as a lodger. The Attorney-General and the Vice Society soon enabled me to support the place without any lodgers, and I put Mr. Edwards off with the assurance that I should not rent any part of it. He was in the habit of coming into the shop to purchase my pamphlets, and I soon conceived the idea of having him model for me a figure of Thomas Paine. He expressed himself as quite anxious for the job, and observed that, being a great admirer of Paine's principles, he would be satisfied with a small price for it. On my wishing him to set a price, he proposed £5, which would just cover the expense he would be at, without including his time or abilities. This happened in the latter part of February or March. A few days later Edwards expressed a wish to have the money beforehand, and observed that it was usual with modellers. I hesitated, refused, and then offered him £1, which he accepted. A head, or bust, was soon ready, and I gave him three guineas extra for the copyright; but I could get him no further with the figure, although I had gone to the expense of the pedestal and other requisites for it, until the fall of the year. During the whole of this time he seemed to be in the most abject poverty, was obliged to give up his shop, and was never to be found at home. I urged him by continued messages to proceed with the figure, and in the month of September I got him to finish it, much to my satisfaction, and that of every other person who loved and revered the principles of Paine. Edwards was paid for the figure long before it was finished and set up, and altogether considerably in addition

to the first agreement. From this time he stuck very close to me on one pretence or another, followed me twice to Blackheath for the purpose of modelling my likeness on his own account, which he completed in the King's Bench Prison, without any apparent idea of making anything out of it. He pleaded great poverty, and twice solicited the loan of money from me. After finishing the figure of Paine, I as often refused, because his whole conduct had convinced me that he was both dishonest and ill-disposed. I had never the smallest idea that he was a spy. And as I knew him to be in the habit of running after Thistlewood and his party, I often asked him 'what project they had on foot', by way of a joke. It was Edwards who informed me that the person who visited me in the King's Bench Prison, in company with Davidson, was a spy, and that it was he who conveyed all the information to Lord Sidmouth and the Lord Mayor. Edwards was the fourth person who entered the room, and it struck me forcibly that there was a strange coolness and distance between these three, who had often met before. I never for a moment suspected Edwards to be anything further than an idle and dissolute fellow. I have some recollection of being accosted by Adams, the other spy. I was in the company of a Mr. Watling of the Strand, close by Mr. Sherwin's printing office, where I had been on business, when a tall shoemaker, with pieces of leather and other articles in his hand, accosted us, and said that nothing would afford him as much pleasure as our going to drink a glass with him, and hoped that his workman-like appearance would not disparage him in our eyes. I answered him that his appearance was by no means a disgrace to him, but that I never drank malt or spirituous liquors. If we would only sit in his company for a few minutes he would be satisfied. We entered the 'Shakespeare Tavern' at the corner of Smith Street, Northampton Square, when Adams introduced himself as having lately left the Horse Guards, and wishing to find out a society of good fellows, that he was a Yorkshire man, and had learnt of his friends the distress of the country, and the disposition of the people. He knew Mr. Watling and myself, but neither of us had ever seen *him* before. I should never have recollected the man or the circumstance had these trials not brought him to light, as we sat with him but a few minutes and heard what he had to say for himself. I saw him no more."

Carlile writes further on this matter on February 28th, 1820:—

"All that I can hear or collect on this business, for it is not worthy of being called a plot, is that a number of persons met armed in a certain hayloft, stable, etc., in Cato Street, St. John's Street, Marylebone, and that it was intended they should issue from thence and attack the house of Lord Harrowby in Grosvenor Square, where a Cabinet dinner was about to take place, and that someone communicated the particulars to the Earl of Harrowby in the morning of the day on which it was to have happened. I believe all this and much more. I have further heard that a party of police and military were ready to cope with these dreadful conspirators, by which a police officer was killed and many others wounded on both sides; that a coroner's inquest was held on the body of the policeman, and a verdict of wilful murder returned against Arthur Thistlewood and nine others, with many others by name unknown. I have also learned that one of the party has turned evidence for the Crown. The first thing which struck me forcibly was the conduct and character of R. Davidson, the more particularly for what has transpired between this man and myself. I had not been very many days in the King's Bench Prison after my trial before I received a letter filled with strong professions of attachment, the drift of it being an offer of 60 or 70 men of the same mind as the writer to affect my rescue, even at the hazard and sacrifice of their lives. It was signed 'R. Davidson'. The writer endeavored to make himself known to me by saying that he was the man of color who had sat with the committee consisting of Thistlewood and others for the purpose of managing a public entry for Mr. Hunt on his return to London from Manchester. This letter I burnt, and mentioning it to Mrs. Carlile, she immediately said that there had been such a man to the Fleet Street shop, who had said that no prison should long confine me. I had previously seen this man for a few short moments when visiting this committee to hand in a small sum of money which had been left with me for the purpose of helping to defray the expenses of the contemplated public entry of Mr. Hunt. I confess to great suspicion of this man, who claimed to be employed by Lord Harrowby; while in the room I heard this man say that Lord Harrowby frequently threatened to discharge him on account of his being 'a damned seditious fellow'. Not liking the appearance of things, I left the room as quickly as possible, though pressed to stay by this man and others. I had never seen this man before, and wondered at it as my situation in business made me acquainted with every man at all active in reform work of any kind. He called on me at the King's Bench and asked me what I thought of the project to liberate me? I told him I thought it was a very foolish project and no object could be gained by it, and that he and his companions should reserve themselves for a more useful and important purpose, and added, 'that if ever a real struggle for liberty should take place, I would not shrink from taking part in it'. He came again in company with a ruffianly-looking fellow, who breathed nothing but the most sanguinary destruction to his enemies or any one else who did not agree with him in his views. I gave them five shillings towards the expenses of a meeting to be held in Finsbury the following Monday, and with an awkward apology for taking money from a prisoner, and on finding themselves interrupted by someone coming in the room, they left the room as Edwards entered. The latter expressed his surprise and suspicion of these visitors after they had gone, and I heard nothing more of them till this new plot of Cato Street was discovered (?). As soon as the terror which these things excite has subsided a little, and the alleged conspirators are put on their trial, the public will begin to see the whole thing in its proper light. It it well known that the Ministers had the means of bringing Thistlewood to trial for a seditious conspiracy fifty times since his acquittal for high treason, but this would not suit their purpose; they have encouraged him to go on, continually surrounded by their agents. Mr. Stafford, of Bow Street, made an observation in 1817 or 1818 to the effect that they could lay hold of Preston or Thistlewood at any time, but these were not the men wanted; there were others of more importance and more danger to the Government. Although I have not the most distant idea that Thistlewood ever took a farthing from the Government, yet he has made himself just as useful to them as if he had done so, and the Ministers, by sending their own instigators amongst these men, have quite directed the conduct of Thistlewood to suit their own purposes on whatever charge they were tried. I hope for their acquittal, and any statement made here is not intended to operate against them, but to show that the Ministers themselves are at the bottom of all the 'plots' that have lately made so much noise. Some other facts were brought out at the trials which caused the case to look dubious, to say the least, one of which was that there was but one entrance to the place, and that though surrounded by both police and soldiery, some one or two were permitted to escape, while one or two others surrendered at once. One man alone was killed, and that one a policeman who rushed upon a man who had a drawn sword, and who warned the policeman to keep off."

It is said that Thistlewood himself escaped through the only door; however, he and seven others were afterwards apprehended and arraigned for high treason. Thistlewood, Davidson, Ings, Brunt, and Tidd were hung for their part in the conspiracy, and it is but just to their memories to say that they met their fate bravely and coolly.

After the unfortunate ending of this miserable affair and the deaths of the misguided men, Carlile addressed the following letter to the wife of Davidson, expressing his regret for having possibly wounded her feelings in his remarks about her husband which were printed in the *Republican* (Vol. 3, No. 2).

A letter to Mrs. Davidson, widow,

"Madam,—I feel it a duty incumbent upon me to endeavor to make you a reparation for the painful feelings my late observations on your husband must have occasioned you. To the person who accompanied your late husband to me in the King's Bench Prison, I shall address a private note, as his name has not been made public, I consider it sufficient. In making the observations for which I now feel the deepest regret, I mentioned that a fourth person entered the room whilst your husband and his companion were present, and that this fourth person expressed his surprise at the presence of my visitors, intimating that they were strongly suspected of being the spies and agents of the Government. This fourth person was the infamous Edwards, whose object, no doubt, was to lay the same trap for me in which he has been but too successful with others. As your husband was quite a stranger to me, and as I had noticed his zeal towards me on two former occasions with suspicion, that suspicion from the suggestion of Edwards became very strong, and led me to look at him in a very different light to what I now view him in. The bursting forth of the unhappy affair of Cato Street filled me with the same surprise and astonishment with which it must have filled every other person, and I was most anxious, and felt it to be most important, to avert the stream of horror which flowed from it, and to throw it back on those who had planned and instigated the whole scheme. I knew Ings from September last up to the time I left London. The man had unfolded his distress to me, and I knew at that time that he was totally unconnected with any political party whatever, and almost a stranger in London. I was sorry to see him drawn into that hopeless condition, as I was convinced some friends had taken advantage of his hopeless condition and despair. But little did I think that villain, Edwards, was the spy, agent, and instigator of the Government, and Mr. Davidson his victim. I now regret this error, and hope you will pardon it as an error of the head without any bad motive. Be assured that the heroic manner in which your husband and his companions met their fate, will in a few years, perhaps in a few months, stamp their names as patriots and men who had nothing but their country's weal at heart. I think as your children grow up they will find that the fate of their father will rather procure them respect and admiration than the reverse. Accept the small sum of £2, as an acknowledgment of my injury to you. It is all that my present circumstances allow me to offer you. Should it be my lot to fill any situation in life where I might be able to render any service to you or your children, you may at all times command my attention. With a due feeling for your distressing situation,

"I am, Madam,

"Your obedient servant,

"Richard Carlile."

This shows the kindliness of Carlile's heart towards a poor widow, whose husband, a poor colored man, had really no claim whatever upon him save that of sympathetic humanity.

CHAPTER X.

HOW THE BATTLE WAS FOUGHT

During the imprisonment of the batch of shopmen who volunteered to enter the service of Carlile and sell the prosecuted works, many letters passed between him and them. I have, however, only those of Mr. H. V. Holmes. The correspondence, from which I make extracts, continued long after the persecution ceased; but here I have to do only with those that shed some light on the events which were then transpiring. Not one of these letters was intended for publication, yet every one would bear it as far as the writer was concerned. Carlile had no secrets of his own, but was the custodian of many of other people's.

The subjoined extracts show the spirit which animated both chief and men.

"Dorchester Gaol,

"January 15th, 1822.

"Mr. Holmes,

"Sir,—That your name and former conviction is known to the Bridge Street gang I have no doubt, and that you will be in the power of the enemy as to banishment agreeable to their 'Six Acts' is equally certain, if they get another verdict. Your plan must be the same as Dolby's, to challenge the whole panel or array of jurymen on the ground that they were returned by Alderman Garratt, one of your prosecutors. The same thing must be done on the part of Berkely, Rhodes, and Byerly whenever the attempt be made to bring them to trial. I admire your spirit, and will endeavor to support it as matters stand now; but had I known the peculiar situation of yourself and wife, I should have hesitated before I accepted your services. My business is precarious and not to be depended on, considering the strength of the enemy against whom we fight. I will stand my ground as long as there is another man, woman, or child to stand by me to be found; but if Castlereagh makes new laws I can say nothing more till I see what they are. I am stronger now than at any period of the war, and have no fear but that even under present laws I shall increase in strength. Respecting your defence, I have only to say that I like best the open avowal of principle if trial becomes inevitable. But I have no objection whatever to you pursuing the course prescribed by your friends if you think it will be more advantageous. If you are the first banished I shall envy you, as I had made up my mind to that honor, although I must have two more trials first. If they could banish me by the first trial, I should be had up immediately, as I have information that the matter has been canvassed in the enemy's councils. Whatever way you make your defence let it be bold and energetic. I think the open avowal of principles will be best for you, as anything short of that cannot excite the same interest in the public mind. You have a wide range for defence in the pamphlet, it embraces every topic; if I can assist you let me know. I am at command, but not upon any principle called Christian.

"Yours respectfully,

"R. Carlile.

"Mr. H. V. Holmes,

"Newgate, London."

"Respecting your recognizances, if any fee was demanded from me here, I should refuse to pay it; I successfully refused it when I left Giltspur Street Compter. It must be that which Stevens alludes to when he says 'I did not behave like a gentleman', for I paid him 4s. ($1) a day for as plain a board as I ever saw on table. At that time I was continually being arrested, and I thought it prudent to spend as little as possible under such circumstances. He expressed himself as perfectly satisfied with what I gave him, though I did not give him a gratuity as turnkey; I saw no occasion for feeing the turnkeys..... Since you have left London, Griffin has gone to prison, and is shut up in Holborn, and the *Dwarf*, you will have seen, is dead. We must not die, and as to prison we have had enough of it. I am fully sensible that you will have to struggle hard to enlighten the people of Sheffield; I know that the present generation of them are a dull mass..... I am glad to hear that Mrs. H. had resolved to brave prosecution had you been again prosecuted. This is the only way to succeed. Had Mrs. Carlile flinched, my business would have gone to wreck, for I verily think that there would have been no volunteers but for Mrs. C. and my sister going one after the other. It gave a sort of zest to the thing, and everything has gone well since.

"I am afraid you will be prosecuted from the rage carrying on in London. Young Hassell has gone up from this neighborhood; I understand the fourth was arrested on Monday last for No. 17, vol. 9, of the *Republican*. The fifth entered on Tuesday, but I have not yet heard of his arrest.. On Tuesday a seizure was made for taxes, but the thieves were soon dismissed with payment. So you see that we shall want a mint of money to stand against them. The plan we proceed upon in London is to withdraw the article from sale for which the last (volunteer) was arrested, so as to make them prosecute each person for a new article. This is better than having them all prosecuted for the same article, though three of them are already fixed for Paine and Palmer. If in Sheffield you have any volunteers to go to London, let me know."

"Dorchester Gaol, March 22nd, 1822.

"I wish to know if any difference is made between your treatment and that of Rhodes. Hard labor in this gaol means nothing at all, particularly before they had a treadmill up for grinding corn, and that is not hard labor in my eyes, as I have seen, and felt, what hard labor is. I do not think there can be much to do in Giltspur Street Compter, although I know they have a mill of some sort there. I can only hope that the doors of your prison will be open to you before 1824. I think they will; a revolution in France would produce one here immediately to a certainty. Our friend, the Devil, will work one here. Be so good as to state what the prison allowance of food consists of for a week with you. As your work is mere play or pastime, I think it will not be worth while to complain of it at present. However, I will do it if you wish.... I return you 'The Solace', I would advise you as I have just advised my friend Smithson, of Leeds, to check the poetic muse; I do not like to see good common sense in rhyme. It does not need it. I intend to exclude all poems from the columns of the *Republican* after this volume. I am not a poet and have no taste for it; but I know that it requires something very good on this head to please the public.... I see by the papers that Boyle has again refused his name to the Court, and again been remanded. I cannot get a lawyer to do anything for me on my plan, and to let them take their own course is the Devil! I even fear I shall not be able to get a motion made for the sale of that property of mine by auction which is in the possession of the robbers."

"May 14th, 1822.

"You will see your 'Reasons for Disbelief' in the Republican this week. I expect to put your name to it, for such a creed, when you speak of having been a Methodist preacher, will not do without.... Should I lessen my expenses by the release of George Bere, I shall add two shillings a week to your, Rhodes, and Boyle's income. I was no party to the first fixing of it at five shillings, and never thought it enough. Wedderburn I believe to be a worthy character as far as principle is concerned, and after such a severe imprisonment as he has had, I feel it my duty to help him on to some of the comforts of life, if possible. If I were in London I would act very different to what I do now toward those who stand by me. I have now others to please as well as myself, and I find difficulty in doing justice to all and pleasing all at the same time.... If you were once to look at the weekly mass of writing that I do, you would never complain of being neglected. I do believe that your heart is bound up in the cause I am advocating, and you shall see that I will do everything possible to enable you to act upon those feelings when a better opportunity arrives."

"July 22nd, 1822.

"Say to Boyle that I am glad he refused to sign the petition. It was only an intrigue of some individual to acquire a little *éclat* in the House of Commons upon the matter. Let them come manfully forward and move for the release of all prisoners prosecuted at the instance of the prosecuting association; and then an assistance or interference would be worth giving. I have often wished that Dr. Watson would turn bookseller and defend some important work in a Court of Law. He will never get out of his poverty in this country without some such step. Gale Jones, who is such a brilliant orator, has dragged through a life of poverty entirely from the want of resolution to exhibit his talents where they would serve him. There is something original in your critique on the '39 Articles', because I am not aware that they were ever handled in that way before. I have been obliged to notice them in Mrs. Wright's speech for November, but I have gone on an entirely different strain to yours. After you have seen that speech it may induce you to re-write your critique and introduce some of those contradictions. For instance, the first article says, 'God is without a body' and composed of a substance, and the indivisible Trinity is divided twenty ways in the course of the articles. We read of 'parts' of a partless bodyless body. Such an abuse of language is scarcely to be found in the Bible as the 39 Articles contain.... This God without a body, parts, or passions, took flesh, bones, and everything appertaining to the perfection of man's nature into Heaven, and made a fourth part of what was before a 'Trinity'. Oh, Christians and Christianity! It is really, and speaking seriously between you and myself, the grossest mythology that was ever practised upon the credulity of mankind. A really free press and free uninterrupted discussion would annihilate it in one year throughout Europe."

"September 19th, 1822.

"Your chaplain is, I think, taking considerable pains to convert you back to his creed. There are half-a-dozen of them belonging to this gaol. They took considerable pains with Mr. Wedderburn, but have been very shy with me. I have published almost every word that has passed between us. I shall leave my prison more thoroughly impressed with the truth and importance of my principles than when I entered it."

"August 26th, 1823.

"Nothing will afford me greater pleasure than to see you all who have been imprisoned on my account turning out bright men. The first thing required is a resolution to be strictly moral, the second to fill up your time well, and be industrious at everything useful. I have no fear but I shall be able to make quite a change in public opinion about myself in another year. I am fully determined to write myself out of prison by my pen, if I do not get out otherwise. I am now carrying on some pretty work with the parsons. I have written to five since Sunday morning in answer to different points. I shall let none of them rest."

"September 8th, 1823.

"I should have no objection to buy Burnett's History if you can assure me against one thing: that they are the real property of the person who sells them, that is to say, if they are honestly come by. This is a necessary caution, as no bargain would induce me to deal with a man who had been sent to the Compter for theft.... Respecting the new prison act, I am sure that my savage keepers cannot alter my treatment for the worse. I am harassing them to make it better. I sent an invitation to Peel to come and see how I was treated; I also sent an invitation to old Eldon to bring the Bishop of the Diocese with him, or any clergyman he liked, that I might give him proofs that no man could defend the Christian religion as a matter of morality or law. They are both in this neighborhood. I will soon publish a heap of the squibs that I have thrown at the priests and others in this neighborhood. Some of them are quite amusing. I feel myself master of them, and they tacitly acknowledge it.... I have been informed that some one has been fishing for more prosecution, but I doubt whether they will take more after Frost and Jones are tried. The gangs are evidently sickened, and now they talk of writing me down. I wish they might be resolute enough to attempt the matter. I think a great deal about Reig; sometimes that he will be destroyed, again that he will not be. But if he is, some of the Faith men will pay dear for it on a future day."

"December 9th, 1823.

"I have not a doubt but that the smuggler Waters was purposely sent to London with a report of my madness. A viler gang of villainous aristocrats is nowhere to be found than this country produces. I very much desire to know who carried this tale among the prisoners, as the rule in this gaol is to keep everything secret, not to let the prisoners of one yard know what is doing or being done in the others.... I am sorry to hear from Boyle that Mrs. Holmes did not like going to Sheffield. This will be the D———l if she continue in the same mind, for you can only succeed by both pulling hard in one way——— Mrs. C——— has often opposed my projects; but I will say this for her—that when she saw I was determined, she would assist after her fit of anger was over."

"I expect to hear every day that you are arrested in Sheffield; but it is possible this London battle may be decisive. Rather than give in I will send for you and Mrs. Holmes too, as if I cannot stand in London there will be dire persecution throughout the country. I have sent your last to print in a most daring address to the old Chancellor, but such as becomes him and me to offer him. Excuse haste; I am writing defences" [for the shopmen then under arrest].

"June 5th, 1824.

"Enclosed is what Mrs. Ellison wished. I have now a fine head of hair—it has been growing all winter—and I can supply a hundred such locks if they are worth anything, or gratifying to anyone. I never set my mind on trifles like these."

"August 2nd, 1824.

"Mrs. T. R. Perry is now in the shop, and after her is another female ready, with men in abundance."

In speaking of a placard about him that had been posted up in Norwich to advertise a tract against him, he says:—

"The author found that he had sold 14 in a fortnight. There is nothing in it that impeaches my conduct. My little egotistical vagaries are only matters to be laughed at, and, as I have just been telling our High Sheriff Garland, are put forth theatrically, to produce an effect upon the audience."

Holmes wants to become a printer of liberal works, and Carlile tells him how to go about making himself one; then, speaking of the *Newgate Magazine*, he writes of applying some money sent to him for the purchase of paper for this magazine, and says:—

"This work is to be wholly their own. Hassell will make a prime fellow with the pen. Clark is an animated Bible. He has compiled the 'Scripturious creed', which I will give to you to print the moment you have types. Another pamphlet I have for you is the 'Life of Paine'. In addition to what others give you to do, I will fill up the time of a journeyman until you are a perfect printer. I sent Sheriff Garland and Abbott (Chief Justice) a *Republican*. Garland came with his niece and daughter and sat down with me for half an hour, the gaoler remaining in the back-ground all the time unnoticed. Garland wanted me to get out by making some little formal apology; but I told him, 'No! I was determined to fight it out'. 'Well,' said he, 'I suppose we must consider you a political Luther.' I thought the gaoler would have spit fire at me this morning for my compliment of last week. Such a look for Cruikshank!"

Speaking of his printer and the difficulties he finds in getting the *Republican* and other work done, he says:—

"I have a tickler in this week's for a visiting magistrate, only Moses (his printer) generally accommodates me with about forty errors to an issue."

This Moses was a man whom Carlile taught or had taught in his own office, and he it was who printed the whole of the *Republican*, though his name never appeared. So in view of the good work he helped on through his printing of the prosecuted volumes, we must forgive him the small (!) matter of "forty errors to an issue", though it must have been a fearful and most aggravating annoyance to Carlile.

November 25th 1824.—Carlile says in a letter of this date:—

"We have had a hurricane on this coast such as never was known before. I felt quite comfortable at being in such a strong building. Parson Richman, the chaplain of the Dorchester Gaol, and his wife were killed in bed by the falling in of the roof and chimney. The damage done to the houses immediately before the sea is incalculable. It has nearly destroyed every beauty of Weymouth. Several hundreds of people killed by falling houses or drowned, and yet the Christians call this a dispensation of

Providence. I am glad that I am out of such a concern. But we are on the wrong side of good luck at 84 Fleet Street, though the Christians are quite savage that we are not nearly so bad off as our neighbors. I fear we shall be jostled out of 84. The City Surveyor is set to work to condemn our house as unsafe. The second I conjecture was a Christian fire....

That second fire was certainly planned for the purpose, because the fire engine belonging to the office in which our house has its insurance had left, and as soon as it had left the fire broke out. I really think the house is in danger, as long as it stands alone as it now does.... I have very little hope of keeping 84. The Saints are trying every scheme to get the house down, and I fear they will succeed; if so, we shall be out of the shop by the New Year."

"May 4th, 1825.

"I have just had an interview with my gaoler to witness my signature to an agreement about my house and liberation.

He is the most foul fellow that I ever looked upon. He ought not to have been born outside of the pale of the Inquisition."

"June 14th, 1825 [On the Rev. Robert Taylor.]

"I noticed the Vice Society advertisement, sent and bought their book, and am about to print it in the *Republican*. Rumor says they are consulting about prosecuting Taylor (Rev. Robert). He is a handsome fellow, a first-rate orator, and bewitches by his face and his tongue some very smart ladies. His meetings are crowded with fashionable ladies, and he is doing a deal of good."

"October 3rd, 1825.

"I doubt you being indicted at the Sessions. If so, you can traverse to Epiphany, and perhaps for a pound or two remove it to the Bench, that is to your county assizes. This would be better than being confined at present; you should not have admitted the law as being against, to the curate. There is no such law. It is all a fiction. There cannot be a law for anything of the kind, for it is not an offence against public morals. Should you come to trial, don't forget to say that the British Government in India sanctions all such exhibitions. I saw an account of some speechifying at a missionary meeting lately where they begged money because Indian children made images of clay, etc., and cried them about as 'Gods' a penny apiece. We have proofs that Haley has sent in a crying recantation to Peel. I see plainly there is nothing too base for this fellow to do. If Peel liberates him we shall have a pull upon both by showing that no one but a rascal can find Christian mercy and grace."

October 11th 1825.—In this letter we can get an idea of how Carlile kept things stirred up in the gaol for both the inside and outside authorities, for this reason I give a little longer extract than usual.

"I shall be very glad to see Mrs. H. at Dorchester, yet I doubt if I could get her free admission. I had a hard fight to get Mrs. Wright admission. The gaoler tried to interrupt it. I wrote to a magistrate, he to the gaoler saying he saw no impropriety in it, but left it to the gaoler. The fellow yielded after saying, 'It was not to be a precedent'. He would not let her write her name to me in the office of the gaol, she had to go back to town to do so; I don't believe you yet when you say he was civil to you. He is the greatest ruffian I ever saw in any kind of office. There is war and rumor of war in the gaol just now. This is session week, and I am about to make a report to the magistrates against the gaoler. I sent up the complaints of the smugglers to the Lords of the Treasury in August. I found out on Saturday that it had made a noise all around, and back, and forward. Their lordships sent it to Peel, and he down to the Magistrates. Mine was a most curious letter to the Treasury; if I make any more noise out of it, I will print it. To be revenged they turned away my favorite turnkey and his wife; they told them they might thank me for it. I was sorry to see them go, but they have been going on their own account for a long time, and I know they would not have stayed after I left. After it was known that he was going the goaler would not let them come to see me, out of his sight. To-day I sent out an open letter calculated to mortify the fellow if he looked into it, inviting the turnkey and his wife to visit me as friends and visitors.

"There are about twenty *Republicans* a week well read in this town now, which I consider a smart circulation for such a place. This is a great mortification to the enemy, but not a word of complaint is heard of it, though the turnkeys have to deliver several of them.... There is a great deal of difference between moral and physical courage; I consider myself a hero on the former ground, but never having been tried, I hardly know what I should be as one storming a breach, and yet sometimes I think in a good cause I could raise enthusiastic courage. I certainly never felt anything more than prudent fears or the fears of prudent caution; but circumstances often form courage as well as the other qualities of the man."

CHAPTER XI.

FIRE AND INSANITY

Some time after Mrs. Carlile's release, while living at 84, Fleet Street, a fire broke out next door to them, and communicated to their shop and warehouse. Mrs. Carlile and children were taken out of the house from the second storey window, and escaped injury except the fright and nervous shock. The stock of books and pamphlets, though injured by water, were mostly saved and carried into St. Dunstan's Churchyard near by. The fire spread all around them, but their building was left standing, and after the excitement subsided, Mrs. Carlile moved back again. It was almost the only building left standing on the street. As soon as the fire engine had left the scene a deliberate attempt was made to burn Carlile's house down; a fire was actually kindled on the floor of the warehouse, but was discovered in time to prevent further damage. His enemies seemed to be enraged that his house should escape when so many others were destroyed. This seemed to be one of those occasions when Divine Providence was on Carlile's side. However, they did finally succeed in getting him out of his quarters by getting the house condemned as unsafe, as, indeed, Carlile himself deemed it. Standing alone that way, they were in great danger from some fanatical incendiary setting fire to it in the night. So that in the beginning of the year they leased new quarters.

The last effort that was made by Carlile's enemies to destroy his power was to send out a report of his having gone raving mad, and while this attempt was as futile as the rest, the report caused terrible anxiety on the part of his friends. Carlile had more than once warned the readers of the *Republican*, his family and his friends, that in case he were found dead in his room never to believe any report of suicide, for on no account would he take his own life. In this way he headed off any villainy of this kind that might be contemplated. This ruse of violent insanity was an afterthought on the part of the officials.

During the latter half of Carlile's term of imprisonment he received many private warnings of plots which were hatching to dispose of him quietly, and so relieve his enemies of his charge. The most notable one was that of Francis Place, who becoming aware that the subject of his removal by poison had been canvassed, wrote to Dorchester Gaol and begged Carlile to eat nothing that was not prepared by himself or in his presence. Carlile rather scouted the warning at first, saying that the prison authorities would not dare to do such a thing, and deeming himself too strong a man with the public for his persecutors to defy them, and attempt his assassination. Francis Place in the next letter asked Carlile significantly if he thought himself a stronger man than Napoleon, or stronger in public favor than Queen Caroline, thereby intimating his opinion of the cause of the deaths of these two celebrated characters. Mr. Place begged him to procure a pint of antimonial wine, and to take a dessert spoonful on the least sign of anything in the way of distress or pain in the stomach. Carlile did this, and also prepared all his food with his own hands. The precautions made it difficult for such a measure to be carried out even if attempted. This, however, was not the only danger of the kind which Carlile had to incur. There was a conviction abroad that measures to finally dispose of him were canvassed in the secret councils of the Government, and that a volunteer for this dastardly purpose was called for and found. The failure of the attempt was due solely to the coolness and calmness of the intended victim. Carlile had been always prepared for destruction in some way, and knew also that the importance to the authorities of his destruction was such that they could not fail to reflect upon it. A very slight pretext was found to be sufficient on which to make a very bold attack upon his life. It was carried out in the following manner. In the first place the reader must be informed that the rules of the prison were that every prisoner should have sufficient "air and exercise"; and again confinement to their own cells, with permission to walk in some courtyard singly, is the degree of solitary confinement the *most severe* in the ordinary discipline of the prison. But Carlile's imprisonment was more severe than this most severe discipline through a period of four years. In making an effort to get these unlawful severities modified, Carlile, in a letter to Robert Peel (afterwards Sir Robert), made use of the following expression: "Unless my treatment is changed in this gaol, I must make war," which simply meant in his case that he would appeal to those higher in authority, or else to the people at large through the medium of the *Republican*, for it is not to be supposed that he was going to kill the turnkeys who waited upon him, with whom he was on the best of terms; and, too, the expression itself was a common one with him, "making war" meant with him attacking, exposing, and denouncing unjust men or measures publicly, by his pen only, and it was out of the question that it could mean anything else. The only thing beside this that he could do would have been to set fire to his own room, which would probably have only resulted in his own death; he would indeed have been insane to do this. However, his words were fastened upon to serve the purpose of his enemies. The next day word was sent up to London and the report was printed in all the morning papers that "Carlile had gone raving mad", and had to be put in irons for his own safety and that of others, thus preparing the minds of the people for any account of his death that might be likely to follow. It was a pretty scheme, and struck terror to the hearts of his family and friends, but the details show that he was more than a match for his persecutors and their wiles. On November 24th, 1823, Carlile was visited by the chaplain and a visiting magistrate, who told Carlile that the sole object of their visit was to get him to make some suggestions as to what he considered a proper place to be allowed to walk in in the daytime. Carlile told them he would be content with the smallest courtyard in the place. The chaplain commended the reasonableness of his expectation, and assured him that the sheriff was coming to satisfy it.

The next day the gaoler entered Mr. Carlile's room accompanied by the high sheriff, Henry Charles Sturt, in manners and appearance a mere boy—a "strutting puppy", an "ignorant aristocrat" as Carlile described him—who, after the customary "How d'ye do?" turned to Carlile and said, "You would have been liberated long ago, Carlile, if you had submitted". "Submit to what?" asked Carlile. There was no reply, but the Sheriff showed signs of rising choler. He drew a chair and sat down; the gaoler sat himself down on the sofa-bed, while Carlile sat at the side of the table opposite to the Sheriff. The Sheriff began by remonstrating about what Carlile had been saying outside and inside of the gaol about his treatment. He grew warm as he proceeded, expressed offence at every observation made to him by Carlile, and soon made him aware that he had come on anything but an amicable errand. Carlile kept his temper and sat perfectly cool and collected, and calmly awaited the storm that was about to break. Sturt, after proceeding gradually to his object, drew a paper from his pocket in which was an extract of Carlile's from a letter written to one of the officials. He then asked Carlile if he considered his life in danger, and if he would act upon the threat there made of "making war as a consequence of that treatment ". Carlile replied, "Yes!" that was his resolution. Then he saw the arrangements which had been made. The Sheriff nodded to the gaoler, saying, "Call them in!" Two turnkeys entered. The Sheriff then ordered them to "secure Mr. Carlile, and put handcuffs upon him ". The turnkeys did this, Carlile offering no resistance, merely saying, "I see your object, so shall not resist; I know you cannot keep me long in irons". He knew that their object was to irritate and urge him on to some unguarded act of violence. Carlile never moved from his chair, but sat calmly eyeing them, and altogether unruffled. The order was given to search the prisoner and the room. The gaoler, Andrews, was now in his element, and everything was ransacked. Nothing was found but what every prisoner of state might be supposed to have about him. The Sheriff and gaoler were evidently disappointed, even to confusion. Carlile sat calmly looking on; he expressed his satisfaction at what they were doing, saying that it was the villain alone who trembled to have his designs investigated. Saucepans, coffee-boiler, frying-pan, snuffers, hearth-brush, tin oven, pie-irons, penknives, tableknives and forks, dumbbells, razors, nearly everything—even to the veriest trifle—was taken away. Carlile pointed out to them, as a proof of their purposes, that the iron fender and fire-irons were left, which were the only really offensive weapons in the room. This occupied three hours, and after all was done the handcuffs were removed. During these three hours the gaoler spent the first and third hour in the room; the second hour was devoted to the burial of his mother, who was lying dead at the time. This shows the character of the man quite sufficiently, and lends a ludicrous appearance to a very solemn matter. The rest was simply fun for Carlile, and served to lighten the monotony of prison life. He declared the excitement did him good. Determined, as he said, to make the fellows look the greatest fools possible, the next morning he set to work and got a bill of fare for the turnkey: beefsteaks, onions, pepper, mustard, potatoes, raisins, flour, suet, and eggs-He ordered them to bring him those things, and bring them uncooked; he had been living on bread and water as an experiment after his sister had left him, but he wanted to try if the gaoler would refuse him the means of cooking. The turnkey brought the things with his letters and newspapers as usual. The chaplain came up to pump him a bit as to what he was going to do, and recommended "a light wire broiler to dress his steak". "No!" said Carlile, "the gaoler shall send me the cooking utensils again ", and he did one by one, the turnkeys bringing them and standing guard while he used them. He told them he must have all the saucepans, for hereafter he was going to live like a gentleman and have half-a-dozen meals a day, at least as long as this game lasted. Nothing was said about a knife and fork. The saucepan from lying unused had grown rusty, so one of his guards was dispatched to get it mended, while the other watched the frying-pan. He set about making a plum-pudding, chopping the suet with an ivory paper-cutter and mixing the ingredients on a plate; but he had no pudding-cloth, and had to choose between a night-cap and a shirt. The night-cap was preferred, and he claimed that no one could object to eating a piece of that plum-pudding. The process of cooking occupied three hours, during which time he had two guards in attendance. Had he not been afraid himself of over-eating, he said he would have kept them twenty-four hours. He kept up this amusement for a week or so; it was fun for him and aggravation to the gaoler and Sheriff, and yet strictly within the rules of the prison.

The report sent to London gave out that Carlile had gone raving mad, and that the Sheriff, Magistrates, gaoler, and turnkey were gone to his room with ropes to tie him down; even stating afterwards the particulars of how the ropes were placed in the tying down process. Carlile anticipated this rumor of insanity, by a sort of instinct, and walked out early next morning through the gaol yards, and showed himself to the other prisoners, so that they could testify to the falseness of the report. It so happened that the smuggler who carried the report to London was housed at the Newgate prison, where the shopmen of Carlile were serving their various terms. They were almost panic-stricken at first at the terrible fate of their chief. But a characteristic letter from himself to his wife was speedily forwarded to London, and allayed their fears. After a day or so, not receiving his cooking utensils back, he addressed a burlesque petition in behalf of the various articles seized, and addressed it to Henry Charles Sturt.

This petition was written in order to make the authorities look foolish, as they no doubt felt after the fiasco just enacted.

CHAPTER XII.

FREE DISCUSSION.

Simple as is the sound of the words "Free Discussion", there is not in our language, or in any other language, an expression that has so many important relations. It embraces everything that comes under the denomination of reform, and indicates everything in the way of improvement, or desire to improve the condition of mankind. If there be any talisman applicable to the question of reform it must consist in the words "Free Discussion". It is of necessity the initiative principle of all genuine reforms, and the neglect to obtain that right first has been the main cause of non-success in all the reforms hitherto attempted. It must be the focus of all genuine morality, as well as all the advantages which man possesses over other animals; for human speech is nothing but human discussion, and free discussion is nothing more than complete liberty of speech. Upon what fair and honest principle can one man, or set of men, claim the right to restrain and suppress the power of speech in another, or even the power of speaking upon paper, whatever that other may think right? If such a practice there be, it is the practice of tyranny; yet very few people seem to have any idea of the importance of free discussion. Few speak of it, and many do not think of it all, yet it is a simple point which every one should understand, if he have any idea at all of the utility of speech. Every man ought to openly and boldly advocate it, and there is scarcely a possibility that any one would so far expose himself to public shame and ridicule as to rise in a public assembly and deprecate the claim in plain words. Yet it was often urged on Carlile himself by the clergy and others that he could think what he liked on the subjects of government, or religion especially;

but he had no right to make his thoughts public either by speech or pen. To the fact that he did so was due the whole of his various imprisonments.

Where there is no law there can be no transgression, and there was no law to cover his case. He simply set the pace of liberty of speech, both oral and written, for others to follow, and to use the words of a prominent gentleman of Chicago in a recent letter, "Richard Carlile established the Freedom of the Press and the Liberty of Speech for more countries than one ".

He said of himself in this relation:

"In maintaining the war of discussion to accomplish its freedom, I confess that I have often had to resort to personalities. My case was peculiar, and I cannot see that I was wrong in so doing. I was personally assaulted with all the venom that religious fury could apply. The Society for the Promotion of Christian (!) Knowledge has frequently designated me as a wretch! Almost every Christian has paid me the same compliment. Instead of calling me a wretch, the Christian should acknowledge that I am a bold, fair, open, and generous enemy, ready to converse in the most polite manner with any of them, utterly incapable of being the first to give a personal affront in conversation; always desiring to be instructed or to instruct, and ready to conciliate wherever it can he honorably done. Christians! I am not a wretch."

Never in the history of the world was there an imprisonment so fruitful, so productive of knowledge of almost every kind. The opportunity never before offered of a thorough and free discussion of every subject calculated to educate and instruct mankind. It gave an impetus to desire on the part of the learned to teach, and great inducement and encouragement on the part of the people to learn. The extent and breadth of the character of the studies entered upon were surprising, and the eagerness with which they were seized upon no less so. It showed that there was a great amount of intelligence lying dormant in the populace, which only needed the coming of the awakener to be aroused to permanent activity. To this day, and even to America, can be traced small settlements and many individual followers of Carlile, who hold to his teachings and honor his memory with a constancy and tenacity which is immovable. It is a matter of gratification to be able to say that these are all intelligent, highly moral, strictly temperate, and in every way model American citizens.

CHAPTER XIII.

LIBERATION AND AFTER

At the end of the sixth year of his imprisonment Carlile was most unexpectedly set at liberty, and the following humorous account of the circumstance, as given in the columns of the *Republican*, is in his characteristic vein:—

"November 25th, 1825.

"To the Republicans of the Island of Albion.

"Citizens,—The sixth anniversary of my entrance to Dorchester Gaol, the 18th, has brought me outside its walls. The King in council on the 12th was advised to remit so much of my fines as were unpaid, and on the 16th he was further advised (*mirabile dictu*) from some favorable circumstances reported of me to him (God knows from whom, for I do not) to remit that part of my sentence which required me to find recognizances during my natural life, of one thousand pounds ($5,000) and of two hundred pounds on that of other persons. On the 18th inst. I first heard of my good fortune in the sight of a King (?) and in case any of my friends suspect that something unknown to them might have passed between me and the King or his advisers, I pledge my word, never wilfully mispledged, that nothing has passed on my part but that which has appeared in the *Republican*, and the favorable report, if anything more than official verbiage, has astounded me! To be sure I did tell his Majesty lately that he was my only idol, but that to him I would not pray nor offer flattery. This remission of that part of my sentence which required me to find recognizances during life must mean one of two things: either that on my part free discussion is fully established, or that on the part of the King's Government it means to renew prosecutions and to pursue me to expatriation. I am, of course, ignorant of State secrets, but my own course is determined. Onward! My future behavior will be precisely what the past has been with this one exception, that if prosecutions cease, I shall war with systems and not with persons. I shall conduct all discussions in future with a mild firmness and with an absence of all personal offence where none is given, still resolved to pursue redress for the past. When I heard that my recognizances had been abrogated, I acknowledge that I felt and pronounced it a finish to my triumph, but in every other respect my quitting the gaol was to me mentally but as a change of lodging. Yet I am fully alive to what I have done and what I intend to do. If free speech be accomplished in this country it will be a point gained toward human improvement, of which the history of man in no country maketh mention-.

"In some countries all public discussion is suppressed; in this country [England] the maxim has been for two centuries to punish the foremost. I saw this eight years ago, and resolved to make war with it. I also saw that by my going to extremes with discussion and speech, I should remove all fears as I removed all danger of prosecution from those who had been foremost, or who might be disposed to follow me at a safe distance. On this ground every free-minded literary man ought to have given me his support, for my long imprisonment was in fact a sort of penal representation for the whole.

"I confess that I have touched extremes which many thought imprudent, but which I saw to be useful with the view of habiting the Government and the people themselves to all extremes of discussion, so as to remove all idea of impropriety from the media which were most useful. If I find I have done this I shall be a most happy man. If not I shall have the same disposition, unimpaired, with which I began my present career, a disposition to suffer fines, imprisonment, or banishment rather than that any man shall hold the power and have the audacity to say and to act upon it, that any kind of discussion is improper and publicly injurious.

"I was in a manner swept out of the gaol bag and baggage. The gaoler being in London sent word that I was to be got out with all speed, which would have been done had I not in a measure been built up in my room so as to leave no passage-way for my sofa-bed without taking it to pieces. This and this alone gave me time to send a notice to London on the day of my discharge. An hour or so after the chaplain had brought me the news, and the clerk had shown me the warrant for my release, the gaoler returned after having driven from Salisbury to Dorchester in a gig to get back in time. The gaoler entered my room with all his servants (as he called them) and said, 'Now I have your discharge, and the sooner you go the better'. He then bid the men clear the room, and he scarcely lost sight of me till I was outside the gaol in a shower of rain. I did not give him any opportunity to witness any kind of emotion on my part at the sudden liberation from a six years' imprisonment under as detestable a gaoler as ever filled that office in England. In Dorchester my reception was decidedly good, and many persons expressed their good wishes who had been systematic in their abuse of me while I was in the gaol. Up to this moment I have not received the slightest insult, and I flatter myself that there is a growing spirit for what is called religious toleration in this country superior to that which is to be found in any country at this time."

On his journey to London he met with the following amusing incident:—

"The weather being fine, I preferred the outside to the inside of the coach; but was sent inside by a shower of rain before we reached Bridgeport. Here I found two ladies, both travellers, and both intelligent; the one young, the other old. It appeared that they had not heard my name at the stopping-place of the coach; and the old lady, though she subsequently protested that she was not a politician, and that as to Republicanism she had not an idea of it, made a fair trial upon my seditious qualities by endeavoring to call them forth in reprobating the conduct of the King and Ministers in not giving the uncultivated land to those who left the country to seek such land elsewhere. I assured the lady that the King was better than his Ministers, and that the Church more than he kept the land uncultivated and expatriated its children to seek a cheaper land free from tithes and other enormous taxes. This was assented to, but the old lady, determined that I should not defend the character of the King, brought up the case of the late Queen (Caroline), and made me so seditious as to confess that it was bad. I had a friend with me at this my first motion on top of the earth after my new birth, my new regeneration, my salvation, my being born again with fire and water and inspired with the spirit of the Logos—as we first-class Christians can say, as well as those of the inferior classes— and I informed him that I had met with a lady more Republican than myself, to whom I intended to make myself known. On re-entering the coach, the most Liberal and most agreeable political conversation took place. I was all perfection in my views, and by the apparent excitement and attention of both ladies I supposed myself a most charming companion to both. But lo! the fatal moment came, my ambition induced me to announce my name, really thinking that I had found friends and supporters; but alas! I found my mistake—one face went up at one window of the coach, the other to the other, and it appeared to be a question of propriety with them as to their going further with me. All that I could do in the way of compliment for their correct political views availed me nothing. The old lady protested that she was not a politician, thought it very wrong for ladies to meddle with politics, and as to attacks on Religion, she abhorred them.

"A long silence followed, though I endeavored to look most humble and explanatory. At length the elder lady began a sort of indirect lecture on the impropriety of shocking religious impressions. I appealed to her impressions of me before I announced my name, and it required all the art I was master of to redeem an atom of good grace before we arrived at Exeter. Every attempt to defend or explain what I had done sent the old lady's face up to the window; but by the next morning, on her leaving the inn, she sent her compliments to me by my friend.

"I was much surprised at my reception at Exeter. I had not intended to stop there but a day, just to show myself to some of my old acquaintances, that they might see that I had not been metamorphosed into the old dragon about which they had heard so much. I find it impossible to get away as soon as I expected. This town is rapidly improving in knowledge, yet I mark with sorrowful emotion the hideous, unsocial, uncheerful and unhappy faces which religion generates, and I see anew the importance of what I have done, and what I intend to do for the improvement of the female mind. It is knowledge alone that can give real beauty to the face, as merely fair outline without knowledge to give it expression is but a cold and lifeless statue, and can charm none but weak minds; nor can dress make up for the deficiency which an ignorant face exhibits. It heightens them and forms a double deception. It deceives the wearer and he who is attracted by it, and decoys both into a snare that inevitably generates an unhappy life for which no external appearance can atone."

This sudden and unexpected liberation gave rise to some erroneous ideas. Some of Carlile's weaker-kneed friends did not hesitate to accuse him of some unworthy truckling to those in power in order to gain his liberty. This was his reply to these accusations:

"I gather from the correspondence of friends in various parts of the country that some wild notions are current as to the cause of my liberation. I answer all queries on the subject by referring friends to my past conduct, to that which has been visible, and by desiring them to listen to no tales about changes in my conduct. My path has been long marked out and straightly walked in; I shall neither go back nor turn aside after so complete a success as that which I have brought about."

At this time it became quite the fashion to impute to Carlile the blame of everything, almost, that happened in the way of misfortune of whatever character. For example, when shortly after his liberation there was a collapse in certain stocks, and consequently a panic in the money market, there were many who openly imputed the cause to "Carlile's liberation"! Another example was that of a man condemned to be hung for forgery, and some one or two others who had committed some brutal crimes. The judge, in pronouncing sentence, said "they had no doubt been reading some of Carlile's pamphlets "!

During the last half of the year 1826, Carlile had been contemplating and arranging for a new weekly publication, with Richard Hassell as editorial assistant and manager. He had also arranged for an extended tour throughout the country, lecturing and speaking to the people everywhere, but unfortunately he was taken ill in November, and was prostrated for an entire year with rheumatism and asthma. Every one who saw him predicted his early demise. This was the after effect of his six years' close confinement. His system made sensitive and unused to the changes of temperature, gave way to the damps and fogs of the English November, and made the year 1827 the only unprofitable one of his life.

It would seem as though the effects of these severe confinements were not always felt at once, but slowly and insidiously undermined the constitution, rendering it unfit to cope with changes of temperature unnoticed by those accustomed to out of door life. There was probably never a man who bore imprisonment so well as Carlile on the whole, still it killed even him at last. It killed Richard Hassell and Thomas Davison, both much younger men than Carlile, and it most certainly affected the mind of Robert Taylor during those horrible months in the Horsemonger Lane Gaol, for on a close reading of this grand orator's masterly efforts, a disparity is surely noticed between those which followed his second imprisonment and those which preceded it. An over-straining of his fine mentality, as it were, leading to much that was erratic and unlike his former self. Carlile, though able to return to the encounter again and again, became so used to the prison life as to be obliged to imprison himself afterwards in his bedroom most of the winter, and, while mentally unaffected, suffered severely from the contact of cold air upon his lungs. This year's illness was a great drawback to Carlile's prosperity, for immediately upon quitting Dorchester Gaol he had taken premises at 62 Fleet Street, and fitted it up as a "Temple of Reason" which should be worthy the name. This new shop was also to be the headquarters of the Joint Stock Book Company, formed to further the object of printing and publishing Liberal works, under Carlile's supervision. In this enterprise he was ably assisted by his friends, amongst whom Julian Hibbert was the foremost. A great deal of money was expended in fitting up this place, some of which had to be borrowed, and which, with the added interest, impoverished Carlile to repay. To add to his troubles, his wife also was seriously ill during this year, and so they were both incapacitated from attending to the business. However, this state of things cleared up at the end of the year, and Carlile recommenced active life in good earnest. It was in 1827, on the 10th of February, that Carlile received notice that he had been bequeathed an annuity of fifty pounds a year by a Mr. Morrison, a surgeon of Chelsea, who had just died; a man whom Carlile had never seen but once, when he called on him quite suddenly, and in a very few words and with great difficulty—for he seemed in very bad health—said, "I have come to tell you, Mr. Carlile, that I have been very attentive to your conduct since the time of your trial; that I am very much pleased with it, and that in consideration of what you have gone through, I have made a provision for your family in my will". Carlile having thanked him, he added, "I shall not now give you my name and address; but I have some manuscripts which I wish you to see and to publish, and I will see you again". He never came again, as he was too ill to leave the house, but he had done as he had said, and in due time Carlile benefited by the bequest, which he appropriated to the purpose spoken of in a previous chapter. The executors were Henry (afterwards Lord) Brougham* and James Evans. The will was very curiously constructed, the bequest to Carlile being put in the following words:—

"Bequest 7th: I give and bequeath to Richard Carlile, of Fleet Street, London, bookseller, his wife and present family or the survivor of them, the annual sum of fifty pounds, by quarterly payments, for the term of their natural lives, as an approving testimony to the character of correct morals, given of the said Carlile on his late trial, holding as I sincerely do that such a character is of infinitely more utility to man, and consequently more creditable, than the profession of any creed whatsoever, since all religions have hitherto rather tended to debase than to improve good morals; and also in testimony of my abhorrence of persecution for opinion, so contrary to the tolerant spirit of a free constitution."

At the 10th clause the testator says:—

"And finally I give and bequeath to the Church, Pagan, Jewish, Christian, and Mahommedan, my anathema for the horrible murders, cruelties and crimes committed thereby in all ages, under the color of religion. And if this anathema against the abuses of religion should raise the spleen of a selfish hierarchy and impel them to refuse my mouldering carcass a cemetery in the usual way, I will that my executors buy the fee simple of a rod of earth (no matter where), therein to deposit the same, and there may the standard of Infidelity, as it is contemptuously called, that is, the standard of Truth, Benevolence, Virtue, and Philosophy, be raised to the final extirpation of bigotry and superstition."

At the close of the year 1826 the __Republican was stopped, Carlile thinking it had accomplished the purpose for which it was commenced. This was, as the dedication shows, solely to maintain a periodical devoted to establishing a Free Press in England despite the opposition of its enemies, and the desperate efforts made by them for its extinguishment. It was kept up till there was no further effort made against it. This was the principle on which Carlile acted throughout his whole career, and that was never to suspend a publication of any kind while a threat was heard against it, at any cost. It was not till the beginning of 1828 that Carlile commenced his weekly periodical, which he named the *Lion*, and which proved a worthy successor to the *Republican*. This was not allowed to go on unmolested however, for before the first volume was completed a notice was served on Carlile to appear by counsel in his Majesty's Court of Exchequer and defend himself against some trifling charges under the penalty of a fine of £100 ($500). Says Carlile:—

"I should have danced with joy—the server of the process would have thought me mad—had Mr. Attorney-General sent me a notice that he had filed an information against me for blasphemy in the Court of King's Bench, but an information in the Court of Exchequer! (The words devil, hell, are very commonly and very properly associated to convey some ideas.) What is to be done now? *Nil desperandum!* The cause of free discussion cannot fail; Babylon must fall before it! So I wrapped myself in my much worn philosophical temperament, and walked to Somerset House to see my new friend, Godfrey Sykes, for though he had honored me with several letters, he never gave me an invitation to call on him before, and even now he forgot to ask me to dine, though he made himself very pleasant. I cannot conceive of a more comfortable state of mind than that of a man who is about to pick your pocket according to law, without any fear of gallows, transportation, imprisonment, or whipping. And I presume that if his Majesty and his Parliament would extend the same sort of protection to the pickpockets in the street that is extended to the royal public officers, the former as well as the latter would do their business in the most polite and most civil manner; there would be no acts of violence committed on the person, nor an unpleasant word offered beyond 'Stand or take this!' meaning the contents of a pistol, which is also the royal mode of doing the business."

The complaint was based upon about one inch of paper, more or less, which gave ground for a quibble as to whether it was liable to stamp duty or not. This was the ostensible reason given, but in reality the paper gave offence, though they did not dare say so outright. It was an old and useless statute which had never been enforced, but was now unearthed for his benefit. Carlile openly defied the authorities, and threw down the gauntlet, saying, "If another six years of imprisonment be necessary for the furtherance of the great and good cause which I am advocating, I shall bear it with patient fortitude." The prosecution was, however, abandoned, and Carlile went on his way rejoicing for a while longer.

"INFIDEL MISSIONARIES."

Very shortly after the Rev. Robert Taylor's release from Oakham Gaol, he and Richard Carlile started to tour the country as missionaries together. Though not entertaining the same ideas of Deity, they were both of the same mind in regard to the errors of the Established Church, and the need of educating the people to think for themselves. They visited all the leading towns in England, as Carlile had done before, challenging the-ministers of every denomination to meet them in friendly conflict, which challenge was seldom if ever accepted. Taylor's strong point lay in his great knowledge of astronomy, and his demonstrations that all mythology was fabricated upon astronomy and all religion upon mythology. He was also a fine scholar, proficient in ancient languages, and a gifted orator. His renderings of poetical passages from Shelley, Shakspere, and other poets were fine beyond description. The name "Infidel Missionaries" was given to them and accepted by them as good as any other appellation.

CHAPTER XIV.

THE "PROMPTER" AND THE ROTUNDA

On the 12th of November, 1830, a new publication was issued which Carlile called the *Prompter*, because, as he said, "THE NATION NEEDED A PROMPTER". It had also for its object to make known the work of the Rotunda—

"A capitol of public virtue, the nucleus for a reformation of abuses, the real House of Commons—in the absence of a better—the palladium of what liberty we have, phoenix that is immortal and pregnant of more, the birth-place of mind, and the focus of virtue's public excitement. This establishment affords the most rational and cheapest way of spending an evening that has yet been presented to the public of any country, and since threats are held out against it, State warrants and indictments talked of, and plots—vile plots—planned, but foiled, the *Prompter* summons the Press to its aid and pledges a brave and glorious struggle and a successful war under its tri-colored banner against the aristocratical or clerical despotism, corruption, and ignorance of the whole country."

"THE ROTUNDA.

"This establishment is at No. 3, Blackfriars Road or Great Surrey Street, the third house from the bridge on the right hand side coming from the City. It was built by Sir Ashton Lever as a museum of natural history and curiosities. It is a curious coincidence that the Museum Tavern at No. 1 takes its name from the original institution. It is also a curious coincidence that the Museum Tavern should also bear the sign of the Cross Keys or St. Peter's Keys, and that the first purpose of the present occupation of the Rotunda should have been the possession of a theatre in which the Rev. Robert Taylor should pursue an interpretation of the sacred writings of Christendom upon the important allegory of those two keys—the keys of the mysteries of the physical and moral nature. Why the building was discontinued as a museum we are not informed, but there succeeded that which was called the Surrey Institution, being an institution for literature and science, which contained a good library and in which many eminent men lectured. The aim of the present occupant is to bring it back to that character, with the addition of freedom of speech and discussion in political and theological matters. The Surrey Institution is supposed to have failed for want of funds, and a thousand pounds a year will now be required to support it, with its attendants, as a generally useful and respectable establishment. The founders of the Mechanics' Institute in Southampton Buildings applied for its terms, but found it too heavy for its now (it is hoped) thriving establishment. Failing to let it for any literary or scientific purpose, the proprietors yielded it up as a place of public entertainment, having a coffee-room, wine, and concert-room, and afterwards an amphitheatre for Cook's equestrian performances, to which succeeded a panorama."

This change from that which was really an honor to the neighborhood, gave great offence, and opposition was carried on till the parties were all ousted and the premises thrown on the hands of the assignees. They had been some time vacant and in a state of dilapidation when Carlile entered into possession of the buildings, which then consisted of a neat dwelling-house, two large billiard-rooms, with apartments, a vestibule or extensive bar, a coffee-room, a long room, or that which was the library; a small circular hall, which was originally the theatre, having a gallery supported by marble pillars and balustrades, and a dome on which the Signs of the Zodiac were painted, as illustrations of the Rev. Mr. Taylor's theologico-astronomical discourses. The theatre was used also for political meetings.

Hither came all the public speakers of the day, and here every man could express his opinions upon any subject so that it was done in an orderly manner. The Rotunda was the first place in Europe where this could be done, and it is interesting to note the names of the speakers or lecturers.*

It is needless to say that this place was an eyesore to the Government, and was watched with suspicion. Spies and informers were constantly on the ground, and many were the attempts made to break up the place. Many attempts also were made to draw the supporters of the Rotunda into premature and naturally abortive schemes of revolution, from which they were saved only by their own good sense.

The last effort to raise a tumult occurred on the 9th of November, 1830. It was a regularly planned effort, and all the parties received their instructions early in the day on the condition of nothing else turning up. The civil force, with a military reserve, was directed to attack the Rotunda; but all turned upon one point, and on that point the whole scheme failed.

News came to the Rotunda that the place was to be attacked that night, and the manner in which it was to be done was so accurately stated that everything was afterwards found to correspond with the information given. Mr. Carlile took his measures accordingly; first, by barricading the door of the theatre through which the charge was to have been made, and beyond which everything was cleared for action;

secondly, by lecturing on such a subject and in such a way as to bid defiance to magisterial interference. At eight o'clock the theatre was filled. Among the company were the magistrates of Union Hall, with a body of officers, and Sir Richard Birnie described himself as having been in attendance at the theatre. Partitioning boards were torn away from another entrance, for which there could have been no other reason than the projected attack. No policemen were seen about the building or doors of the theatre; the mob and its orators were allowed to collect, and to make what noise and to do what mischief they pleased until the whole plot was found to be frustrated. Then at twelve o'clock that night the police came to disperse the crowd, after a whole hour's effort had been made to break into the passages of the Rotunda and to get out the proprietor. Mr. Carlile entered the theatre at eight o'clock, and took as the subject of his lecture Sir Robert Peel's explanatory speech in the House of Commons on the Monday previous. The effect of his lecture was universal conviction on the part of the audience, and their declaration that the Ministers had been plotting against the people and that the people had not plotted against the Ministers. There was not a sentence in the lecture of which the Union Hall magistrates could make a handle for a warrant to arrest the speaker; and they must have sneaked away in utter confusion at the temper of the audience and the frustration of their plot. The company left the theatre at ten o'clock, and a few minutes afterwards the doors of the Rotunda were closed and everything quiet. This was a matter of intense astonishment to the concealed forces that were impatiently waiting to be brought into action. Rumors had been spread through the City that a tumult was to begin at the Rotunda at eleven o'clock. Mr. Carlile had been challenged out just before that time by a young man with a moustache, apparently an undressed military officer, "to head the insurrection" and to lead the mob! But he smiled and shut the door, to the great annoyance of the plotters outside. He retired to bed soon after eleven, but was aroused by what seemed to be an effort to break into the premises by a mob, and by a succession of harangues of a most violent kind. This was the disappointed crowd of plotters who tore down the bell of the house and would have forced the doors if they had not been more than ordinarily strong. Mr. Carlile was prepared for their entry, and allowed them to waste their vengeance on the doors and the knocker—a war upon which was kept up for an hour. All hopes of the desired tumult being over, the policemen began to order the accumulated passengers to walk on, and Sir Richard Birnie, if he stopped until two o'clock, must have spent an hour and a half in the agony of disappointment after the whole scheme had become hopeless. The calculation was that, as Mr. Hunt's meeting on the night before lasted till half-past eleven, the meeting on that night would not break up before eleven. In case of failure to arrest Mr. Carlile on the platform, the plot was to have been completed at eleven. The subject of the evening and the breaking up of the meeting at ten frustrated that step which, more than the votes of the House of Commons on the 15th instant, was the death-blow to the Wellington Administration. The last hope of all their little schemes for a premature insurrection among the people had been vanquished, and from that moment they felt that they could no longer hold office.*

This is an exact copy of the article in No. 3 of the *Prompter* which was selected for indictment, and which, with a little rough handling of the jury, ended in giving Carlile three years' imprisonment in the Giltspur Street Compter:—

"A list of officers in the King's Household is the most ludicrous and ridiculous thing that can be read. It will not bear mention in the present day, and is of itself an evidence that a constitutional monarchy is a most ridiculous state of government. More than mimicking absolute monarchy and perpetuating all ancient follies and abuses, everything conspires against a king to tell him that he is something more than human, and all that sort of flattery is calculated to unman him and to make him less than a man! We want no mummeries and nonsense wherewith to please savages and fools in the present day. We want public officers who shall really be men of business. We want laboring men to carry on the affairs of government, who shall be paid for their labor and their labor only. Let us see what the Whigs will do to make their constitutional monarchy appear decent to the brightening eye of the public."

The Whigs were supposed to be the Liberal party as opposed to the Tories, and what they did was to immediately proceed against this article and the following, and clap Carlile into prison with heavy fines and sureties:—

"To the Insurgent and Agricultural Laborers—

"You are much to be admired for everything you are known to have done during the last month, for as yet there is no evidence before the public that you are incendiaries or even political rebels. Much as every thoughtful man must lament the waste of property, much as he country must suffer by the burning of the farm produce now going on, were you proved to be the incendiaries we should defend you by saying that you have more just and moral cause for it than any king or faction that ever made war had for making war. In war all destruction of property is counted lawful. Upon the ground of that which is called the law of nations, yours is a state of warfare, and your quarrel is the want of the necessaries of life in the midst of abundance. You see hoards of food and you are starving you see a Government rioting in every sort of luxury and wasteful expenditure, and you, ever ready to labor, cannot find one of the comforts of life. Neither your silence nor your patience has obtained for you the least respectful attention from that Government. The more tame you have grown the more you have been oppressed and despised, the more you have been trampled on; and it is only now that you begin to display your physical as well as your moral strength that your cruel tyrants treat with you and offer terms of pacification. Your demands have so far been moderate and just, and any attempt to stifle them by the threatened severity of the new Administration will be so wicked as to justify your resistance even to death and to life for life. Persevere in your moderate and just demands! Go on as you have begun, and learn—not only in precept, but in your own example—that great political sentiment of Thomas Paine, the greatest political friend of the laboring man that ever put pen to paper for his instruction, that *For a nation to be free it is sufficient that she wills it!*"

It was only the mildest part of this address that was chosen for the indictment, but we cannot but feel that it was what was left out of the indictment that really gave the offence.

After Carlile was in prison very large meetings were held at the Rotunda and elsewhere to voice the popular indignation at the conduct and outcome of that really disgraceful affair. The very fact that these large meetings were openly attended, and as openly addressed, without any governmental interference, showed a marked progress in the minds of men and the lessened power of those men in authority since the first trial in 1819. Then no one dared openly to say one word in his favor.

Subscriptions began to pour in unsolicited, and one was addressed to him as follows: "This subscription is the

127

spontaneous record of hostility to a corrupt and tyrannical Whig administration, to a corrupt judge, and to a corrupt and slavish jury." The subscriptions amounted to over £100 ($500) per week for many months. Carlile, in writing to a body of friends who had sent him money and their sympathies immediately after his third trial, said:—

"I was cheered by your letter and its fifty-eight names which reached me last night. It seemed an anticipation of that encouragement which some men would require in my present situation, but which is not really necessary to push me forward. It may seem strange, but whether from habit, or what else, it is no less true, that in the course of our great political struggle I like a gaol, and am more happy here than I can possibly be anywhere else, until the time of our final triumph. To me it seems like a place of political enchantment, and that I am made the great political diviner of the State, to whom the reformers will look for encouragement and direction."

July, 1831, found the Rev. Robert Taylor in Horsemonger Lane Gaol for blasphemy, and subjected to the most rigorous treatment. This imprisonment was severely felt by the rev. gentleman, much more so than that of the previous one at Oakham. Carlile had great difficulty in keeping him in reasonable bounds, owing to Taylor's excitability and nervous temperament, which received a great strain by this vindictive punishment. Carlile urged upon Taylor the necessity of some engrossing work. In this situation "The Devil's Pulpit", "The Diegesis," and "The Syntagma" were produced. Had it not been for Carlile these would never have been written. Carlile also moved heaven and earth, to use a common expression, to get Taylor's condition ameliorated. He got the people all through England to send petitions to the House of Commons on his behalf, and kept up such a verbal cannonading that his gaolers could not help but better his condition somewhat. The following (private) letter will show what sort of a task Carlile had in hand:—

"Compter,

"July 20th, 1831.

"To Rev. R. Taylor,

"Sir,—My first duty to society is to seek the preservation of your life; your first is to preserve it as far as in your power.

If you die, we shall not fill the chasm for many years, if all the genius of England were to unite its efforts.

"I have just received your letter of this day's date. I heard at twelve o'clock that your friends were excluded for the day; at three o'clock by the medium of the vile old Osgood that there had been a fury between you and your gaoler. You say Walter the gaoler insults you. That is your fault. It is not in the power of man to insult me. The world could not do it if it were to try. Assault is one thing, but insult is another, and there can only be insult where there is a disposition to court it. Human nature is capable of a dignity that will not leave room for the word insult. Unfortunately you have the temperament that encourages villainy to be insolent. Let us try if reason cannot cure you of this disorder, which to you, at this moment, is as bad and dangerous a plague as the cholera morbus. To begin, let me remind you of the question of the Greek philosopher when asked why he did not resent the insolence of a vile fellow? He answered: 'Friend, if a jackass were to kick me, would you have me kick him back again?'

"By the statute law of gaol management the gaoler is required to go into every cell in which a prisoner is confined every day. Let him do so. If he must see you it is no reason why you should see him. I have been placed under much greater difficulties in Dorchester Gaol than those under which you are now placed. My gaoler would have given his fingers to have worked me into such a temper in which you were seen this morning. I never so gratified him; and pray do not you so gratify yours again. I know that reason is one thing and passion another; and that neither one nor the other can at all times be commanded. In the first place, let us have no more tricks. They greatly embarrass your friends and thwart our efforts and means of assisting you. It is now with you no time for poetry, for rhapsody, or for jest. You have and we have for you a serious game to play. At trick, our Christian enemy will beat us. I heard on Sunday that a Surrey magistrate had said: 'Taylor is playing some tricks with us about his pretended wife. We know all about it, and will out-trick him.'

"They will beat us at any game but that of open honesty. I have always seen this. You know my word. No secrets, no smuggling; nothing but that which will be fair and above board. My politics would have hung me twelve years ago if I had been a politician anywhere but through the Press and in the course of such lectures as I have delivered to public companies. No plots; no schemes; no tricks; no purposes but those which are openly avowed. I do not write in the spirit of reproach; but of salvation, of plan of warfare, of a determination to conquer the common enemy; and in this spirit, allow me to say that your friends, Mr. Hibbert, Mr. Prout, Mr. Ewen, and myself, are sorry for much that has been written, spoken, and done during your horrible fortnight past. There has been trick and impropriety in it, and it has not succeeded. It cannot succeed. Yours is a glorious situation if you will but fight your battle well. Having gained the necessaries—the physical necessaries of life—you should now make every shot tell among the enemy, and not allow another shot of theirs to reach you.

"I am more than a brother—I have an estate in your life. I shall lose and not gain an estate in your death. Not one word but a word of comfort should you hear from me did I not think some explanation necessary to the salvation of your life.

"If you were going out of the harbor in a ship to fight an enemy in another ship, would you not put your wife and children ashore if they were aboard? Let it be so now. Don't say to the enemy, 'Don't fire, because my wife and children are aboard,' but let them stay ashore, and you may safely say—'Damn you, fire away! I will rake you fore and aft, and give you broadsides between wind and water, and you shall not put a shot into me.' You may have it so if you will, and if you will not you will be beaten and die a thousand deaths. Your life is in your own hands, and not in the hands of your enemies. For the means and the disposition for annoyance, you cannot be worse situated than I was at Dorchester Gaol through four years and more of the time; yet I came out through it triumphantly, and I am of opinion that a similar game will never be tried or attempted on me again.

"First, then, I advise respectfully, regard fully and in the most friendly and brotherly spirit, that you send your wife and children ashore and say not one word more about them while the battle rages. Too much has been said, but my mouth has been sealed until I received your letter this evening. I will communicate the spirit of that letter by the first messenger that I can command to-morrow, and will, while I can, protect and comfort your family. But I will not, till I see a better reason for so doing, permit one more word about them. Too much has already been printed. Your friends—those whom I know to be your friends—are grieved, doubly grieved by that circumstance which doubly grieved you. It has been hitherto your fault to present your weak side to your enemy. You have in you the spirit of a divinity that is invincible. You have the spirit of humanity also that is weak and to be conquered—now which will you present to your enemies? They are not to be subdued by appeals to their sympathy or by any moral force. You must subdue them by making them afraid. They will beat you at any game that is wrong, they will be powerless if you avail yourself of your best and fairest means of warfare.

"If I could tell you of my motives, my feelings, my calculations, my every action in Dorchester Gaol, it would be a useful lesson for you. Blackguard, vile and wicked as was that gaoler, I made him fear me, simply by looking at him; yet I never expressed myself toward him that he could describe it as an insult or a threat, I conquered him by virtue. Leigh Hunt was once confined in your gaol and was much illused at first, but afterwards he obtained something approaching to decent treatment, and had his wife and children with him and free admission for his friends.

"You have everything to conquer, and you must begin your reform at home and first conquer your own self-command. Patience is not so necessary as a cool methodical warfare. Write such letters as your last to Lord Brougham. Let Lord Melbourne have one such every week. Address the King in every way of matter of fact statement that your case will admit of. You shall have a good specimen in my forthcoming one to Lord Melbourne.

"For the sake of our glorious cause, let nothing come from your pen about the gaol that can be contradicted. You have

132

not been sufficiently careful. It is not a time for joke; your enemies will call your jokes lies, and to the world at large they are lies. Mr. Hibbert made it almost a *sine qua non* as to his further assistance that your letter to-day for the *Morning Chronicle* which came to our hands should not go forth to its destination. My taste is to print every word that you write in your present prison; but that taste has been swayed by that virtue (Hibbert's) to anything below which I never would yield my motive of right and mode of action— I mean the virtue of Mr. Hibbert and one other such friend.

"Let me appeal to that portion of your spirit which is reasonable. I know that you care nothing about liquid spirit at this season of the year, other than as it is forbidden you. Now, is it fair, manly, or generous on your part that you should for a mere half-pint or so of brandy expose your friends, your generous friends, their generosity itself, their willingness to die to serve you, to every species of insult; to searching, to generate suspicion as to every other circumstance, to the certain exclusion of many other comforts that might allowably pass the gates of the prison, to such exclusion, and yourself to such excitement as occurred yesterday, to the risk of fine and imprisonment, and subsequent seclusion; in short, to an increase of your own mental anguish and to that of your friends? If you smuggle that which is forbidden, if on that head you glory in violating the law, you have no ground left on which to complain, and our complaints will be as the idle winds that passeth by unheeded. Give your gaol enemies but one real ground of complaint against you, and you give them justification for their worst intentions. I wish I could pour an opiate over your irritability and say, *be composed*. You want composure, coolness, dignity, patience, fortitude for your present situation; but I know it is not to be commanded. You must reason with yourself, and write down laws for your own government in prison. You will do

133

this coolly and they will keep you cool. Beyond what you print I would have you keep a journal, as you have the taste and application for journal-keeping. I shall have an admirable *Prompter* this week in your behalf.

"Richard Carlile.

"Thursday morning.—My messenger has gone off to Rathbone Place.

"You missed a fine lobster yesterday by the exclusion of your friends; but it will come.

"Beware of old Osgood; he is a wicked enemy. The wretch has dared to call on Mr. H. because he found his address in the *Prompter*. He was at hand yesterday to trumpet forth your alleged indiscretion. I warned him off my holy ground; but if he trespasses I shall most certainly kick his share of the Holy Ghost downstairs; and I expect that his share all lies in the seat of honor rather than in his *carib skull*."

This letter, though rather lengthy, I have given entire as throwing a light upon the characters of the two men then heading the "glorious cause", as Carlile puts it. The truth of the "wife and children" matter is that Taylor never had been married at that time; this was one of those very foolish tricks of which his friends accused him. Carlile knew Taylor had neither wife nor child, but knowing that his letters were in danger of being read by the gaol authorities, would not give the lie to these foolish statements and so put a weapon in their hands; he trusted to the power of his reasonable arguments in the letter to have Taylor give up such silly stratagems. The Osgood spoken of was, we believe, one of the chaplains of Horsemonger Lane Gaol, and was both meddlesome and treacherous. The letter itself has never been printed, though most of the correspondence of Carlile and Taylor, while they were both in prison, was printed in the *Prompter*.

On hearing that Julian Hibbert was contemplating the release of one of the imprisoned men by the payment of his fine, Carlile wrote to Hibbert as follows:—

"I think that mischief will be done by any proposition to pay the King a fine in this struggle for the liberty of the press and of speech. I should count that man my enemy who would pay such a fine for me, and set me free against my will. We cannot have too much money, but we can all make a better use of it than to pay fines."

Lines written by Carlile.

(On the 4th month, 29th day, of imprisonment, 1831.)

Response of Julian Hibbert.

"Well pleased, I read, and reading must commend Man's true and honest, persecuted friend. Nor you refuse the praise my muse bestows, Free from an uncorrupted heart it flows. Oh! would mankind but pause awhile and think, From persecution as from sin they'd shrink, Such simple reasoning must their souls awake, And from their thoughts blind superstition shake The empty dreams that filled their mind before, No more should fight them or disturb them more. Sweet heartfelt pleasure should their fears succeed, Sweet tranquil pleasure, sweet the thought indeed. Write always thus, Carlile. Oh! may your tyrants yet repent and save Man's truest friend from living in the grave."

In 1833 Carlile's prison doors were almost unexpectedly opened and he passed out into the open air once more a free man—that is free corporally, he was always free as to mind and pen. He was not daunted or dismayed by threats, or the little matter of a year or two's imprisonment. As in the case of Dorchester Gaol, he had turned his room into a bookshop and warehouse, edited various papers from the prison, and carried on a large business by messengers and correspondence, and had accumulated such a mass of stuff in the way of letters, books and papers, etc., as to require a large van to remove them. The facts relating to his release were very amusing. His sentence required two years' imprisonment, two sureties in £250 each, and a heavy personal fine. In the first place a warrant was sent down to the governor of the prison to release Carlile, and remitting *one* part of the sureties. This Carlile would not accept. A month later a warrant came down for his release and remittal of the fine. Carlile sent word back that that would not do yet, as the fine was remitted on condition that he put in his personal recognizances of £500. He instantly wrote back to Lord Melbourne that "he would do nothing of the kind". Then a third warrant came down; nothing was left but the personal recognizances, and this third warrant removed that, so that Carlile had everything he stood out for at last, and left the Compter in triumph. As he said: "I came out with flying colors without yielding a single point". Carlile met a large congregation of 2,000 people on the following Sunday at the Rotunda, and was given a fine, hearty greeting. Here, too, the Rev. Robert Taylor made his reappearance, and met with great enthusiasm. This was Carlile's last appearance on the floor of the Rotunda, for the very next day it was leased to Mr. Davidge, an actor, who was to open it up once again for theatrical purposes. Mr. Davidge, in his announcement to the public of the change in its management, "hoped that they would congratulate themselves on the remarkable advantage a first-class theatre would be to them over this sink of profligacy, etc., etc., which had been a focus for the concentration of the worst characters, from whence had emanated the most demoralising and destructive doctrine both in religion and politics, etc., etc., operating at once as a shock to the good sense, good feelings, and as a serious detriment to the interests and comforts of the entire neighborhood, etc., etc.," then, privately, penned the following note:—

"5, Charlotte Terrace,

"August 29th, 1833.

"To Mr. Carlile.

"Sir,—If you are disposed to purchase the lease of the City Theatre (once Mr. Fletcher's chapel) I will sell it to you for £600. The rent £200 a year—about sixteen years unexpired—with immediate possession.

"I am, sir,

"Your most obedient servant,

"C. B. Davidge."

Carlile printed both the announcement and the private letter in the *Gauntlet*, without comment. Davidge evidently was not afraid to lease any property of his to Carlile, for all of his high sounding charges in the public announcement. So it was in almost all the affairs of Carlile's life—publicly enemies, privately friends.

CHAPTER XV.

SCATTERED THREADS

ON WOMAN.

"An amiable woman is one of Nature's perfect works, unspoiled and uncorrupted by man. Any number of men brought together without women could not be kept together in any other character than as slaves or under military discipline. Therefore, as women form the groundwork of society and civilisation, their presence and influence must be beneficial in the same ratio as the civilised is preferable to the savage state. All history gives us proof that the degree of virtue and amiableness in women is in proportion to the freedom they enjoy or the degree in which they can move and act independently and uncontrolled. The freedom and independence of woman is the best proof and guarantee for the freedom and independency of man. A despotism never exists in one degree alone, it is expansive and dangerous. If it exists in the head of a family, every member of it will be despotic according to the degree of power of some other member or members. With women there is no medium; they are neuter in nothing. It is, then, the duty of man to make virtuous the soil where woman treads, and she will be found to blossom in purity and Nature's most splendid and perfect work—a radiant and unclouded constellation, illuminating all within her sphere. Philosophers in general have not paid that deference which is due to the female in society; in speaking or writing for the improvement of society they have passed by woman as a secondary or insignificant object, whereas she forms the most important channel through which virtue can be propagated and the social state be rendered peaceable, prosperous, and happy. Every impression that is attempted to be made on the female mind that she is an inferior being, every step that is taken to degrade her, is a bar to virtue, an inlet to vice. It interesteth the welfare of society to raise the female character to the highest possible pitch in the scale of intellect, even to a competition with the male in all the fine arts, science, and general literature. A free and unlimited discussion on all the merits of this and all subjects is the sure harbinger of improvement. When we reach this climax the age of virtue as well as the age of reason will approach. Let them make themselves acquainted with the science of government upon the simple basis of republicanism or the representative system of government, and particularly to examine and weigh well the dogmas and pretensions of all priests.

"If I have read history correctly the best of women have been most virtuously bold and have been seen as public teachers. All public reforms are moral proceedings. All useful public teachings are moral proceedings, and in all such proceedings women, while their manners are mild and becoming, can never be wrong. The propriety of the thing will rest upon the way of doing it. The great fault I find in woman is that inanity in character which places them below the line of equality with men. Alive to female influence in the propagation and maintenance of opinion, I find my reason in paying them every proper compliment and attention, and I hold in contempt that contracted mind that would so narrow their sphere of usefulness as to represent them as criminals in publicity, or make it a crime to appear in public with them. This state of things has partly arisen from the circumstance that past politics have consisted of an advocacy of men rather than of principles, that there has not been in reality any code of morals existing, and that religion hitherto has been a prevailing and epidemic disease among the human race. It is impossible to describe what the high state of man and woman will be without religion, with

139

a good code of morals, with good laws, with good and cheap government; and when party contentions are swallowed up in the advocacy of good principles. Female efforts can never be more usefully applied than toward the improvement of the human race. And nothing can be effectually done in the way of moral and physical improvement without the assistance of women.* I feel the necessity of a constant appeal on this point, and am not for treating women as the mere breeding machines for the human race, and men as the directing lords of the aggregate machinery. There is no kind of equality more deniably advantageous for the welfare of the human race than the equality of the sexes. The present (1828) general character of woman is that of a gaudily dressed doll, a toy made up as a plaything rather than as a companion for man. In the aggregate there exists no such a quality as female mind. There are men who think this is the most fit state for the female race to be kept. I think differently, knowing that woman is the mother, the nurse, the general instructress of the man, knowing that the mind of the man is in a great measure formed by that of the woman. I would have the woman most perfect as an essential preliminary to the greater perfection of man. I know no proper regulation with relation to the principle of knowledge, but that of the most unlimited acquirement that is possible to the acquisition of either sex. To say that this and the other point of knowledge is improper for the attention of woman, is to assume a tyrannical judgment and to put her below the pale of human equality. For a woman to be content under that pale of equality is to exhibit mental degradation."

FREEDOM AND FRANCHISE OF WOMEN.

"Will the new Reform Bill allow women who are householders to vote for members of the House of Commons? I have just thought of this matter. If no express exception be made, female householders will be entitled to vote. And what existing law is there to reject a woman if she were returned to Parliament? I have no such high opinion of men as to think them intellectually superior to women. There are not a hundred men in England to be matched with Frances Wright;* and I know none superior. That woman is qualified to be a member of the House of Commons. We shall not make this leap at once, but I am sure we shall come to this: women will claim and exercise the elective franchise and sit in Parliament. In ancient times such was the case in this country. I can see no evil in a Parliament of women or in the mixing of men and women in public affairs and offices; I would have them put on a perfect equality with men.

"The ladies may be assured that whenever they will stir to assert the rights of women I will assist them; and be assured that the rights of man will be best secured in the maintenance of the rights of women."**

Prejudice. "Like all others I am most interested about myself, but as I am made up altogether of public politics, in some cases myself is the public. Here is a note to correspondents from the editor of the *Times* about which I shall have a few words to say of myself in the only space left to me in this week's issue of the *Gauntlet*: 'To Correspondents.—As the letter of Richard Carlile would do him injury we decline to publish it. His stupidity and ignorance cannot fail to make him an object of contempt with all reasoning people, but we have too much generosity to turn the man's folly against him. He is what Mr. Coke called Mr. Joseph Hume—'a muddle-headed fellow.'"*

In answer, Carlile said he had borne injuries enough of this kind, and the *Times* had shouted—"'At him, give it to him, spare him not, kill him, crucify him, away with him, he is a pestilent fellow'; but I sometimes steal a march upon the editor of the *Times* by getting a friend to copy an article, and then it passes, and brings me the compliment of being a talented correspondent. No correspondent that it has had, has been more complimented for talent by this editor than I have been when unknown to him; but if he discovers the writer's name is Carlile, then he condemns, rants, swears and curses." We have abundant evidence that this was true in other cases besides that of the *Times*. A most prolific writer, Carlile contributed many leading articles and editorials to the Press of the country, and was for many months a regularly paid contributor to the *Durham Chronicle* and other papers. Over the *nom de plume* of "Theophilus Clay" or the "Hermit of Enfield", he did a vast amount of miscellaneous writing, and towards the end of his life supported his family almost entirely in this way. But it was the name—Carlile.

If we may take the liberty of paraphrasing the lines of the immortal bard.

SECRET ORDERS.

Carlile, with his constitutional dislike to everything secret, exposed all secret societies and orders from Freemasonry down. The members of the various orders who had outgrown or grown tired of the ceremonies of these different associations, furnished all the information to Carlile. These books were on sale for many years and attracted widespread attention. As usual Carlile was inundated with both praise and abuse, as the feelings of his critics leaned to one side or the other.

The Rev. Richard Carlile

The fact of Carlile's adding the title of Reverend to his name came from the efforts made by the authorities to prevent him speaking to the people on Sundays in the open air, claiming that none but licensed clergymen were entitled to that privilege; Carlile met with this objection throughout England. This led him to the examination of the necessary qualifications for this privilege, and he found that a belief in God and an English half-crown (about sixty-two cents, of American money) would purchase the title of Reverend and give him the right to address the people on Sunday in the parks as well as everywhere else. This cheap honor was easily procured, and stopped all opposition on that head. So, as the *Reverend Richard Carlile* he could speak anywhere and at any time, and, as he said, "With the Bible in my hand I can go anywhere and preach without the slightest diminution of my former principles". The transaction was simply a *ruse de guerre* to gain an advantage over the enemy, which he did; yet it took a long time and many explanations to make people see why this was done, and to convince them that he had not gone over to the enemy.

"PUFFENDORF."

In the course of one of his lecturing trips he tells the following story of himself:—

"My visit to Buxton was one of retirement. The only great man whom I met there, or rather took with me, was 'Puffendorf'. Having read much of the House of Commons debates in which there has been copious mentionings of Grotius, Vattel, and Puffendorf, I bought the great man for a couple of shillings in Manchester, and intended to study him in Buxton. To my surprise, I tried but could not read him; I tried again and again, but my perseverance failed me here, and I threw the book aside resolved to take no more books upon the recommendation of the House of Commons members. By reading 'Puffendorf' I thought I might qualify myself to be a member of the great council of the nation; but if nothing but Puffendorf will do I shall never get among them. I found this author, like Dugald Stewart since, deducing his theory of morals from the theory of the superstition of the age in which he lived, and exacting some most outrageous observances as moral and national law. It is but fair to say that my copy was translated by an English priest and was a professed abridgement, so that it is possible that the real original Puffendorf might still be as Macintosh, Burdett and others would have him to be."

Carlile went to Buxton at the solicitation of Miss Burnett, the writer, who was an invalid, and wished to see and converse with him. She was greatly interested in his work, and had for him personally the highest respect and esteem. Her letters to him are still preserved, in one of which she writes of his "fine, expressive face", and declared it would have been a great privilege to have been present at his trial in the Recorder's Court and listen to his noble defence.

HIS RULING PASSION.

The ruling passion was so strong in Carlile that he invariably sized-up every man or woman that he was brought into contact with to see if they had the stuff in them of which martyrs are made, or if they had a taste for philosophy, or capacity for the construction of a lecturer or an orator in the cause to which he himself was devoted. His influence on people of all classes with whom he was brought into contact was simply marvellous. His gentle affability and the genuine interest he displayed in other people's troubles and difficulties won all hearts. Privately he had not an enemy. It was wonderful too how the tradesmen he employed stood by him through thick and thin, his landlord especially never failed him through all his seizures and other troubles.

ELIZA SHARPLES CARLILE ("ISIS"). From a Crayon Copy of an Oil Painting.

PART II.

CHAPTER I.

"THE STORY OF ISIS"

THE LADY OF THE ROTUNDA

In the town of Bolton in Lancashire, England, early in the present century, lived a family named Sharples. It was a tradition in this family that a Richard Sharples, or Sharpie, came into England in the train of William of Normandy, and was given considerable land in the neighborhood of Bolton, in consideration of the services which he rendered to William at the time of the Conquest. However, we will leave the verification of this to those who care more about such things than does the writer. Our Richard Sharples was a manufacturer of quilts, bed-quilts, a peculiar kind of heavy white quilt with little white tufts or knots on them which were in the early days in almost universal use, and will be recollected by many of the mothers of to-day. They were called then "counterpanes", and lasted a lifetime or longer. Richard Sharples and his wife Ann were very much respected by their neighbors and lived in very comfortable, even affluent circumstances. They brought up and educated a family of four girls and two or three boys. Of the girls— Sarah, Anne, Eliza, and Maria—Sarah, the eldest, died from a decline in her young womanhood; Anne was married to a Mr. Tunnah, and Eliza became the "Isis" of our story. Maria was younger than Eliza by some seven years. Of the boys we have but little account except that one was drowned in his youth while swimming, and that another one, William, is mentioned by Carlile and Isis in some of their letters. Mrs. Ann Sharples was herself a very beautiful woman, and was described as a beauty by one who saw her at eighty years of age. Her hair then was snow-white, her eyes blue, her cheeks rosy and her complexion like a baby's. Our informant adds that she looked like "a Dresden china doll". It is possible that Eliza, who was the beauty of the family, was indebted to her mother for her good looks, but took her height and her disposition from her father. She was indeed, her father's favorite child, to whom also she was an anxiety on account of her beauty. He kept this daughter at a boarding school till she was more than twenty years of age, thinking that it was the safest place for her, and when he could keep her there no-longer she spent most of her time in the seclusion of her own room, sewing and reading. Her first sorrow was the loss of her father, to whom she was deeply attached, and it is probable that had he lived a few years longer there would not have been this story to tell. During one of the school vacations she was invited to visit a younger school-mate, who was the daughter of a banker of Liverpool. Whilst there this gentleman, whom we shall designate as Mr. A., told the young ladies that they would have to dine in their own room that day as he had a friend coming to dine with him and to discuss various matters, and wished to be alone with him for that purpose. In some way or other the name of Carlile leaked out, and this name Miss Eliza knew to belong to a very notorious man of whom she had heard dreadful things. The plans of the girls were soon laid, for their curiosity was greatly excited. So when the gentlemen had dined and the servants absented themselves,

147

the young ladies sought positions where they could hear and see everything that was said and done. The dining room was in communication with both front and side parlors by a door in each, and kneeling down on the rug at each door, with first their eyes then their ears at the keyholes, they heard every word and gazed their fill at the awful guest, who proved to be a very mild and amiable person, apparently quite harmless, and certainly handsome. I have nothing to say as to the dignity of the proceeding on the part of the young ladies, being content with certifying it to be the truth as told by Miss Eliza in after days. About a year after this, while calling on a cousin, she was surprised to find her reading a volume of Carlile's *Republican*. She remembered him as the gentleman she had seen in Liverpool. She then conceived an immediate desire to read some of his writings. The library which contained them was pointed out to her, and she began reading them with avidity, unknown to the family. She had seen the author under peculiar circumstances. His person and his manners were before her mind as she read his writings. She read with instructive astonishment. In those writings the ignorance and the errors of her past life were told to her as by a magician. We find her after a while making regular weekly visits to the bookseller who dealt in his works, and entering into conversation with that gentleman, a Mr. Hardie. At that time it was a rare thing for a young and beautiful girl to be interested in philosophical reading, particularly where that reading tended to freethinking, and Mr. Hardie in one of his business communications to Carlile made mention of the case. By this time both Carlile and Rev. Robert Taylor were in prison, and it looked as though freedom of speech had seen its best days. On the 5th of December, 1831, Mr. Hardie wrote again to Carlile saying:—

"You are requested to address a letter to Miss Sharples, care of A. Hardie. N.B.—She is a most amiable young woman, expects to be in London shortly, and will call and explain her views to you. I can say so far, that they are in the missionary line, and her *début* will create a sensation, as she is really a very beautiful girl. Do not, I beseech you, neglect this part of the business."

This aroused Carlile's curiosity, and he wrote her the following letter:—

"To Miss Sharples,

"Care of Mr. Hardie

"Madam,—I, a bachelor,* locked up in prison, and requested to write to a young lady to whom I have had no other introduction than that of having been informed that she is young, amiable, beautiful, and has a mind to become a Messiah. I will believe in this case without seeing, having more faith than St. Thomas. The Devil tempts me almost to doubt the good tidings; but I am so much interested in the first English lady who will publicly advocate those truths, which are a light needed to remove the present Cimmerian darkness, that I swear eternal fealty to her before I see her. I had much rather have answered a letter from Miss Sharples than to write comparatively in the dark; and if it be a serious request that I should write as the opening of an acquaintance, I hope to be favored with a letter by first post in return. My unabating zeal to encourage any lady that shall aim at the character of Hypatia and of Frances Wright, shall wait on every effort made. Such a lady shall be my daughter, my sister, my friend, my companion, my sweetheart, my wife, my everything. I should become a poet if my wishes on this head should become realised. Blessings will crown that head, and virtue's essence swell that bosom with noble dignity, when a woman shall be found bold and open enough to publicly instruct mankind in philosophical truths.

"Richard Carlile. London, December 8th, 1831."

To this he received the following reply:—

"To Mr. R. Carlile,

"Giltspur Street Compter, London.

"Sir,—Your esteemed favor I duly received, and am extremely sorry that I have only time to acknowledge the receipt, and thank you for the ready compliance with my request In consequence of a severe indisposition under which my mother now labors, and my being her sole nurse, my time is very much restricted. I trust, in my next, that circumstances will allow me to be more communicative. In the first place I must undeceive you as to an error into which you have been led in regard to my personal appearance. I am neither young nor beautiful, merely an every-day sort of a person. My age is upwards of twenty-five, my height rather above the middle size. However, be this as it may, you in a very short time will have an opportunity of judging, it being my intention to be in London in a very few weeks on a visit. I am a strenuous advocate of your cause and will do everything in my power to support and assist the Rev. Robert Taylor and yourself. I feel exceedingly sorry for that gentleman, and sigh when I reflect upon his situation, and think of the deprivations to which he is subject. How often have I wished that it was in my power to soothe, cheer and comfort him. Do you, I pray, endeavor to stimulate him. Tell him not to let his noble courage fail, it will be such a triumph for his persecutors. If my abilities were upon an equality with my

150

inclination, I should indeed make a shining figure in the world, or if my researches into philosophical truths had equalled my instruction in gospel errors, many years of unhappiness had been spared me; but more of this hereafter. I look anxiously forward to the time when we shall become better acquainted. Let me hear from you through the medium of A. Hardie, and with your permission

"I will reply.

"Farewell,

"E. Sharples.

"Bolton, Dec. 10, 1831.

"P.S.—Surrounded as I am by strict religionists, I have no one to whom I may impart my thoughts. If you will condescend to be my instructor, I shall feel proud in being selected by you as an object worthy your attention. You tell me that I should be everything to you. So be it. I once had the pleasure of seeing you in Liverpool and you have seen me, but you have no doubt forgotten it. Adieu."

This letter being written hurriedly, was followed by one more at length, and explanatory of her views. It was dated from Bolton, December 11th, 1831.

"Mr. Richard Carlile,

"Giltspur Street Compter, London.

"My Dear Sir,—Excuse the appellation. I have in some of your works read of your antipathy to such an expression from man to man, yet a lady may be allowed to make use of

151

a term of endearment, when it flows spontaneously from her heart, to express in some degree her approbation, preference, or attachment, without creating sentiments of indifference in your bosom. My scrawl of yesterday would intimate my readiness to enter into a correspondence with one on whom my thoughts have for a long time been fixed, and having just now a few moments to spare, I think I cannot do better than to devote them to improvement. Your extreme penetration will easily perceive my ignorance in letter writing, but if you will only condescend to be my instructor and make allowance for my weakness and errors, you will find me anxious to learn and to make some progress in philosophy. Believe me, my dear sir, I am very much interested in the cause. Although educated in the Church, I never felt so happy as now with regard to my principles, now that I am purified by a little knowledge from some of the errors of my education. Twelve months ago I had not even read or seen a critical work on Theology. Since then I have obtained and perused them as often as opportunity would permit, but, surrounded as I am by friends who are strict adherents to the Church, and being destitute entirely of friends to whom I may impart my thoughts and whose participation in them would elevate my enjoyment, my wish to form an acquaintance with yourself over-rules every other consideration; yet still I wish to act with discretion. While at home I am under the absolute necessity of acting the hypocrite, indeed I am becoming quite an adept. Circumstances oblige me to act contrary to my wishes, consequently my situation in that respect is not very enviable. I have, however, thrown off the fetters of superstition, and begin to find it as difficult to disguise my real sentiments as to assume those I do not feel. You may form a faint idea of my character and disposition when I tell you I have thought for myself for about three years; previously I had adhered as much as possible to the doctrines of the Church. In fact, I was quite an evangelical being, sang spiritual songs and prayed myself into the grave, almost. Accident brought me into acquaintance with A. Hardie. I have since perused your *Republican*. I cannot express to you the pleasure I enjoyed in meeting in every page sentiments exactly my own, but infinitely better expressed. I am sorry to be under the necessity of addressing this letter to a prison. Do not allow his Satanic Majesty to gain an ascendency over you! It was my intention to have spent Christmas in London, but in consequence of my mother's severe indisposition I must defer it. I am anxious to see, converse, and to become better acquainted with you. Give my kind respects to the Rev. Robt. Taylor if you have an opportunity. Tell him he has one female admirer, one female friend, and although a Deist, which in this place is a most dreadful word, particularly for a lady, yet one who never encouraged a thought inimical to virtue and honor. Hoping to hear from you very soon and with best wishes for your health, happiness and prosperity,

"I subscribe myself, my dear sir,

"Yours truly,

"Eliza Sharples."

Many other letters passed between Carlile and this lady, who became fired with the enthusiasm to become a volunteer in the good cause, and devote herself and whatever talent she might possess to the work under the direction of Carlile. The last, or the last but one of these Bolton letters was written on the last Christmas Day she was ever with her mother and her sisters, and we must pause for a moment in sympathy for that poor mother who was so soon to lose her brightest and best daughter. The time was close at hand when she would mourn this beloved

153

daughter as one lost to her for ever. For, sad to say, she was one of those marble-hearted Christians who could forgive anything but unbelief; and though our sympathy goes out to her for her sorrow at that time, it is restricted by the fact that she never forgave Isis for the step taken. No, not even to death itself nor to the children of Isis after their mother's death. Here is the letter written on old-fashioned foolscap paper that feels like parchment, and is to-day in most excellent preservation, though all these letters (of which only the preceding ones have been before printed) have travelled many thousand miles and been exposed to many vicissitudes for more than sixty years. This next letter was written to Carlile on Christmas Day, and we can see how quickly the idea of helping in the work of reform had taken root and was carrying her on to the new and unknown life, and how her quiet and peaceful past was falling away from her, like loosened garments from her shoulders, to be left behind her as she steps into the new life.

"Bolton, December 25th, 1831.

"ISIS POSTOPHORI—MY POSTOPHORI OMNIA,—

"My dear sister having just left me to attend her devotions at church, reminded me of my obedience to you. Under this impression my thoughts are committed to paper and transmitted to London; her thoughts are wandering—God knows where? Words are inadequate to express my feelings in being allowed to correspond with one who possesses such an exalted, noble, and generous mind. Would that our acquaintance had taken place years ago. I should not have been the ignorant girl I am. My aim in future will be to make up for time lost by strict application to study. Do you think I can be of any service when I come to town? You may depend upon my perseverance and attention. Nevertheless, I am fearful of being found dull and stupid, because deficiency and imperfection are natural, at least constant attendants upon all my undertakings. Oh! that my humble endeavors may be crowned with success. Every exertion shall be called forth, every effort, every attempt made to enlighten myself first, and then to diffuse that knowledge and instruction to mankind which is so universally wanted. I am an enemy to every kind of subordination and persecution. I am an enemy to 'kings and priests and lords'. I am a female reformer; but a consistent one. I am also a philanthropist, in an eminent degree an admirer of Carlile's and Taylor's characters. The opportunities that have been offered me in making my enquiries into theological truths were exceedingly limited. Those opportunities were not lost; I am convinced that all religion is vice; experience has taught me to believe so, and it is not in the power of even the Archbishop himself to convince me to the contrary. I feel proud in being called an Infidel, and wish that all mankind felt as I do. What a reformation, what a glorious reform we should have! If I remember rightly it was I that retired from the room into which you were shown at Mr. A————'s? Had our introduction taken place at that time, what years of happiness had been mine; my desire to be introduced was very great, and I particularly requested the favor, but all in vain. I am greatly indebted for the interest you are making in my behalf; assure those friends that their kindness and attention will not be bestowed upon an ungrateful object-The inducement to my conduct in this correspondence proceeds from an unquestionable nature, an inducement to render myself useful to society generally. My pretensions to knowledge are at present very few indeed, but under such a master I am sure to improve rapidly. Mother and sister are quite ignorant of the particulars of my journey to town. I have an antipathy to everything connected with intrigue, but under the present circumstances am obliged to act cautiously in consideration for my mother's feelings, for which I have a very great regard. I am quite at your service, so you may appoint any time you think proper for my departure. Everything relative to my family and friends shall be made known to you verbally; they are respectable. My dependence is entirely upon my mother, but she being very feeling and considerate, gives no reason for dissatisfaction. My anxiety to commence my new career grows stronger every day. My wishes to prove the sincerity of my assertions are equally so-Will you add to your kindness by pointing out the best method of conveyance? My travelling has been rather confined, so the least information will be very gladly received. This letter is quite unconnected. I think if I have been called off once, I have been called off twenty times. Sunday is generally a gossiping day, and more particularly being Christmas Day. I must conclude by wishing you the compliments of the season. My kind wishes to Mr. Taylor. Grant me the indulgence of a letter very soon. I quite expected sending you a very long letter very closely written, but am disappointed. Ere your next arrives you will have come to a decision, perhaps, as to the time of my leaving here. I went up to Hardie's yesterday to meet my letter, which came safe to hand, and took opportunity of sending you a few lines (which have been or will be received ere you receive this) from there. May you be blessed with health, happiness and prosperity, and continue to increase in knowledge, and may you have every succeeding day an opportunity of defeating your oppressors and of imparting your sentiments to mankind, and be able to induce them to turn their thoughts on that which conduces to their happiness, their honor, and their prosperity.

"Eliza or Isis."

The summons she awaited was not long in reaching her, and so we find her on the 11th January, 1832, starting for

London, which she reached safely, and lost no time in getting into active service. She called on Carlile in the Giltspur Street prison, and after a lengthy consultation with him, set about opening up the Rotunda again. It is needless to say that Carlile was more than pleased with the beauty and intelligence as well as the courage displayed by the young lady, and he accepted her as a veritable Joan of Arc for the cause to which he was devoted. Almost her first act was to go to Lord Melbourne and procure his permission to reopen the Rotunda on her promise that while she was in charge of it, there should be nothing but philosophic lecturers and discussions take place there. To Lord Melbourne she made known her name and family connections, as also her object, viz., to assist as much as possible to support both Carlile and Taylor while they were in prison. It is fair to say that the gentleman treated her kindly and granted her request. Isis delivered her first lecture at the Rotunda on the 29th of January, a little over two weeks after her arrival from Lancashire. From consideration for the feelings of her family, her mother most particularly, her name and connections were carefully concealed from the public, and she became known as the "Lady of the Rotunda". Isis, the name Carlile had given her in his letters, was adopted as the name of a weekly publication which was started in February and kept up for about two years. Naturally, the novelty of the proceeding, combined with the beauty and talent of the lady, and the mystery surrounding her, drew many hearers. She was the first woman to take the platform as an independent thinker and public speaker in England. Almost, as a matter of course, she was inundated by letters of adoration, curiosity, approbation and so on, and proposals of all kinds. Any of these that seemed to carry a double purpose in it were answered publicly in the columns of the *Isis*. She preserved her *incognita* completely so far as the public was concerned, and also kept herself free from all private

157

calumny. On Sunday and two or three times a week she lectured at the Rotunda and various other places by invitation. The study necessarily incident to these frequent lectures occupied the whole of her time, and except for her visits to Carlile in prison in Giltspur Street, and the Rev. Robt. Taylor in Horsemonger Lane Gaol, she had no diversion of any kind. There is no doubt at all but that Carlile outlined all her lectures for her, for it would have been impossible for an inexperienced country girl with the ordinarily narrow education of her time and class to have been able to have pleased a metropolitan audience of reading and thinking men and women. As it was, she delivered the lectures in a very quiet and dignified manner, and at their close quietly left the platform, leaving to others the task of discussing or defending the arguments used or the merit or demerit of the discourse itself. Frequently her exit had to be made through a long double-lined passage of admirers. Flowers were offered in profusion. She would sometimes accept a few simple ones with an inclination of the head or a "Thank you", but never stayed her steps for an instant. She busied herself in procuring for Mr. Taylor a modification of his sentence, or at least some mitigation of the severities practiced upon him. Writing to Carlile from Horsemonger Lane Gaol, January 12, 1832, the Rev. Robt. Taylor says:—

"I am much delighted with your 'new born hope'. 'Isis' is the very name. The Goddess, I am already an idolator. My eager adoration anticipates her ephiphany! She is indeed Isis Omnia to our cause. If she should realise your description and my fancies, the path of immortality is open before her."

He adds a postscript:—

"I have just seen Isis, who beyond all I had dreamed makes me happy. She will, she must succeed. I have seen her star in the East, and am her worshipper."

A little later she addressed a petition to Lord Melbourne in Taylor's behalf, wherein she makes mention of his "proneness to jest" on what are considered sacred subjects, and that his best friends regretted that tendency of the rev. gentleman, who was really the finest orator and deepest student in the country, and a man of wonderful genius, ect., ect. But the prisoner took great umbrage at this, and would have no pardon of this getting. The petition itself was innocent enough and was really of Carlile's framing, and Taylor had no better friend than Carlile. But the rev. gentleman was very much of a spoilt child, and it was always difficult to keep him in good humor. It was two or three of Taylor's jokes which gained him the two years' imprisonment he received on the last trial. A little note in Mr. Taylor's handwriting, but without date, showed how keenly he felt the reflection on his good sense.

"Mr. Taylor begs to be spared the superfluous pain of seeing a person who has injured him so grievously, and has made the pretence of presenting a petition on his behalf a means of insulting him more than his bitterest enemy could have done. Mr. Taylor would have rather terminated his existence, with his own hand, than have accepted his deliverance upon that degrading and atrociously insulting promise and condition with which Miss Sharples has taken upon herself to implore it. Mr. Taylor has written to Lord Melbourne to counteract as much as possible the mischievous and scandalous falsehood of which Miss Sharples has been the instrument. Mr. T.'s only hopes of a lessening of his term of imprisonment rested in the doubt that existed in Lord M.'s mind as to the nature of the alleged offence. Miss S. has removed that doubt and justified the imprisonment to any extent.

"To Miss Sharples,

"Editress of the *Isis*."

Following this, in a few days, after Carlile had written to Taylor telling him that "he ought to apologise to Isis on his knees for grieving her thus, when she was turning every stone to do him good ". Taylor replied:—

"Ah, Lord! you talk of romance and recommend wisdom and reason. Nobody loves wisdom and reason more than I do; but my knees are now too stiff to undergo the operation you recommend. I would rather and better support the consciousness of being altogether in the wrong, than to rescue even my life itself by kneeling. If you should find me as I intend you shall, on good terms with Miss Sharples, they will not have been achieved by kneeling. Mark! I will achieve my peace without you. Humiliations never yet healed grievances,

"Yours affectionately,

"R. Taylor."

Later still we find him lamenting from the bottom of his heart that he should ever have been the cause of bringing tears to those lovely violet eyes, and asks forgiveness for whatever has seemed excessive in the expression of his grief, which has indeed been intense, and "assure Miss Sharples that I am sorry in my soul for the weight which my mental anguish has thrown upon her".

Several months passed away and the further acquaintance and constant daily interviews of Miss Sharples with Richard Carlile, which were necessary to the business and the cause in which they were both so earnestly engaged, developed a very strong attachment between them. It would seem, almost, as though Miss Sharples had been reserved for this union, it being more than singular that she should have arrived at the age of twenty-six without having met anyone who had made any impression upon her heart. Yet she had many admirers, and indeed, one would think that so beautiful a girl had been formed for love alone. We cannot find, however, a single instance in her history which would show that her heart had ever been touched before she met Carlile. It seemed as though she was waiting for the summons to take her part in the allotted task, and when he wrote to her in his delight at hearing of a young and beautiful woman who wanted to wield a sword in the battle of free thought, saying that such a woman should be everything to him, she was not surprised, but expressed her complete willingness in her simple "so be it". But when she was brought into close relationship with Carlile and had the opportunity of seeing the genuine superiority of his character, the generosity, the unselfishness, the amiability of his temper, his kindness to everybody in his employ, his great love and patience with his children, and his unfailing sense of justice in all the relations of life, she found one who was worthy of all the love and appreciation she had to bestow, and he received it: a love that filled the measure to overflowing. Unfortunately, Carlile had been and was still paying the penalty of the mistake of his early manhood, his unhappy marriage, although after twenty years of unhappiness he was as free as he could be when no divorce was possible. So, in this state of affairs, Carlile did all that was left to him to do, and that was to explain every particular of his situation to her, for her consideration and reflection.

CHAPTER II.

ISIS TO RICHARD CARLILE

The first shock to the happiness of Carlile and Isis was caused by the receipt of a letter from her brother which induced the following:—

"Health and Tranquillity! A letter from Bolton has at length found its way to London, and my bosom is bursting with indignation and sorrow, with indignation for the contemptible and satirical style and manner in which the letter is written; and sorrow for a parent's suffering. My God! what shall I do? Leave you, my dear Richard, I cannot, it would be death to me and your hopes, and your and my cause. My own hopes are that mother is not so ill as represented, and that they have written in such a strain to induce me to give up my purpose. What must I do? Oh! how I wish that you were at liberty to advise and comfort me. I am quite alone in this large place. David wished to go out with Thomas, and I could not refuse, 'tis the first time the request was made. Mrs. Hudson merely gave me the letter and then went out again; all is shut up and I feel to want your presence so much. Oh! Richard, I think my heart will burst, that cruel, taunting, unkind, insulting letter. I could have forgiven him if it had not contained the distressing intelligence of my mother's illness (inconsiderate, unfeeling wretch, you have not written in haste, but must have sat and premeditated every word, so-that you might doubly wound, doubly wring my over-whelmed heart). My dear Richard, what must I do? You are

162

all the world to me, yet I cannot divest myself of those feelings which are now almost too much for me to bear. Were I to return home to-morrow it would perhaps avail nothing, and the idea is madness itself to me. You must forgive me, Richard, for troubling you with my grief and sorrow; but methinks my brain will turn if I do not give you a little of them. Remember you are my friend, my husband, and never did I require your love, your care so much as now. My brother has probed to my heart's core, by heaven, I think I shall never forgive him. I will never again write to him. He shall never hear from me. I will write to my sister to-morrow; how I feel for her, poor Maria. My heart is torn with contending emotion. I long to go home for mother's sake and Maria's, but for my own sake I wish to remain with you. I feel quite assured that if I return home that I shall never see you again, and what say you to that? Are you willing to relinquish your Isis, your bride? Oh Richard, do endeavor for my sake to obtain your liberty. I will endeavor to be all that you can wish. I will strive to equal Miss F. Wright. My eyes are quite swollen with tears, the first I have shed since I came to town. I wish much to breakfast with you this morning, but really I am afraid the Governor will think my visits too frequent. I, however, hope to see you some part of the day and to hear from you early in the morning. I am afraid, my dear Richard, you will think me very weak, very unlike a philosopher. It was only to-day I was boasting of courage and firmness. I cannot but think that empty vessels make the greatest sound.

"Good Night."

After this it was agreed between Carlile and Isis that she should return home for a short visit and satisfy herself as to her mother's condition, and to ease her mother's mind as to her own well-being, which certainly was the wisest thing to

163

do. In the following letter she takes leave of Carlile for a time:—

"Of all men the most intelligent and the most beloved! When you receive this note I shall be in person many miles distant, but united in heart, in thought, in corresponding sentiment, in mind, in soul, in mutual love and affection. These are the two first days that we have been separated, that we have been taken away from each other; and although I am writing this before my departure, because there will be no opportunity of sending during my absence, I can very easily anticipate what my feeling and disposition will be on. Sunday morning. I shall be surrounded by friends anxious to make me comfortable, and they will wear a smile upon their faces; but my bosom will pant for him whom it has-been accustomed to meet, and whom it adores. It will pant for its accustomed embrace from him on whom my eyes gaze with pleasure and delight, him whose features shine with perfect integrity, with confidential affection, with intelligence, with candor, with conscious dignity, with friendship, with reciprocal love, and with manly beauty. My attachment becomes stronger every day. The more I see and know of you the more I admire, love, and esteem you, and the more reluctant I am to be absent one moment from you. Oh! may it be always thus. In twenty years may we embrace each other in tried affection, and again renew our engagement of everlasting fidelity, honesty, and truth. I sincerely love you, and flatter myself that my absence will be a little regretted to-day, the day on which I shall request David to convey this note. Let us be happy in the kind assurance of each other's love; let us bless each other with a free, affable, and corresponding deportment towards each other. Let us strengthen each other so as to be able to contend with existing evils, but let us never deviate one moment from our principles. Let not the presence of the Misses Laws on Sunday make you to forget me. Remember, my love, that now I have a double claim to your protection, to your assistance, to your kind protection, to your solicitude, to your love. Oh! do be faithful, be constant, do not encourage a thought to arise that will, in the least, stem the torrent of affection with which my bosom is overflowing.

"I hope ere this your cold is better. Do, my dear Richard, take care of yourself. The name of Richard is doubly dear to me; my father, my beloved father's name was Richard, and now my husband's, my lover's name is Richard. I love to dwell upon it. Adieu, most valued, most beloved of men. God bless you, my philosopher!"

This little visit to Bolton relieved the mind of Isis of some anxiety in regard to the mother she had so abruptly left, and convinced also the mother that the determination to follow the course she had mapped out for herself was no idle purpose, but one of principle and duty. Besides, she was wholly linked to Carlile in spirit, in principle, in the object to be attained, in business, and in the strongest bond of all—that of love. As she said herself, "Her spirit was wedded to the spirit of her husband before she had spoken to him". With him was life, without him was death. Probably never before had a prison witnessed such an exhibition of awakening love and almost perfect happiness. To Isis it was not only the opening up of the fountain of knowledge, but that of love also, and seldom have those two all-powerful streams been more beautifully and more fittingly blended. Their agreement was that they should make the best marriage contract that could be made at that time, that she should unite her name with his and be known as Mrs. Sharples Carlile, her private signature to be Elizabeth Sharples Carlile, and the public announcement of their moral marriage to be made immediately upon his liberation from the Giltspur Street Compter, which was then in early prospect. But the action of the authorities in refusing her admission to the gaol caused an earlier explanation of the facts of the association to be made, and was understood by all their private friends. It was not, however, till May 29th, 1834, that it was publicly announced in the dedication of the first volume of the *Isis*. An outbreak of cholera in the city of London gave to the authorities of the gaol an excuse to keep out all visitors. This was truly an unexpected blow to both, but to poor Isis it was almost a killing blow. Carlile had to find courage and fortitude for them both. The letters that passed daily between them were of the most affectionate character, and Isis poured out her soul in love and adoration through them. Unfortunately for the better sequence of this correspondence, many of Carlile's letters have been lost, but enough remains to show the character of it. It is very difficult to arrange these letters in proper order, owing to the fact that they were not dated, being exchanged by bearers or messengers making regular trips once or twice a day. It is only by a searching out of dates and of facts, otherwise known, that it is possible to place them with any degree of accuracy or fitness.

This love which Isis poured out so lavishly was of the old-fashioned kind, of happily an old-fashioned time: the time when women had no other avenue for their pent-up feelings or ambitions, the only avenue which opened up for them except their church, their sewing, or their household cares, their dresses or their gossips; when they were wholly dependent upon their relatives for their support; when no diplomas awaited their eager studies; when the luxury of self-earned money was unknown to them; when the curse of Puritan propriety was laid on them, when a skip or a jump was a crime against young ladyhood; when all the possibilities of the present age were undreamed of, and women were bound by the iron rule of precedent and respectability. Even our poor Isis was only in a transitional state, and had much to unlearn and overcome.

Here are some extracts from her letters of that time:—

"Your letter to me of to-day is really a most delightful one. I have read it over and over again, pressed it as frequently to my lips and blessed its author. I feel the value of your friendship most fervently, and feel myself happy in your choice. How kind, how very kind and considerate is your behaviour toward me. Believe me, your acquaintance is duly appreciated, and expect and hope that twenty years hence our feelings and affection will be still the same. I feel that mine will never change, whatever fortune may allot me. I am very much in arrears with you in letter writing. I believe a bankruptcy will have to take place, at least a compromise. I send you an *Observer*, loaf sugar, and a little tea, as much as can be afforded this evening. Heaven bless you, my love, anchor of my affection and my hope, solace and comfort of my life, inferior to none and without an equal."

"The light-fingered goddess to her friend and beloved companion. You desire me to be happy; and you, my friend, a prisoner. Be really happy, you say. Think of my situation for a moment, and then you will be led to exclaim, 'No, poor girl, I must make her happy, her happiness will depend upon me '. I am waiting, oh! how anxiously, for your liberation, and then, and not till then shall I be able to say, 'I am happy'."

"Happiness!

"There was only one object wanting to render Mr. Owen's institution a perfect paradise. The company was very numerous, being, I suppose, about 2,000 individuals in

167

attendance, upon whose countenances joy, health and happiness seemed to beam. Oh! what folly to look beyond this world for heaven, I thought, as I gazed upon the happy throng. Oh! that man would become rational, make, for it is in his power, a heaven upon the earth; instead of which, like the dog in the fable, he is grasping at a shadow and losing the substance. Oh! that man would cease to be inconsistent, that he would cease to act so contrary to reason and common sense by soaring above his comprehension and understanding in search of that which is in his immediate possession. My evening's amusement was greatly enhanced by the introductions which took place between myself and several of the delegates, particularly those who came from Lancashire. I was introduced as the 'Lady Isis', and was indeed warmly, and I may say affectionately, received. My fame, they were pleased to say, had spread abroad in Lancashire, and the co-operators were anxiously awaiting the time when you and I could pay them a visit. Your name being introduced, and with so much ardor and respect, afforded me additional pleasure. Two or three were requested by the society to see you, if possible, and are calling to-day at Fleet Street in order to be taken by me to prison. What think you, love, must I attend them or send Mullins? You must decide. Do say yes, because remember I did not see you yesterday. I promise not to stay a moment with you; and I really have a great deal to say, for I have seen a gentleman from Bolton who heard a sermon preached in our church on the Farce day, and all about me. Now must not I come just while I tell you the news? The hour appointed for the two gent.'s to call here is one o'clock. Now, love, if you think it will be more prudent to remain at my post, I will submit cheerfully, although to-morrow I may not see you. My visit to the amiable Misses Laws must be deferred to-morrow, I cannot go and lecture too. Mr. Smith is going, he told me. I saw Mr. Prout last evening, and had a nice chat with him. I have sent you a number of the *Co-operative Society*. I thought of filling up this bit of paper, but Thomas is waiting. Adieu."

"Now, love, I have just a moment to spare. I assure you that with the exception of the short time it took to prepare your little dinner, my absence from the shop has not amounted to more than half-an-hour. The dinner was rather late, in consequence of my being detained in the shop. I did not fidget about it, because I felt desirous that you should have time to enjoy it. Oh, my dearest Richard, excuse me, but really I must mention the subject that lays nearest and dearest to my heart first, my separation from you; everything else sinks into nothingness in comparison of that greatest of all evils and troubles and trials—my separation; overcome this point, and I will be happy and cheerful and gay. On the contrary, I am sure, I shall not survive a month. It is nonsense to preach patience and philosophy, I'll not hear it, my patience is exhausted and all my philosophy falls to the ground. All my thoughts, all my hopes tend towards seeing you on Sunday. If I am disappointed, I shall bid farewell to all hope. You must insist upon seeing me just once to explain matters of business, etc., etc. Oh, dear, I will see you. Indeed, I must! Now, love, the second trouble. I have sent to Standige's, and they very politely said £15 would satisfy them until next week. I have sent the £15, so let your mind be at ease on that point. Do, do, Richard, if you love me, obtain me an interview; it will reward me for a world of pain and suffering. You know not how this separation presses upon my heart, and to-morrow—But I will not anticipate anything unfavorable, you, I know dear, you will do your best. I wish I was Miss Newell* for a day or two. Copeland is waiting, love. I send you a *Crisis* and two oranges, in haste. Bless you. Good night, my beloved, my honored Richard. I hope we shall yet be happy."

And now comes another style of letter.

"Isis to her well-beloved Richard—'Happiness'.

"I was surprised by a visit from two ladies last night after nine o'clock, and who do you think they were? Mrs. Robinson and Mrs. Brooks, they wondered what had become of me, and felt anxious to know. Mr. Owen has likewise been very punctual in his enquiries, and wishes much to see me."

Phrenologically speaking, her head was said to be the exact counterpart of that of Lafayette, and the similarity was often alluded to by lecturers on the then new and fashionable study of phrenology. While this has been said frequently, the writer thinks a mistake has been made, for having recently seen photographs of the death mask of Lafayette, she can detect no similarity. The head of Isis was purely feminine in form; one cannot say this of the head of the French general, if these masks be genuine.

Mrs. Robinson mentioned Friday for my first visit, and I inadvertently agreed to go, where I shall have the pleasure of being introduced to other members and Owenites. Let me be wherever I may, my heart is always with you. I never am so happy as when with you, and allow me, again and again, to assure you of my love, friendship, and esteem. My hope is, Richard, that you will survive me, after twenty years' engagement, that you will receive my last sigh, that my latest breath will be received on your affectionate bosom; the firm reliance that I have on your honor and character gives strength to my love. I feel that you are the best man in the world, and I the most favored woman. I want my lecture for this evening, to study. When may I expect the one for Sunday? You are really worked to death, and I am ashamed of myself. What can I send you, love?"

"Pardon for my neglect. I have been busily engaged in reading the discourse for last Sunday evening, which has afforded me infinite pleasure. I really think, love, it is superior to any of the former ones, and much regret that I had not an opportunity of delivering it. How beautifully sentimental in all its passages. I am pleased beyond measure. The paragraph, particularly, commencing with 'Let me again and again impress upon your minds that there can be no error in a well-spent life', I admire. I am glad to hear of your good health and spirits. May they always remain tranquil. Copeland is waiting with the newspapers, and I must not detain him. Must I visit you to-morrow? I hope so; if not, I will ask Mrs. Smith to accompany me in a walk to-morrow afternoon. My heart is aching."

Carlile wanted Isis to become a philosophical lover, and had written her something to that effect, which called forth the following letter:—

"Why, my dear, this very paragraph alone is sufficient to turn the argument in my favor. You say that you should have by right given me on the first onset five or seven years of hard study in philosophy; and then again you say, perhaps had you done so, I should ere this have run away, you not being so situated as to be able to lock me up, or I should have died. Does not that prove that there is nothing charming about philosophy; or why fear me? I am enamored with love. I love with all my heart, with all my mind, and with all my soul, and with all my strength. I very soon found out the beauties of love; I have experienced the delightful sensation that love produces. I have felt its power; I have received its cheering influence, and have drank deep draughts from the fountain of love. In vain have I been endeavoring to find out the charms of this divine philosophy. The charms of love presented themselves immediately to my view. But no, like the glorious

171

Constitution of England, its charms are lost, are hidden, and the more you become acquainted with either the more anxious are you to run away from both. Such is the impression that remains still upon the mind. And your letter, believe me, has advocated the cause of love more ardently than even mine did, for one word in favor of philosophy you have bestowed twenty in favor of love. 'Tis true, indeed, the first sheet of paper was entirely occupied with the subject of love. The commencement of the second sheet, says, 'How charming is divine philosophy, not dull and crabbed. It is the perfection of love, and to this I want to bring you.' Then again you fall into full strain and sing the praises and glories of love. I confess myself that I have never been a philosopher, because I saw nothing in it to admire. I saw everything in love, and I want to become a scientific lover—not a philosopher, but an unequalled lover, a paragon of perfection, of constancy, and of faithful love—pure, uncontaminated, unsophisticated, unmixed, natural love. Love sincere and true wants not the aid of philosophy; does not want any restraint and will not bear it, it cannot long exist in thraldom. It must be free as the air we breathe. It will not be told that it must love thus far and no further. No, no, that will never do. I do not say that it is to be indulged in to the injury of other duties or claims; that it is to satiate itself. No, that would be a mere carnal passion, an animal propensity, and a profanation to call it love. It is not the love I feel, not the kind of love that I am pleading the cause of: I want a love, virtuous and pure, but still unbounded. When we talk of moderate love, philosophical love, etc., it amounts to nothing. There is no such a thing as a moderate true lover. Pray tell me how do you like a moderate reformer? 'Tis just the same. A Whig, a half and half sort of a Radical. Nay, the subject will not bear the comparison. I am an out and out Republican, an enemy to kings, priests and lords, and have not patience to hear anyone talk of being a politician when his head is stuffed up with superstition. And how in the name of wonder can you preach philosophy to me in my present situation, surrounded as I am by almost insurmountable difficulties? If I had only one very large one to overcome then I might listen with some degree of patience to-your preaching and entreaties. But then I have a thousand little troubles, real troubles, besides all my imaginary ones, and they are numberless. And I have one as huge as a mountain, our separation. Ah! none of your philosophy for me, I make no account of it, Diogenes (I don't know if I am correct in spelling the name, but you will understand to whom I allude). He might very comfortably preach philosophy he having nothing to do with the practice of it—no-cares, no troubles, no nothing upon his mind, and really he had nothing to engross his time but to roll an old tub about and write moral sentences and philosophy. I tell you what, Richard Carlile, I will make this agreement with you, that if you will consent to my going into the country and taking up my abode in some sequestered spot, far from the busy haunts of men, I will become all you wish me to be, quite a philosopher in petticoats; I will write pastorals. I shall then have no annoyances; I will even try to forget you for a time. I think a few years' study would make me perfect, quite inanimate. You say, 'imitate me'. I cannot, you're a man, and Richard Carlile. Can the ass ever inherit the strength of the horse? Can weakness ever become strength? Can woman become man? Can I change my nature? I respect, I admire, I esteem, I love where I find it impossible to imitate. You are an exception, and where you point out yourself as an example you do not give me fair play. We are now in the nineteenth century, and you cannot find me one dignified woman as an example. I only ask you for one. I shall enter more fully into this subject again, if I am allowed. I have not written well today. I was much pleased with your effusion of love. I will not accept you as a father, as an example. I am almost inclined to think that I am

173

jealous of your superiority of character over mine, and am aiming at being a more jealous lover than you. Love is a delightful study; I feel and know it to be so, and shall never be less a lover than now. I find the passion to grow upon me, and I am not a wild-fire. You say let there be no more nonsense, and that you do not like that foolish kind of love, wild and romantic. It is not good nor lasting. Why, then, did you arouse, by your kindness, by your attention, by your example, by everything but precept, my affection to such a pitch of love? You have endeavored by every inducement that lay in your power to implant the seed of love in my bosom, and now, when you see the fruits, you are alarmed, you are distressed. What! did you not know human nature better than to expect patience? Ah, you may talk, you may preach, you may pretend, you may assume an angry appearance, you may threaten; but it will not do. Now pray tell me, if you can, I say mention but the name of one individual in whom the two passions have been encouraged, in whose heart philosophy and love have taken up their abode at one and the same time. I am young in philosophy, and yet you are angry because I am not a sage. You are angry and distressed because I have paid more regard to your example than to your preaching. I knew a priest once that said: 'Do not do as I do, but do as I say.' Now there was honesty. Well, well, you are, you may be a philosopher. I know that in every affair that concerns us in the way of business and in the generality of human affairs, that you are bold and honest, just, calm and patient under the most trying circumstances. Cool, courageous, and mild under disappointments and perplexities and difficulties, in fact that you are a philosopher in everything but love. You may smile and say I am mistaken. I tell you that I am right in my calculation, in my conjecture; come, come, be honest on this point, give your love a favorable answer. Yes, say, love me in your own way, that is, tenderly and affectionately; love me and never mind philosophy. You blame me. How in the name of heaven can you expect me to be reasonable in such a dilemma, between snow and heat, between two such extremes, and one is pulling me one way and the other is dragging me in an opposite direction? Decide, Richard Carlile, will you have your Isis, a wild, romantic, erring, loving, kind, affectionate creature, sometimes weak and making you a little angry at times, hoping, fearing, sincere, faithful, changeable, warmhearted, kind, generous, thoughtful but grateful, thankful for your kindness and sensible of your worth, say, will you have me a woman, or will you have me a philosopher? Whichever character you prefer, I will become that one. As a philosopher I will not smile, I will view every change with philosophic indifference and exclaim with Pope, 'Whatever is, is right'. My heart shall never be overburdened with care, my countenance never change, I will neither laugh nor cry, sorrow shall not make me weep, misfortune shall not affect me, and when I again behold you I shall be a stoic: no expression of love or of pleasure, no exhibition of feeling, no, no, that would be disgraceful, my character would suffer. Charming philosophy! No, love, I tell you again I cannot be both, that the two characters cannot be associated in the same person, and I defy you to point out one example—say 'Imitate this philosophical love, encouraging, admirable woman!' And should you do so, should you happen to have hit upon one female in the course of your deep reading and researches, I would immediately tell you that she had not a lover in prison, and if she had that she was not prohibited from occasionally beholding and conversing with him; and if she was, that she was not within a few days of being a mother, and if she was that she did not live at 62, Fleet Street; that she had not to fear a despicable Whig Government; that she did not fear for her lover's safety, and if she did, that her love did never equal mine; and if, after encountering all these perplexities she could boast calm fortitude and philosophical love and indifference, I do not envy, do not wish to be possessed of such feeling. Ah, Richard, have not wisdom, strength and power fled when love gains possession of the heart? Of what use was Solomon's wisdom or Samson's strength? Where then was philosophy? 'Tis nonsense to talk of both. Such a doctrine fails when it comes to be put in practice, and you know it only you want honesty, philosophy and love. You must be both. I will be both, but it must be when our child is born; it must be the hero; I still must remain what I am, a mere woman.

"Living in a retired, quiet spot of ground, having your mind at ease, your wants supplied, and your wishes gratified, that is the hour, then is the time to talk philosophically. I got into a little fit of love this morning. I begged Miss Philosophy to help me over it, but the cross old maiden lady used me very ill, just as you would fancy a cross old maiden lady treating a young, lovely girl of twenty, did this maid treat me. I thought of you, and then I was uneasy. I thought again philosophically; then by way of a little stimulant, I rummaged for that very ugly letter you sent me the week before we were separated. You must remember it. A 'to be burnt' letter you called it. It assisted my bit of philosophy most wonderfully. Do you remember the contents of that letter? Oh, this letter has assisted my philosophy most wonderfully. I almost think that if I received a note for admission in the compter to-morrow morning, that I should have magnanimity of soul sufficient for a Seneca's wife. Now what say you? I will have you make a choice. No both. Must I practise love? I will adhere to either of the two characters but not to both. I shall spoil myself and be neither one nor the other. Make a choice, oh! make a choice. Pure nature's feeling for me, altho' I may err 'tis not of the heart; let me be thought weak and irresolute. I perhaps am so, but I never hoped to be called unfeeling. Must your Isis love you or must she not? that is the question; or must she assume an indifference that she does not feel: a cold, calculating, philosophical, dignified indifference? Come, make a choice; oh, make a choice; philosophy or love?"

CHAPTER III.

LETTERS TO "ISIS"

A little later comes this letter of Maria, the younger sister of "Isis". It was written because of two open letters which appeared in the *Isis*, the publication of that name. We neither criticise nor defend these letters, they were no doubt outlined by Carlile in his usual habit of publicity and with the best of intentions, but there is also no doubt that they startled and wounded the feelings of the family deeply. In those days to have your name in the paper was a disgrace, unless under the heading of Births, Marriages or Deaths.

"1832. Her sister Maria to the Editress of the *Isis*.

"My Dear Eliza,—

"'Isis,' I suppose I am to call you, since you have renounced your Christian name, and taken one instead which I can find only in the heathen mythology. I have received both your letters, and indeed in a form which I should least of all have expected, and least of all wished for any member of our reputable and respectable, but always retiring and obscure family. You are the first one that ever had the ambition to appear before the public, and I must confess that that ambition, extraordinary as it is, appears under circumstances that raise it above all suspicion of the influences which are the ordinary incentives to ambition. It cannot be any ordinary pursuit of riches, nor any very particular regard to reputation that has placed my sister in a situation of such peculiar attachment to an individual whom the law of his country has-placed in a gaol.

"But as I am no philosopher, as you profess to be, and therefore unable to judge of things (as you would) save as they really are, I am obliged to confine my judgment to the nature of things as they appear to be, and as the judgments of society are necessarily governed by appearances, we surely claim too much from society when we expect its good opinions and its bestowal of confidence, without paying the compliment of our attention and regard to appearances. An authority which you ever respected, and which our dear departed father would have us both to respect through life, has counselled us: Whatsoever things are pure, whatsoever things are lovely, whatsoever things are of good report, if there is any praise think on these things. And this, I presume, would have been no counsel to regulate young women's deportment in society, even though she had come to discover that the faith in which her father lived in virtue, and died in hope, was a mere being, held bound or tied fast to a system, a dogma, a ceremony, a discipline. But at the distance to which you have pleased to remove yourself from us, a distance I fear greater than miles can measure, we, your religious family, have no means of judging of your conduct but by report, and it is with an aching heart that I find that the frightful corroboration of your own report against yourself. In your first letter, which I read in print in the *Isis* No. 34, purporting to be edited by a lady, and that lady to be my sister Eliza, you are pleased to expose to the world what certainly the world could have as little curiosity to know as I had inclination to discover, and it is hardly making me amends to publish at the same time the uncalled for acknowledgment that you were a young woman when I, you say (and I thank you, madam, for the advertisement), who am calculating on some early settlement for future life, 'was yet a child'. I am willing to give you as much honor as you would wish for the advantage you have over me in the point of age, though there is a sort of heroism in the extraordinary virtue of a young lady telling the world that she is in the view of thirty, which other young ladies of the same age would feel more disposed to admire than to imitate. But that advantage of quite sufficiently advanced age, on the score of which you are fully authorised to be the instructress, example, and guide of your sister at one and twenty, like all other advantages, involves a corresponding accountability, and gives the world a right to expect and to understand that a lady of such an age does not play with language with the unwary simplicity of a 'Miss in her teens', nor bandy sentences of a construction which may bear meanings to other minds of which her own was unconscious. The composition of a woman of thirty will never be interpreted according to the simplicity of a girl of fifteen. In the stationary and the staid condition in which our father left us, and left us with his best wishes and prayers that we might continue steadfast even to the end, you will not wonder that I should have consulted our minister, the Rev. H. T., in this great calamity, to me, of receiving two letters in print of such a nature as those in Nos. 34 and 35 of the *Isis*. I thank you for the admission that our minister (for so he was once, and I hope he will be again, both yours and mine) is an amiable man, and that you know he is amiable. Your good opinion of him to that extent would not have been lessened could you but have witnessed with what a generosity of soul he received and read the new sort of questions which a wandering member of his congregation had propounded to him. A sort of questioning, indeed, from which the character of Mr. T.'s suggestive influence is written as with a sunbeam. You bid me examines his motives. Well, my dear sister, well, the advice which you give to me is transcendently well. It is a wise, a discreet, a becoming caution in us young women to examine men's motives, especially ere we take them into such places in our confidence as none but a father could or ought to be. I have examined his motives, and to do so effectually I took the plan of doing so rationally, that is, I contented myself with examining those of his motives which came within my extent of power to examine, without going beyond my powers to examine, and which could be known to God only; and as far as humanity, I could find no motive for the advice I received from him of a less holy character than the motives which would have governed the counsels of a dying parent. Eliza, our minister was moved with sorrow for the inferior repute into which your conduct has brought our respectable family. What could be the corrupt motive for bringing upon us so much sorrow? For though you might choose to maintain that your conduct was that of an angel, you could not deny it was of evil repute, and to have been of a family of good repute and to see it fallen and cast down into most vile suspicion, and however your philosophy may enable you to set it at defiance, is to my feelings a very great calamity. For though you are very clever and have become so all of a sudden, yet I, your poor sister, feeling only as common people feel, and thinking only, I confess, as I have been taught to think, cannot help thinking what would our father have said? Would Eliza have turned Pagan had he lived? You say that the purity of my mind would revolt at the first idea of idolatry, as you have done. But how came you not to revolt at the last idea of idolatry, or having revolted at the first, to come at last to such a peace with that you first revolted at as to renounce your Christian name for that of an Egyptian idol; and not content with taking the name of Isis, to take her character too, and let all the world see that Isis could do nothing without her Osiris—'her friend, her comforter, her priest, her saviour and her God'? They are your own words, my sister, and I pray God to forgive you their import, whatever it may be. I hope I do not understand them. You ask me in your first letter 'Will the Rev. Mr. T. bear a 'critical question?' Alack, my dear Eliza, what is it but my sister's love and duty that hinders her from putting a critical question to you? But with a sister's love and a sister's prayer I commend the question to your own bosom, which I long to press to mine; and I bid you adieu, not in the new-fangled meaning which no one ever heard of before, but in the sense of its common acceptance to God. And to God I commend you with the utmost sincerity of soul, as no fear of infidel rebuke shall ever hinder me from saying, 'through Jesus Christ our Lord '.

"Maria Sharples."

This not unworthy letter of itself throws no discredit on the writer, but the postscript attached to it carries a sting which undoes the very good impression the letter itself makes, which in justice to the writer, as well as to the recipient, is withheld, as it only shows that the religious ossification of the heart had set in even at the premature age of 21. Another curious circumstance in regard to this sister's letter is, that it is in the Rev. Robert Taylor's handwriting. The only explanation for this is that Isis may have sent it to Carlile, and he in turn sent it to Taylor, in prison, for his perusal, as their daily correspondence shows them to be in the habit of doing, i.e. exchanging everything that may have been of interest at the moment. Taylor must have copied it, with what object we are at a loss to discover. We find it in a collection of Taylor's own letters.

We left Carlile and Isis exchanging confidence and making arrangement for a permanent and mutually satisfactory partnership of marriage as well as of business. It was not, however, thought wise to make a public declaration of their union till Carlile's term of imprisonment had expired.

Richard Carlile to Isis.

"What shall I do to be saved? was never more earnestly felt than a feeling of mine at present which says: 'what shall I do to restore happiness to her whom I love and whom I have wounded?' As I began an intended long letter just now, Mrs. and Miss Henderson came about six o'clock. They waited until eight for Master Cooper, and left thinking he would not come. They had not left above a quarter of an hour before he and his father came. I wish you would come to breakfast with me to-morrow and have my atonement for the injury I have done you. I cannot write more to-night as my messenger whistles his visit."

"I did, love, indignantly say to Mr. League, do you think Miss Sharples is hiding herself? She is at my house, at her own house, indeed. I told him that his conduct was insolent and unbecoming him, that it was persecution, of which I had encountered enough to know how to deal with it, and that I should deal with it; I did not spare him, but treated him as he was—a low scoundrel. I shall write and tell him that you will visit me as usual to-morrow, and that he will refuse you admission at his peril. Mr. Paine and I are friends. I think it was the whispering of something of the kind that alarmed Mr. Paine and made him uneasy. I am very hungry waiting for my dinner. You shall have the receipts. I think you had better print 250 more *Gauntlets*. There is no other way of increasing the circulation than to meet all demands. This ten pound note must go to the landlord. I shall have another from Edinburgh in a day or two. Copeland is gone to the East for me. Cannot David get the paper from Shelding and Hodges?"

"If you were to complain to me of an insult from Richard, I should forbid him the house; but, love, I do not think it lessens you, but think it very much heightens the public view of your standing with me to see my boys about you. It shows that your ground is moral and good. If Mrs. Carlile did not feel this, she would never consent to the boys sleeping there or being there, and there is no more danger of your being undermined in my love, esteem, affection, and good opinion by any member of my family than there is of my taking back Mrs-Carlile, than which I had rather shorten my life. Such are my feelings on the subject, that I shall never shrink from meeting Mrs. Carlile anywhere in your company, nor from meeting the boys, nor from proposing to take either of the boys out with us, or to ask them to dine. In every respect I shall treat you as if there were no other Mrs. Carlile, and as if you were my lawful as well as my good wife. I fear nothing about you but your own temper, you own susceptibilities, which, though in some degree admirable, are very apt to be carried beyond the verge of reason and justice for the moment. I will always endeavor to set you a good example to rise above you in character and temper and goodness if I can. From me you shall never receive injustice, from no one will I bear it patiently. Now, love, I pray you, if you have written me any unpleasant letter to throw it in the fire. It will only spoil my working and make me unhappy. Why should you do it?

"I consider David France has done wonders for me since he has been in town, and notwithstanding that I intend much alteration in the management of the shop-when I come out."

But now a little shadow has fallen between them, but it is a shadow. Isis is smarting at her exclusion from the gaol, while every other lady is admitted; she is evidently a little jealous, and has so expressed herself. One cannot but be impressed at the dignity and firmness of his reply. Yet how tenderly considerate of her he is. He will not let her have his reply till morning. He does not wish to spoil her night's rest or his own.

"I am as chaste towards you in mind and body and thoughts, as the infant at your breast. Toward you I have been honest and will be honest; but remember, I am not a man to be trifled with, to be jeered at, nor to be easily duped. You have seen my promptitude in resenting an insult from Mr. Taylor, and my resolution in carrying out the resentment. I shall deal with you precisely the same if you so deal with me. And I am sorry to say there is a much nearer resemblance between your temperament and Mr. Taylor's than between yours and mine. You have his weaknesses and waverings, and much of his impatient, suspicious irascibility, without his genius and study. Instead of growing in philosophical improvement you are diverging from it. You do not now act up to the promise of your Bolton letters. It is no sufficient apology to say you love me too well to be at ease; I should prefer the love that would allow you to be at ease. My soul burns with a steady and pure flame of desire to see and be with you; but I cannot degrade myself so far as to exhibit folly and madness about it, and to be food for the sport of my enemies; nor do I upbraid you on account of our separation. This letter has been all my evening's work, I shall not let it spoil my sleep, and I do not intend you to have it until the morning. After the apologised error of Saturday I did not expect another so soon. I feel nothing but love for your love, and pity for your weakness, and ill-health, and separation from me. The letter which I began about the husband was intended for a pretty letter, but the pie (the dinner) came unexpectedly, before I could finish."

In the Preface to the first volume of the *Isis* the Editor made the following statement in relation to the matter; it is her first statement to the public of their union:—

The Preface to the "Isis" (1st Vol.)

"When a gap was made in the philosophical business of the Rotunda by the imprisonment of Messrs. Carlile and Taylor, I volunteered the best assistance I could give to preserve the utility of that establishment. A stranger to all public business and public men, I came alone from Lancashire, fortified in my resolve by nothing more than the goodness of the principles I espoused, and the kind, generous encouragement and assistance given to me by Mr. Carlile, to whom and with whom, I rejoice to say, I have since allied myself in matrimonial engagement, and find no disappointment in the possession of happiness in the third year. I have seen Messrs. Carlile and Taylor restored to public business, and under every engagement I felt that my task was complete. If I have not done all that I might have wished, I have done my best, and should rejoice the more to see an Englishwoman doing more than I have done. I am proud in the conviction of having set a good example, somewhat proud of the success of my effort, but prouder still of the honorable and useful position which I still fill in the community in aid and assistance of the true spirit of reform for whatever is corrupt and wrong. There are those who reproach my marriage; they are scarcely worth notice, but this I have to say for myself, that nothing could have been more pure in moral, more free from venality. It was not only a marriage of two bodies, but a marriage of two congenial spirits, or two minds reasoned into the same knowledge of true principles, each seeking an object on which virtuous affection might rest, and grow, and strengthen; and though we passed over a legal obstacle, it was only because it could not be removed, and was not in the spirit of a violation of the law, nor of intended offence or injury to anyone. A marriage more pure and moral was never formed and continued in England. It is what marriage should be, though not perhaps altogether what marriage is in the majority of cases. They who are married equally morally will not find fault with mine; but where marriage is merely of the law, or for money, and not of the soul, there I look for abuse. My spirit was wedded to the spirit of my husband before I had spoken to him. My soul craved him on the love of good political principle, and for his endurance of its martyrdom through many years of imprisonment. I have not yet repented. We fairly won the bequeathed flitch of bacon to a year's happy marriage.* And long may it continue. We remembered that we were human, and have not fallen into the error of pledging love for life, hoping in the absence of that pledge to make it last the longer.

"The contents of this volume, in conjunction with my life's career, I submit to the judgment of all charitable beings. I court not the judgment of those who have no charity; but I can boldly say I brave and defy it. I live to please myself, and to serve the cause of virtue and honesty. Rail who may, I am not to be dismayed or discouraged; praise who may, my career must still be guided by its principles, rather than by that praise, though I am neither alien to gratitude, nor do I boast of being insensible to just approbation. I have intended well, and I am satisfied, conscientiously satisfied, that whatever I have publicly done has been well and usefully done, and will not license complaint until some Englishwoman does better.

"Eliza Sharples Carlile.

"62, Fleet Street, May 29, 1834."

On another occasion Carlile said, in reply to an attack on his marriage with Isis:—

"On the subject of marriage I have ever been the advocate and the consistent practicer of monogamy, of the honorable and happy and mutual attachment of the one man to one woman, the basis of which must not, cannot be human law, but the divine law of love and affectionate attachment. Chastity is found in obedience to the divine law, and not to the human law. I am now living up to this law in the highest sense in which it can be interpreted, openly, honorably, and with injury to no one, against which reproach has no power, for which the insect has no sting nor has venom poison. I have paid the penalty of perpetual unhappiness, and have still to pay a financial penalty for an error arising from the ignorance of my youth, and for supposing that the priest and the law could unite two hearts. Alas! I found that there was no charm in either the priest or the law to that end, and the experiment was to me the penalty of seventeen years of misery, hopeless and irremediable as to law, and which I have only remedied by the force of moral courage and the sacrifice of whatever property I had accumulated beyond the brain. As far as means were available, I have honorably filled out the character of a son, a brother, a husband, a father, a neighbor, a tradesman, and a citizen. I shrink from no enquiry. All is now better, all is now settled in my family, and I am not aware that a single human being regrets the arrangement. The wife of my bosom, the willing participator in my toils and troubles, is wedded to me in mind, body, and estate; she strong in her confidence in my honor, I strong in the confidence of her virtue, and this promises to be a happy marriage through life. It is so in the third year. It is sufficiently respected in the metropolis and elsewhere. It is pure in spirit, and *is* pure. It conceals neither motive nor purpose. It is open, fair, and honorable, not intruding itself upon the world's attention, but not shrinking from the world's scrutiny."

CHAPTER IV.

IN PRISON AGAIN!

A very few weeks after Carlile's liberation from the Compter he was again under sentence. This time it was for refusing to pay the Church rates, which were unusually burdensome and excessive, owing to extra assessments which had been made. These assessments bore very hard on people of limited means, and many were the cases of consequent suffering which were endured. A seizure was made of 1,200 almanacs to satisfy the claim. In retaliation, Carlile had made three effigies: a bishop and the devil arm in arm, which he placed in one of the windows over 62 Fleet Street; these were designated the "spiritual" brokers, and in another window the figure of a man in ordinary clothes as a "temporal" broker. This drew immense crowds of people to the house, so large as to interfere seriously with business in the street. He was threatened with all kinds of "actions", and several attempts were made by the police and others to drag them from the windows, but he finally "compromised" the matter with the authorities, "for the sake of his neighbors"; he would only put them up on Sunday, that being, as he said, "the bishop's day". He hoisted these effigies to-attract the people and call their attention to one of the greatest burdens they had to endure in the way of taxation. The next week another seizure was made for Church rates, and 800 general book almanacs were taken for a tax of £6 ($30). There were three distraints made in one year amounting to £30 ($150). There were many persons who encouraged Carlile to make this stand, and many offers of assistance were received by him (privately) in carrying on this war. Many people were heartily sick of these burdensome Church taxes and special assessments.

It is a singular fact that the collector of such rates paid two of them out of his own pocket rather than make the levy on the goods. Carlile on discovering this paid one of the sums back, but warned him never to do that again.

Joseph Harris* was fined £1 and locked up one night for being in the shop at the time of the seizure! Carlile was brought up on an indictment before the Court and again sentenced to three years' imprisonment, to pay a fine of forty shillings, and to give sureties of £200 ($1,000) for good behaviour for three years. The spirit of this sentence was to keep him silent out of prison for three years. To this he would not submit, saying that "he would rather be free in prison than shackled outside".

He therefore wrote a note to the Governor of the compter asking that his old room be made ready for him, the one he had occupied so long; and once more he took up his abode in a gaol. However, he was not required to fill out his term, and after being in the compter four months he was released quietly, the authorities themselves becoming ashamed of the affair.

This was the last of his imprisonments, having now completed nine years and seven months on the various charges.

Shortly after the liberation of Carlile from the compter, he and Isis made a short tour in the country, where he lectured at many places. Unfortunately, in some way their infant boy, then about six months old, contracted the small-pox. The mother and babe had to be isolated in a little cottage outside the town, the fear of the inhabitants of the town being so great as to be almost wild in their alarm. Things the patient needed were brought and left at the door; but not one could be had to wait upon them. To make matters worse poor Isis, probably from using the same handkerchief on the baby which she had used to wipe away her own tears, was attacked with a serious affection of the eyes, which made her almost blind. In this situation she remained several days, as Carlile had been travelling from place to place filling engagements, and she was not able to reach him till the end of the week. We will not dwell on this most terrible experience, which ended in the death of their beautiful boy and the illness of its mother. Their grief, and Carlile's mention of it in the *Gauntlet*, was very touching. He was only able to stay with her one week, and then he went to fill up his belated engagements. A public man has not much time to give to private griefs. Neither did Carlile force his sorrows upon the public notice. We get this meagre account of the sad affair from private sources, though his boy's death was published and commented on in the *Gauntlet*. After the death of their beloved son, and birth of another, Carlile leased a pretty little place in Enfield. It was a pleasant home, and Carlile and his little family were very happy. The place, though not large, had a nice garden and many fruit trees, with a fine spreading yew tree on the front lawn, under which tea was often served in fine weather. Here they lived for several years, and here their two daughters, Hypatia and Theophila, were born, Julian having been born at 62, Fleet Street. The many years of imprisonment had seriously affected Carlile's lungs, and had developed a family tendency to asthma. This, with the fogs and dampness of the usual London winter, made it almost impossible for him to breathe in the city's atmosphere. He was almost well at Enfield, but whenever he was called to London to lecture, or on any other business, he would suffer agonies until he got back to the country again. Unfortunately, these calls were frequent, and often required forty-eight hours in bed to overcome their effects, and Isis had frequently to take his place on the rostrum. But he was not idle by any means. In the summer months he made extended trips to the leading towns of the island, and in the winter he wrote much, always with a good grate-fire in his room, for he could not live without a good fire, being so very sensitive to changes of temperature.

In a letter to Thomas Turton, dated Enfield Highway, December 1st, 1840, Carlile writes:—

"I have this afternoon been delighting myself with me correspondence with Mrs. C. (Isis) while I was in the Compter, separating the wheat from the chaff. It will make an interesting volume some future day. Mrs. C. is heartily sick of the poverty of philosophy. You may be sure of that. She has had her martyrdom that way, as often without money as with it."

"Battle of the Church Rates.*

"A country gentleman came into my shop on Tuesday evening, and said he had heard that the Jury at the Old Bailey had just returned a bill against me for the exhibition of the effigies; that the bench had issued a warrant, and that the trial was fixed for Monday next. The Wednesday morning papers have taken no notice of the matter; in the afternoon I sent my son to the office of the Clerk of the Arraigns, whose clerk demanded a shilling for the precise information, and as I have determined not to spend a shilling about it, he came off without satisfaction, though the clerk more than once mentioned that no such a bill had yet been returned to that office, where it must necessarily be lodged. So that up to this moment, Wednesday evening, I know nothing about the matter in fact, and may have to go to press with this number before I know anything, even if there be an indictment. I am quite prepared for it, and shall have nothing to regret, unless I am interrupted in doing what I wish to do for the family of the departed Rowland Detrosier. The moment I am certain of an indictment, I shall prepare the effigy of a lawyer, as one of the temporal brokers and props of the Church. If the Duke of Wellington shall say that he intends to propose the sinking of the Church rates, I will take his word for it, and remove the effigies; but I will not take the word of a Whig for anything.

"*Thursday Noon,*—I have been to the City Solicitor's Office, and have learned that an indictment was to be presented against me this morning. I have since learnt, on returning home, that it has been returned a true bill, and that the Court has been moved, and has granted a warrant for my arrest. All this is mere sport to me. The indictment charges me with having committed a nuisance by the exhibition of effigies in Fleet Street The foreman of the Grand Jury, which has returned this a true bill, is that selfsame notorious Robert Hedger, who is Chairman of the Surrey Sessions, who was born in a nuisance, brought up in a nuisance, and who has turned out a nuisance to society as a profligate drunkard. His father begat him, and made the fortune he inherits in a common brothel and highwayman's house, that was called the Dog and Duck, in St. George's Field's. If the man's character were now good, I would not reproach him for the scene of his birth; but it is notoriously bad and hypocritical. Though I have quarrelled with Mr. Taylor, I have not pardoned Hedger for his conduct toward him. I will go through with this indictment as I have gone through with others, and defy any indictment to put or take them down.

"The trial is fixed for Monday, Dec. 1, in the Old Court of the Old Bailey, before the Judges of the Central Criminal Court. May God overthrow the Bishop and the Devil.

"R. C."

"Oppressive Taxation.

"William Davis, a chimney sweeper of King Street, St. Ann's, Westminster, was called on for king's taxes to the amount of four pounds twelve shillings, on the 23rd of October, by Sharp the collector. Davis asked for three days to make up the money. Sharp refused. Davis then sent out to the pawnshop his best hat, coat, and trousers; his wife's cloak, gown, and shawl, and raised £2 4s., which was all he could raise, and Samuel George Blake, of John Street, Tottenham Court Road, a fellow sweep, had to raise the remainder by paying interest for the loan of the money. David offered to pay the money by a sovereign per week, which was refused by Sharp and the sheriff's officer. He is now threatened with distraint for poor rates, church rates, and land-tax. *What* is a government that is supported by scenes of distress of this kind? What is protection for liberty and property, where the law swallows up both liberty and property, without cognisance of any other offence than the poverty of the housekeeper? It will be well to publish as many cases of this kind as possible, to teach Our Lords who have not the fear of The Lord before their eyes, what is the real state of things; and moreover, that an endurance of such a state of things may be exhausted.

"R. C."

CHAPTER V.

LETTERS TO TURTON

The correspondence of Carlile with Thomas Turton commenced with business, but ended in the truest and strongest friendship that Carlile ever had: and this is saying a great deal, for his life was enriched with the friendship and esteem of many noble men and women. But we have only glimpses of the correspondence of some of these, so that we cannot judge so well of the length and depth of their mutual esteem as we can of that of Carlile and Turton. It is to Mr. Turton that the gratitude of the editor is due for having so laboriously yet lovingly procured and preserved the very complete collection of his friend's and her father's works and manuscripts. Like that of W. V. Holmes, this correspondence commenced in 1822, and was kept up through a period of twenty-one years. The first one was written March 21st, 1822, the last January 24th, 1843, just two weeks before his death. We will extract part from that dated June 23rd, 1822:—

"Mr. Thomas Turton,

"Sir,—I thank you for the subscription, and would by no means wish you to press it further. The same amount spent in my publications would have done me nearly as much good, and I rather think the idea of subscription is calculated to keep many aloof who would otherwise purchase the publications. I am in hopes I shall get on well now, without any further subscription, and I shall write to check it in all the principal towns where it has been kept up. Any new converts who may like to publish their names this way, well and good. I will send a man to Sheffield as soon as I hear of a volunteer who will keep out of the public house. No laboring man is worthy of being trusted who has not this resolution."

From this there is a jump to 1833, when Carlile was in Giltspur Street Compter, for a paragraph in the *Prompter* relating to the agricultural riots which were then in progress.

"London, March 8th, 1833.

"Dear Sir,—I trouble you with a couple of dozen of the *Gauntlet*. I do not invoice them as I wish them to go to the cost of the carriage for the parcel; what I want is to introduce them to Sheffield and to have an agent for them there, if you can find me an honest one there. Every one there, excepting yourself, has failed me in something. The *Gauntlet* is well received. It will be a political paper, now and then making a hit at superstition. I have sent of them this week 1,250 to Lancashire and a hundred to each of the other principal towns. The fourth number will be interesting to Sheffield for the extract from Buckingham's *Parliamentary Review*; indeed, I am sure the whole will give 'high political satisfaction'. You see I am not out of prison yet. You would have waited a long time in town to see me out. But I am in good health and the *Gauntlet* will tell you I am in high spirits. I know you well enough to know that you will do what you can for me."

"London, September 19th, 1833.

"I like your suggestion of reviewing Allen's discourses on Atheism. I will do so. Allen was at Liverpool when we were there meeting Thom in 1829, and I heard he offered to meet us if some one in the Methodist connection would join him. You will see that I have fixed on being at Sheffield on Monday, the 30th inst. Mr. Taylor (the Rev. Robert) does not like the country. I wished him to go to Manchester and challenge the Methodist Conference, immediately on his liberation, but he declined it. My taste is to excite Sheffield in the best possible way. I shall do it better alone than with Mr. Taylor, for his peculiar astronomical interpretation of the Bible leaves no room for discussion, and he does not like discussion. He is brilliant as a scientific lecturer on this ground. I could master Allen in good style now, it is just the thing. I thank you for the suggestion. I can do it so as not to offend any one."

"October 24th, 1833.

"I will leave you and other Sheffield friends to do what you will with Allen. I shall write to him from Manchester on all the points I have heard, and reiterate my challenge so that if he print anything as correspondence with me, he may have something efficient, and I, of course, shall print the letter."

"London, November 28th, 1833.

"Between you and me there is no question but Allen, like every other priest, when pressed to discussion, is a shuffling scoundrel appealing to calumny for a justification. I have paid and have to pay dearly for appealing to law against them, so, some day, I will horsewhip one of these rascals for meeting me with calumny. But if you take my advice you will notice nothing that is published on the subject unless it be an attempt at argument. I have received the knife from Mr. Holmes and every thing your good nature had intended for me. I send you the books I borrowed and a *Prompter*; you shall have a volume of the *Isis* when ready, which I shall never drop, as I pride myself on that work."

"January 14th, 1835.

"It is true, as you say, that I have a formidable conspiracy against me, and the worst part of it is my own family do-their utmost to assist my enemies. I shall beat them all! I am as young and vigorous as ever in this sort of resistance." By this time he was in prison again, for refusing to pay Church rates. He says: "I bear imprisonment as well as ever, but I do not intend to stop after the church rate question is settled. I shall have out a good letter to Peel by the first of February—a goodly pamphlet."

"February 5th, 1835.

"I trouble you with a little parcel and beg your acceptance of my letter to Peel and portrait of Julian Hibbert. I still remember that I owe you a large portrait of Paine when I can get one. Peel has written to me to acknowledge the receipt of my pamphlet. I sent it on Friday evening. He acknowledged it on Monday, and on Wednesday I see a commission announced.

"I am about to memorialise the Court in my case: you will see it in print next week. I bear imprisonment as well as ever; though things go on ill at Fleet Street."

"May 7th, 1835.

"I am simplifying my allegorical interpretation of the Bible to the plainest understanding. Could I get the Sheffield Theatre again? I would improve on the last use I made of it. Robert Owen has announced his intended retirement from public life on account of age. The truth is, he projected in-vain. Nobody understands him, and he does not understand himself as to the practical measures. The philosophy of beating down existing evils is the only practical philosophy. We are all in good health save that I suffer atmospherical injury on the lungs and want more exercise in good air."

"April 23rd, 1835.

"I am somewhat damaged in health, but I am looking? forward to country air for restoration."

This was when the cottage at Enfield was about to be leased.

"May 7th, 1835.

"I am waiting to see what the Whigs will do with the stamp duty before I start another publication. For the mere Radical, as certain men call themselves, I have but little respect, and have found them less honest than any other party. Richard [his son] is now in a shop in 37, Fleet Street, held from the Bishop of Worcester, clerk of the closet to the King, who is greatly annoyed at having a tenant from the Carlile family, but his forbiddance came a day too late."

"November 19th, 1835.

"I am surely a wreck in purse and health. I have this day taken a cottage in the country to recruit my health, and I do not despair as to purse, though it is now a trying struggle. I am now about to advertise my catalogue of books in the unstamped. These things have driven me from the business market. No regular printer will print them, and everyone now has to get his own types and press. This I cannot do, nor should I think the risk warranted, in so far as the principle is of value. Mrs. Carlile and the boy [Julian] are well; all my family are well, but struggling for comforts."

"October 5th, 1835.

"I have nothing new; Mr. Cousins has put my name to his almanac. I am not pleased with this, so I have not sent it to-you. I gave him the title, but he stole the name. I am writing a letter for print to the Bishop of Norwich, who has been silly enough to make a comparison between me and a Mr. Geary, of Norwich, who is building a school, as to which is the best friend of the people? He has given me a fine subject."

"December 10th, 1835.

"Dear Sir,—Though volume three of the *Deist* will contain nothing new to you, I must beg your acceptance of it, on account of the perfect copy of Annett's lectures and in acknowledgment of my perpetuated debtorship to you. I am at another periodical, but the state of the thing is that no regular printer will venture to print an unstamped paper, and I, not having types and machines, suffer for want of a printer and not for want of credit. I shall hope to see you next year, as I mean to be active if I have health equal to it. At present I suffer much from the London winter climate, every now and then feeling as if I should cease to breathe, and finding great difficulty in getting upstairs, and always dying without a good fire."

"May 5th, 1836.

"The place I held last year did not suit my health. I became frightfully ill, and was driven to the country, where I soon rallied. I shall stick to the cottage in future. It is at Enfield Highway, ten miles on the Cambridge Road; garden, etc., low rent, and very neat place. I am now ready for activity of any kind, writing, lecturing, anything. I do not mean to die yet or to be idle, but to follow out the character I have formed. I have committed the folly of adding a daughter to my family. I am now about to end my days in wisdom.

Joseph Harris is doing well in Newcastle, and Alfred [his second son] is well situated in Fleet Street. We shall do business now on a new basis. Advertise much and have no credits. Many of my friends cannot follow me in the pure mythological description of Christianity; I hope you can; I am sure it is the best point in Infidelity yet reached. I have quite resolved on one thing—not to identify myself with the class of men now self-styled 'Radicals'. There is no good to be done on that ground."

"June 2nd, 1836.

"The Bradford people want me down there. If the Sheffield Theatre could be had, I would come to Sheffield; or if any other respectable place of good standing could be had I would come. I want a shy at Allen, and remember I shall take higher ground with him than I did before. I shall publicly declare that these men Allen & Co. are wholly ignorant of Christian Revelation, and challenge them on ignorance of their own subject."

"Manchester, November 11th, 1836.

"I have used the Oldham Theatre here for four nights with pecuniary success. My subject, 'The Application of Science to the Revelation of Mystery,' is very palatable to the people, and very annoying to the preachers. They are compelled to say 'they agree with me as far as I go', but 'I say nothing about a future life'. That is not my fault. I retort upon them that I have no evidence in or out of the Bible on the subject. That I should be an impostor to preach without evidence. But that I do more than they, I make my people sure of that salvation by setting their lives right here. To this they are bound to assent, but they will have the doctrine of a future life. The cultivation of the human mind universally as the catholicity of Christianity is everything.

Every kind will follow and not lead on that point in the way of reform. I am sorry to hear of our young friend's illness [T. Turton, junr.]. Send Tom and Mrs. Turton to Enfield. My priestly authority bid him live and be useful. Cicero's subscription to his friends was 'Jubes te vale'. I order you to be well! Such is mine to your family. I hope to give you a good account of myself yet, but at present I feel just like Simonides shipwrecked; I carry nothing about me but my brain. I think of being in Liverpool in September to meet the British Association of scientific men."

"July 7th, 1837.

"My sister's [Mary Ann Carlile] marriage improves on more information. It is a captain in the army, who has served much in India, that has married her, and I am told his income is not less than a thousand pounds a year. It is curious that he is a Methodist or attends the Methodist church."

"September 30th, 1837.

"I excited Norwich more than I ever did Sheffield, for by going to preach several days running in the market place, I got into a splendid hall, in discussion with a dissenting minister, before the mayor, and a hall filled with the best citizens of Norwich. It lasted two nights, and on the second I stuck my opponent so fast that he could not speak another word. Great good was done; before the discussion three or four were challenging in turn, and I triumphantly exclaimed before the mayor and a thousand persons on the retirement of my adversary, 'Who comes next?' No one came. My new friend remitted me £35 for my expenses here. I spent the week quietly with the British Association. I am about to challenge Roebuck. I have been pretty active this week, and now, like Titus, I feel that I lose a day if I do not preach. I shall get to Halifax for the sake of giving Bywater another opportunity. He is, of course, now the Rev. Mr. Bywater, and my equal in title, except that I am a M.B.A.A.S., Member of the British Association for the Advancement of Science."

"November 22nd, 1837.

"I almost despair of making men anything but the worshippers of men. I do not see that the best of them (with very few exceptions) have any comprehension of or respect for principles. I am recommending associations for scientific pursuits because they will be purely schools, but any political association I still hold to be mischievous and weak, becoming after all the mere voice of individuals. Hetherington's present standing is this: the Tories have bought his paper and Bell's paper, and another called the *Guide*. Who was chairman of Powmell's committee in opposition to Hume in Middlesex? It is a plan to work those Radical papers more efficiently against the Whigs; Radical editors are retained. The *Northern Liberator*, at Newcastle-upon-Tyne, is a branch of the same thing. There is no difficulty in guessing for what purpose Tories will buy Radical papers in the present day. It is quite a new feature in the state of the times among the political parties."

"The Oldham Association for the Advancement of Science commenced on Sunday last with 23 members as a beginning. They will exclude no subject from discussion that the council or committee shall approve. I am very proud of my Oldham friends."

"I consider my little dictionary an important document, but there must be an initiation of mind to understand its force, as Bible language. I am commissioned by my friends to give away ten pounds worth of Shepherd's writings, with a view to forward the interest of the publication."

"Manchester, December 8th, 1837.

"This is my 47th birthday. With care in the winter, I think I shall wear a dozen years longer; but I must take care. Mrs. Carlile will return with me and lecture here and about. It is astonishing how ill men bear discussion. These Socialists are as offensive and dishonest as any religious sect when brought into discussion. Frivolity seems more suited to the present state of mind than any sound, serious, or permanent principle. Notwithstanding, I feel myself right enough for the future, and rejoice in the course I have taken. I am well pleased with your getting me the books for my new friends. I have preached or lectured ten times in the last eight days, and finished my season in criticism on Owenism to-night. I mentioned my missionary friend to stop mouths here who say that all I care about is their pennies. I am improving my audiences in quality. The low catholics came first, but now they do not. I never despaired of working my way in spite of Radicals and the devil. I shall beat them both. Though the Socialists are very rancorous, I make them wince. They are afraid to come near me in Manchester, and this they call beating me. If their principles are sound they ought to thank me for discussing them. I would like you to hear my discussion at Beard's. I treat them all in reverence, seriousness, and solemnity, without any sacrifice of old materialistic principles, and command great attention by the force of my explanations. Your name and virtues are not unknown to, but are fully appreciated by my Gloucestershire friends. I have been three nights, and am to have a fourth to-morrow at Hyde, discussing with Stephens whether we should seek the repeal of the new Poor Law Amendment Act, in preference to going for the tithes and other church property, as an original and still legal right wherewith to supersede the necessity of any Poor Law. I have had nothing but his audience to address, and when I pressed him hard, he knew how to relieve himself by appealing to their ignorance and their passions against me. Stephens has a deal of bilious ferocity about him, but this must be confessed, that he has thrown away the favor of the rich to advocate a better lot for the lowest poor. Taking his character altogether I like him. I have accomplished my purpose of reaching his audience. The class of people who should come to me stand off on account of the old prejudices, while the devil they make of me frightens others. The Owenites are the best class, yet they are sectarian and fanatical, hating all professed reformers who are not Owenites. Shall we ever see mankind, or will future ages see them, working together for common good? I begin to doubt it, still I would have no effort relinquished toward it. To save some, if we cannot save all, is something. This discussion with Stephens is not likely to be printed; had it been anyone else but me there would have been a flaming newspaper to do. I am certainly in a curious predicament as to parties in this country at present, everyone of them is alike shy of me, but I shall work my way out to something eminent among them yet. Ackland and Stephens are at dagger's point; neither of them are theological reformers. I have been trying to school both, and have them both interested in my revelation of the Bible mystery. Both say it is beautiful, but Stephens says he must get the new Poor Law Amendment Act repealed first, and Ackland says, keep it on. They will not use me as a mediator, and I wish to be a mediator between them. Oh, these public men! and oh, for those who are led by the nose through them, and cannot think for themselves! A deputation has been here with a project of a national petition and a national fast for universal suffrage, and after that, not getting it, a national disuse of exciseable articles. The old story revived; the do nothing story!" [This was Carlile's old project of not using exciseable articles.]

"Manchester, April 4th, 1838.

"I have no particular news save that my prospects improve, which I know will please you. Mrs. Carlile will now travel and lecture under my travelling name of Mrs. Clay."*

"May 15th, 1838.

"I am sorry the Sheffield people do not like the *Church*, though I am looking for an entirely new class of readers. The first number converted a fine fellow of a clergyman here in town, who is quite in raptures over it. His name is Claiborne, and he writes over the name of 'The Curate of Swalacliffe'. Claiborne is American born, whose father was one of the strugglers for Independence, and intimate with Thomas Paine. I assure you I am very happy. The few friends I have are worth all the rest of the world."

"December 18th, 1838.

"My chief stand has been in Carlisle this autumn. I find that I kept at it too long, as I broke down altogether in health at Manchester. I must now keep by the fireside for two or three months and nurse myself carefully. *The Tory*, Lord Lonsdale's paper, fell foul of me, and went so far as to say that I undertook to lecture on teetotalism and got drunk and disappointed the audience. A vagabond by the name of Hawthorne had made a boast of doing this. He began to abuse me before an audience in Cockermouth. I mentioned his own statement to the audience, and the Tory paper made the answer apply to me. Mrs. Carlile joined me at Carlisle and lectured on Phrenology, also at Annan, and in the summer at Gravesend and in London. I was really triumphant in Carlisle. The people demanded that the preachers should meet me. Every one was asked and declined. In despair a messenger was sent to Annan to a Mr. Ward, who came boasting into the market-place that 'he was about to meet in the theatre and to silence one of the adversaries of the Lord'. I gave him such a discourse to deal with as he could not touch, but altogether complimented it, declaring in the theatre that he altogether approved of it. I reminded him that I had superseded his historical Christianity. That was a difficulty for which he needed time."

"Enfield, February 19th, 1839.

"You will find by this that I am neither dead, dying, nor asleep, but still in vigorous health and mind, after my six months of vegetable diet. I hope you will live to see me still beating down all opposition yet."

"Enfield, March 2nd, 1839.

"I see there is nothing in a reforming or a political public to be relied on. They may be cajoled, cheated, led by the nose or ears, but to reason with them offends them, while the multitude will follow where immediate interest or even excitement is imagined. O'Brien's (Bronterre) threats all ended in vapor. He is no politician, as shallow as any other Irishman; I never knew one that could reason on any subject except Roger, the father of Fergus O'Conner. Fergus is an empty, shallow creature, and will be found in a ludicrous position in the autumn of this year, from his having set a day for universal suffrage to be the law of the land. I like to see Owenian discussion in print, and this is where, and alone where, the Owenists are doing good. I sent you a *Sunbeam*, with something of mine in it. I shall write more articles for the different papers under the signature of 'Cadmus', which, being interpreted, is the same as Jesus Christ. We want him, but have never had him yet, either in body or spirit."

"Hull, May 13th, 1839.

"The Socialists here will not allow me to use their room notwithstanding that their leader and founder was an old London friend of mine. My subjects are, 'Science in the Church,' 'Science, the Religion of the People,' 'Down with Superstition!' The Socialists are a little frightened at my view and review of Owen's projects. They say that if the preachers get hold of it they will vend it from their pulpits. I am not so bitter with them in open discussion, and would defend them where I saw them unjustly pressed by the fanatics."

"Doncaster, June 7th, 1839.

"Dear Friend,—I made a fine beginning last night to a fine audience, but I so frightened the clergy that they have threatened Mr. Bright to buy no more trinkets of him if he allows me to use the betting room again. I called on the Mayor to ask him for the Town Hall; am to see him at four.

The people behaved remarkably well in manners, and in the-expression of delightful approbation. Had you, my desponding friend, been there, you would have said, 'Go on at all hazards and consequences indoors and out of doors, home or no home, life or death, fortune or starvation'. And so I will go on if I walk from town to town, from village to village, confined to a diet of bread and water.

"Mr. Levison complimented me this morning with saying that he would have walked any distance to have heard the fine philippic I gave the clergy of the Established Church for their neglect of the education of the people. I am all the talk in Doncaster this morning, frightening some, pleasing others; but fright is predominant among those who did not hear me.. Even the people here in the inn are beginning to exhibit alarm. Alas! for superstitious minds. The 'Crier of Doncaster' is a Methodist local preacher, and found himself in a pucker to satisfy his conscience that I was a real convert from infidelity. He was sure I was from the bills, but many out of doors assured him I was not. He went to Levison, came to me and I satisfied him of the goodness of my religion and that I was no infidel. He cried for me, but he declared he would neither cry for the Socialist, Chartist, nor Infidel. I doubt if the fool has slept to-night between his illformed conscience and his interest. I have a letter from Crowly saying that no room can be got for me there [name of place not given] in consequence of the alarm about Socialism. These Socialists will be very much in my way for a time. I see the Whigs have dropped their modicum of education; they are utterly contemptible as ministers. The editor of the *Chronicle* (Doncaster) says the clergy ought to cope with me. Mind, he says this privately; I doubt if he will say anything publicly or perhaps the contrary. I had a pretty group of well dressed ladies at first, but unluckily they did not feel themselves kept sufficiently in countenance, as I, in giving St. Paul's definition of a Jew, had to read something about circumcision, which passes in a church pulpit, but is offensive as a public reading elsewhere. Determine to be happy within yourself and family, and let not the external circumstances annoy you. Proud of exchanging friendship with you."

"Doncaster, June 8th, 1839.

"Have Faith, my good friend! Have Hope! Charity you have in abundance. Faith, Hope and Charity, are blessed qualities in this wicked world. All that the Doncaster religious folks can say to me is to ask how it is that I am the only wise man on the subject of religion in the country? I answer that it is for them to find out how they have been misled? I pity the solidity of the materialists who cannot see my present course to be the most useful and spiritual. Bigotry is universal; it belongs to every sect and party, be you a Catholic Christian! I am very happy in Doncaster."

"Wakefield, June 13th, 1839.

"I came to Wakefield and spent the evening in the Working Men's Association Rooms, which has a good library. They sent the 'crier' round to say that I would address the people in the market place, which I did in good style. At the conclusion, a Mr. Nichols, the principal bookseller here, took me off to his house. This morning he took me over the Proprietary School and introduced me to all the teachers. To-morrow he is to introduce me to Charles or rather Squire Waterton, the Catholic, whom I am anxious to see. Nichols is a religious man and saw lately in London, in the possession of a Quaker, the signet which Pharaoh gave to Joseph!

"*Friday*, a.m.—I had a fine audience last night, even amidst a smart shower of rain, in the market place. I standing sheltered and wrapt up in the spirit, did not discover it till the business was over. The open air work is my forte, as I find I have a more perfect command over even the religious folks. With the Bible in my hand I can go anywhere without the least sacrifice of principle. It is a magic book on human ignorance, and I will try to work its magic among the learned, unravelling those mysteries, which was the promise of my early life."

"Bradford, June 21st, 1839.

"I found Leeds placarded with a challenge from Lloyd Jones to six or seven preachers by name, undertaking to prove that there was no rational evidence to conclude that the Christian scriptures are of Divine authority. No other preacher coming forward, I took up the cudgels against him to maintain there was such evidence. To my astonishment I found Leeds in the highest state of excitement, fifteen hundred people crammed into the music saloon, and hundreds standing about it. This was a fine opening for me, and I made the most of it. I found my old friend Laurence, the showman, there, with his fine bald head, and a more gratifying evening I never spent. I have warm work in prospect. I begin to feel all my powers and extensive reading available in speech. This was not so until of late.. I am getting to be called the 'Prince of Lecturers', Tuesday night I had an electrified audience."

"Manchester, July 17th, 1839.

"I left you to find out by the *Northern Star* where I was for the last fortnight, increasing in usefulness, but not in wealth. I began my first speech with an angry audience, but mastered their feelings and commanded their respect. O'Brien is but a miserable orator with a miserable subject, he revenged himself on me by abusing Thomas Paine, not much to the taste of the audience. I have challenged him to discussion, which, I fear, he will not accept. On Sunday at Leeds I addressed an audience of 5,000 persons, also in Dewsbury. Bradford presented me with over 2,000 people; with very large audiences in Bolton, Rochdale, and Halifax. I must be doing good, for new as is my subject, it delights my audiences. I have well agitated every town I have visited since leaving Sheffield."

"Manchester, August 3rd, 1839.

"My warfare here is a curious one with reformers. They denounce me as a spy and an agent sent down by the Government to divide and distract them. In this neighborhood things are very critical as to the temper of the people. A large quantity of pikes have been openly made and as openly sold. My judgment is that the people here have a real taste to try the use of such weapons. At Halifax on Sunday last the magistrates and constables were there to arrest me if I attempted to preach in the market place, it being private property. A gentleman came forward and offered me a piece of his own property to speak upon. The authorities followed, and after listening awhile, they sent the constables away saying it was no use, they could do nothing. I am, unfortunately, suspected by all parties, so none support me. Yet I think of myself that I am the nearest right of any. I cannot despair, I am in the same temper with five shillings in my pocket as with five pounds. I am sure they are principles and not profits on which I rest."

"Birmingham, September 11th, 1839.

"You must ere this have thought my silence ungrateful, and ingratitude above all the vices is the one I wish to avoid. On the third of August I found the excitement about Chartism and the national holiday to be so overwhelming that I could do nothing in Lancashire. I went to Bolton on the fourth and addressed an immense crowd of 5,000 people, more than the church would hold in the morning, and about 3,000 in the evening.

"My address to the reformers has excited a good deal of interest, and I verily believe saved some property from destruction and some necks from hanging, if not other lives. I found the Chartists of Berry, Leigh, Bolton, and part of Manchester, madly rabid for the destruction of property, life, or something. Almost every London paper noticed the address, some of them quoting largely from it, and I was told that the Tory paper of Birmingham had noticed that the 'Great Satan of the day had begun to rebuke sin'. I satisfied all who heard me last night that it was nonsense to talk about reforming the House of Commons. It could only be reformed as a representation when it ceased to be a House of Commons, separated, mixed with, or distinguished from a House of Lords. They could not but applaud my statements, but I fear they were too stupid to understand them."

"Enfield Highway, January 15th, 1840.

"I shall expect to hear of other Chartist outbreaks, besides this of Sheffield. I am very much afraid that Tom [his son] will, in his desperate circumstances, be committing himself in Manchester. I was told some weeks since, by a Dewsbury man, of a turn out there one night of a thousand armed men, ready and willing to lay Dewsbury in flames. Such movements as these will decide the fate of Frost, and begging pardon moral force Chartism is as pure a piece of humbug as physical force Chartism, and more so. The first cannot succeed, the second may by haphazard and desperation. And as to the Socialists, their propositions for reform are monstrous. Imagine an appeal to all the agricultural, manufacturing, mercantile, and trading interests of this country, to stay their pursuits, and shape themselves by Mr. Owen's parallelograms. If there were unanimity, and no dissent, no adverse interests, it could not be done; with one mind, and successful examples, it would be a work of centuries in one country. Then would come the consideration of the conflicting interests or passions of other countries. I should be unmerciful in satire on the Socialists but for their warfare with the other superstition. They are a shabby, unstable crew of reckless projectors. There is really a moral want in their characters, and such I

213

have found with the great mass of working-men reformers. If ever a man devoted himself body and soul to serve them I am that man; and yet how few of them there are who can find for me a civil word. I shall go on to reform the reformers, and have not a doubt but I shall get up a paying register."

"January 27th, 1840.

"For the first time in my life I have a secret to keep. I am working an *incog.* experiment to market my labor. Do not mention this, for a breath of suspicion would paralyze it. I dislike secrets, but they are absolutely necessary to existence among the competitive tricks of human beings. I have had inflammation in my eyes ever since I returned from Birmingham. The doctors would tell me not to harass them by candle-light, but I must, and say as a doctor said of brandy, that 'he liked it better than his eyes' after warning a patient not to drink it who found him drinking. Our London Chartist insurrection was more contemptible than that of Sheffield. The truth is that Englishmen are not now weapon-fighting men, until they are trained as soldiers."

"February 12th, 1840.

"My going to town in the winter seems to be at the hazard of my life. If I could live without it I would not see London from 1st of November till April. I am quite out of the lecturing world, being neither a Tory, Whig, Radical, Socialist, or Chartist. I find I am nothing and nobody. I am pleased with the Bishop's movements, it will do good. There is nothing like prosecution of opinions to propagate them. The cessation of prosecution was my political death. If I am dead, which I am not, I am getting compliments as an *incognito* writer; some day I will startle you with a curiosity in this way in which I am likely to do more good than before. I have proved that the general public has no objection to my writing, but will not have my name. It is a question if any periodical is the better for a name? I shall send you O'Brien's challenge back, for I have a great repugnance to hoarding anything, though I often sustain wants for which my carelessness has left me unprovided. My nature is a circulatory one, it hoards nothing, is pained by secrets, and wants the human mind as open and visible as the human face.

"T. P. C. [his son] has come to London and renewed his-*Regenerator and Chartist Advocate*, I am a rejected writer!

"The Socialists and Chartists preach at one another, but don't discuss. I have offered to fight the Bishop of Exeter for them if they will guarantee me £200 for five years; it will take that time to settle the question. The Government is bound to prosecute. Lord Melbourne is now in the same predicament as to Owen as he was with me and the Rotunda. He will be goaded to prosecution, though Owen has sent round circulars advising his followers to drop theology. They have nothing else to talk about. I am glad the life of Frost is saved; but I wished to see the Chartists put upon their mettle, if they have any, for I doubt if they have. They are quite down in London. Socialism is the only thing that lives here, and that must go down. It has no living principle."

"Enfield, February 26th, 1840.

"The office I was seeking in London was a place in a good situation for business. They who could or would help me to an official situation are afraid of my name. Heywood, of Manchester, I hear, is prosecuted for Haslam's letters; he cries out and says he would rather give £50 and the stock of publication than stand the prosecution. We shall see what sort of martyrs they make. I cannot tell you my secret yet I pass *incog*, as a man of respected and admired talent; you shall see the proofs of this some day. I fear that I have lost two papers, merely by the knowledge of my handwriting.

It is a case, too, where an amanuensis or copyist cannot be trusted. I have sketched a petition to the House of Lords, if an outcome be found to present it, stating that as the Church is founded upon Jewish history, the way to establish it well is to correct the current errors of that history, return to the original Jewish philosophy, and remove all the heresies of the last eighteen hundred years. I ask the Lords to make the Lords Spiritual a Committee of Enquiry on this subject so interesting to all nations. The Ham Common School (Bronson Alcott's) is a failure. There was nothing generous in it, save that my Gloucestershire friends paid the expenses. I have sadly lost by it in my income. It has from beginning to end been a bad project. In all your preparations for heaven, I hope all your family will find it. I have great need of a warmer climate, but unless I am transported for treason, do not know how I shall ever get there. When the sun is out I am alive, when not I am dead.

"Most of the reformers or pretended reformers that I have known have been flighty men, flying about after everything without solidity to rest on, and accomplish anything. They are, as such, too often deficient in moral character."

"Enfield, March 11th, 1840.

"I see by the *Times* yesterday that memorials are being sent to the Protestant monarchs to combine and send the Jews back to Palestine at this struggle for Syria between the Sultan and the Pasha. Would the Jews go back? that is the question. No! they know better. They are commercial men and could have very little commerce in Palestine. I never knew an unemployed Jew living retired without business. I am now writing leaders for the country papers of Liberal principles. I find I am so far master of all political and theological subjects that I could write-equally well for any party and please them all in turn. I find, too, that there is much good to be done in this way.

All that is required is to support the cues and bent of the paper and party, and you may introduce any good sentiments under that guise. I got a famous letter on blasphemy into the Cheltenham *Free Press*, of February 29th, signed 'Christian'. The editor wondered how a Christian could write so. My politics never consisted of property burning or the assassinating of innocent people, nor did yours; and I would willingly give evidence against any such cases, to serve better political principles."

"July 9th, 1840.

"Cogswell's imprisonment was fully reported in the *Gauntlet*. I supported his family. His wife died during the prosecution, for she too was prosecuted. He afterwards married her sister, who came to look after the children. I have found him a very grateful, honest fellow. I feel content with myself in not having joined either the Socialists or the Chartists. There will be something better coming up by and by."

"Enfield, August 6th, 1840.

"I had not heard of the death of Abner Kneeland, and I have reason to think he is still living in Boston, U.S."

"October 13th, 1840.

"I made a declaration last Sunday that there was a mistake between me and the public, that I had not recanted a sentence I ever published, but had only gone on another tack in my warfare with superstition. When I box up the Gods in the human head as I do, making it the heaven, the earth, the garden of Eden, the ark, the tabernacle, the temple, depend upon it, I will not let them roam abroad in the physical world for superstitious mischief.

"I would be bound to bother Acland, though I confess he is on his best ground. I had a fine triumph over him about the Poor Laws, in the Bolton Theatre, and never before nor since did I hear the phrase of 'Three cheers for Carlile'."

"November 13th, 1840.

"I have been rolling restlessly on the bed all this week since my return from London on Sunday, incapable of lying still any way for a quarter of an hour at a time, with a high (more than usual) inflammation of the chest. This is my first salute for the winter. I am now worse on Friday than on Monday, and have some fear that I shall not be able to go out soul saving on Sunday next. I shall go if there be a possibility to stand up and talk. I find that I have reached a point in my ever sanguine calculation, and that is that the time has come in which I can excite more interest in London than any of the Socialist or Chartist leaders. I have restored a lost audience to the Hall of Science, and have drawn well there; moreover, I have pleased. Have sold my books freely, and have brought home about £5 in four weeks, which is a welcome addition to my slender income. I work now on Sunday afternoons, as I have no evening vacancy. I am enquiring for a place of my own—but my health!"

"Enfield, March 17th, 1841.

"You would have been delighted on Sunday, the 27th, I had a Brindly-like opponent, who, however, could but regret that such splendid talent as he had to his astonishment witnessed that evening should be prostituted to so bad a purpose; and yet he talked himself quite round to me; paid me high compliments, and came to shake hands warmly. Owen, I hear, is veering round to some new point about colonisation, and offending his community party. Sir H. R. Inglis brought up my name in the House of Commons last Friday in the question of Jewish Emancipation. He wanted to know how a Jewish alderman could have met me? I immediately drew up a petition of my whole case, briefly as possible, praying for two things: examination on the question of ancient Jewish history, and compensation for damage and merit as soon as the Jews are introduced among the legal authorities of the country. Peel moves well in the item of scientific schools. I have told him this week that he has only to move into the Church with them to be all right. I will send your books with Baraclory's parcel. I may keep out one for my very good friend Charles Roach Smith, the chemist, of 5, Liverpool Street, City, who came out enthusiastically to lecture at the Rotunda when Mr. Taylor was sent to Horsemonger Lane Gaol. Mr. Smith is a young man much respected among the antiquarians. His papers are read in the Antiquarian Society, consisting of bishops and all sorts; and lately the Marquis of Northampton sent him a card of admission to his soirée as President of the Royal Society; so we swim. I feel myself growing daily in public interest, though the money does not flow in yet. My passion for doing public good is as strong as ever; it is tempered a little with the discretion of experience. I am now a regular correspondent of the *Bolton Free Press*; my signature is—'A Reformer of the People.'"

CHAPTER VI.

CARLILE'S LAST YEARS

Here are two letters of much later date, and the last we have of his to Isis, except the one dated the 7th of December, 1842, with which we commenced the story of his life. By this time Carlile and Isis have come to the settled stage of ordinary married people.

"Richard Carlile to Elizabeth Sharples Carlile, Julian Carlile, and Hypatia Carlile.*

"Loves,—To you, Mrs. Carlile, I know I shall be worth all the more and be all the more lovely as I can earn money, though I grant that you have borne the want of it much better than I might have expected. I hope that I am beginning to turn over the new leaf, but I will not again *talk* about making the hit I have been so long talking about. But I will tell you what I have so far done in Brighton. I have not made one unpleasant step. Beyond the detervation of Mr. Colbatch, I have not encountered one public reproach. You will have seen the letters in the two papers. I wish you to send the papers to your mother, as I shall reprint the letters and syllabus of lectures in a small pamphlet. I found here two of the Owenites whom I knew, a Mr. Wood and a Mr. Stonie. They have been very active and very generous. Mr. Wood wished me to take my meals altogether at his house. He has raised a subscription of several pounds to pay all my expenses of advertisement. Another friend has given me the free use of the best, and best situated lecturing rooms I have had out of Newcastle-upon-Tyne. It is a large new-built shop on the ground-floor of one of the most respectable streets, without any house over it. It makes a room fully as large as that of Shipyard, and quite as good in appearance, with everything that is desirable for entrance and convenience, save a little ante-room for the lecturer, so that I am now set in for a fair trial of my powers in Brighton. I have had but one dissenting minister visit me this (Monday) morning, who has gone off to read the Bill and consider the subject. My letters have produced the same effect here as my pamphlet did in Plymouth. I have not heard of any pulpit abuse. I was stopped in writing the above through a number of visitors, and shall not now get you off this on Monday evening. I must do so to-morrow evening, because when I set in for lecturing twice a day I shall be very busy. However, if I send you some money, you will excuse me in much writing.

"*Tuesday noon.*—Everything promises well. My bills are read with great curiosity and avidity, and without reproach. Depend on it, I have at last hit the right ground of procedure. The fanatics cannot abuse me on this ground. If ever a man was worthy of support in going through a country as a public teacher, I feel that I am. I have not heard from you since I have been here. I shall have to buy a Bible to-morrow morning. You may send in by Richley, to be booked in Gracechurch Street, a parcel containing the small Bible. I do not recollect its being at home. I should like the two volumes of Greek and English Testament, and the American book by Fellows on 'The Exposition of the Ancient Mysteries and Freemasonry'. I first sent you a parcel, then a letter to Mr. Vickery, and two newspapers. The newspaper published to-day has nothing new but my advertisement. I had a letter in the *Gazette* and another in the *Herald*, both of which I hope you have seen.

Kiss me Julian and Hypatia. I hope they will keep in good health, and I have not a doubt but that by the time they can judge and think of the thing, they will see and hear me before large, respectable, and approving audiences; so as to make them proud of the name of Carlile. My heart's desire is that they hear you, too, before approving audiences. I have had no preachers visit me this morning, but I had three yesterday. You might have seen a paragraph in one of the Brighton papers stating that the quondam Miss Wright has been mobbed in Philadelphia for meddling with the banking system. I am glad to see her in America again."

"Richard Carlile to Elizabeth Sharples Carlile.

"Love,—I am exceedingly sorry that you have not kept clear of a quarrel with Mr. Vickery—you ought to have done this, say what he would. His age should atone for a thousand faults, and above all things, I think you should not have said anything to him about his son. As to who visits him in company with his son, it is his business, and not yours and mine to enquire; but as to who shall take up a lodging in my house, it is my business to decide, and I decide that no 'Aurelia' shall sleep under that roof with my consent, and certainly not at all if I were there. Ours is a marriage unlicensed by the priest, but I know of nothing disreputable in it, or I could never have tolerated it for an hour. But where there are avowedly two husbands to one wife all living together, there must be something so base, mean, filthy, and dastardly in all three, as to make them a disgrace to society, and I do feel disgraced in having either of them put a foot in my house. Poor Julian, when I see the children here drawn about the town and seaside in a little carriage by a goat, I wish I had him here. I do not wish to see him a milksop boy, afraid of everything and everybody about him. But then, let Mr. Vickery's age be an apology, he is past reproof and if he cannot be happy with us and the children, we can part with him, but we cannot part with the children. I soberly and seriously think you have been wrong altogether in your carriage to Moses, and it is the fault of you very lively, sprightly people, that there is no happy

222

medium with you; but that you are always in extremes; sometimes too gay for sober observation, sometimes too sad even to be worth pitying. But it is no use, where there is no pursuit of knowledge, what is in the bone will not come through the flesh. I wish you to come to Brighton, not that I want you for money taking, because I think you are out of place there; but I am absolutely keeping a shop with what books I have. I sold an *Isis* for 20s. this morning, and a 'Volney' and other things. I found I could not do without somebody, so I sent for Tom Paine. We are lodging at 8s. a week for two bedrooms. My bed is a large one. We breakfast and tea at the lodging, and we have a standing pressed invitation to every day's dinner with Mr. Woods, the co-operative. Our expenses are small, certainly within 25s. a week. You would add but little if you would be content with where I am. It is a decent house in a good street, and near my lecture room. I am really set in for business here. I should mention that we could not dine in the house, and that would be awkward. But I will take another lodging after you come. I will never consent to be saddled with any person's housekeeping at Enfield Highway but that which you shall appoint. I could be satisfied with the washerwoman's mother if she were disengaged; or if Ann Collis could spare sufficient time from her school to attend to Mr. Vickery—I do not mean in school hours, but after. My present prospect is that I am likely to stay at Brighton some time. I cannot now say how long. I will come up for you any day after Wednesday if you write for me. But I wish Hypatia and Julian to be with some careful person if you leave them. I shall send you as many pounds as I have with this. I have paid £2 17s. 6d. for printing bills, cards, and advertisements. If you send a parcel and there is only fourpence and twopence booking between a letter and parcel, send two volumes of *Isis* and a bundle of the letter to Peel. I think I could sell some of the numbers of *Isis* from 12 to 22, as far as you find them folded. Brighton has never had anything of mine. I am a new man among them. I have picked up a volume that has some of the first tracts I ever wrote, which you have not seen and which will amuse you. You'll say that they are better than the last. I wrote to the High Constable of Brighton to say that I should address the public on the Steyne to-morrow, Sunday; he has just called upon me to say the magistrates have expressed their disapprobation of my attempt and will send a reporter; but I learned from him that if nothing unfavorable was reported, nothing would follow. It happened that the High Constable of the town dined at the City of London Tavern in 1826, to celebrate on Paine's birthday my liberation from Dorchester Gaol. He is a right sort of man. I shall want an answer to this immediately, to be sure it gets to you safe. I think I may calculate on picking up for books and lecturing a couple of pounds per day here for some time. I was uneasy until I heard from you and not easy after. Mrs. Cooper and Elizabeth and your Daniel are here. I called there yesterday, and she was threatening to 'hide' Elizabeth because she did not speak French to a French waiter in the house who cannot speak English. The woman is to be pitied, and the girl much more so. I particularly want as another book for reference one that lately came from America called 'The Phoenix'. It was lent to Mrs. Guiver, but she returned it. I have received the others all safe. I shall send a few things to wash to make a parcel. I intend to get this off by the mail on Saturday with a hope that you will get it on Sunday morning by Guiver. Be a good girl and have no more quarrelling with anybody. I do not intend to quarrel with any person hereafter, I see it wiser not to do so.

The newspapers this week have said nothing about me, save my advertisements. I am selling books very well. By Michaelmas I hope to have money for rent at Enfield and Shipyard, besides many other things. A surgeon has bought the 'Diegesis', and tendered me half a sovereign to give him a private lecture to-morrow evening. I am afraid I shall be too busy money-making to pay you much attention when you come. Send down a parcel—a 'Volney's Ruins' in boards, on the shelf at the top of the stairs. I send you four pounds, which is all I have. I have cleared all expenses except a printer's bill for work just done. Write by return of post, or send a parcel by first coach. Kiss me Julian and Hypatia. I salute you with a holy kiss; but you are not quite a Christian yet."

Late in the year of 1842 Isis went to visit relatives in Torquay, her health was not of the best, and a change of air and scene became necessary to its restoration. Carlile's eldest sister came from Devonshire to keep house for the family during her absence. She spent the holidays there and was greatly improved in health and spirits, and had already written that she would soon return, being much improved by the change. In the meantime Carlile had decided that if he would do business with any kind of satisfaction, he would have to go to London to do it, even if he had to imprison himself in his bedroom during the winter months. The lease of the Enfield cottage having run out, he decided to move to London in preference to renewing the Enfield lease, and he arranged to move before Isis returned, and so surprise her, and at the same time relieve her of all the care and trouble of the change. He had an interest in the premises No. 1 Bouverie Street, corner of Fleet Street. His son Alfred having the management of a book store there in his father's name. Carlile knew the danger of the London winter in his own case, but November and December having passed and January nearly so, he thought that he would be able to hold out till the spring, which was then close at hand; and so he might have done, but that the exertion of moving was too much for him, and combined with the horrors of asthma and a great fright which he received by the temporary loss of his little son Julian, which caused him much apprehension and fatigue. He was so exhausted by all these circumstances that in a letter to Turton we find him complaining of a bad night's rest, of tossing about all night, of being unable to get warm, etc., always, however, looking forward to being better in a few days, always hopeful and cheery to the last. Unfortunately, he did not get better, and it was soon seen by the family, all except Isis, who was still in Torquay, that Carlile had only returned to Fleet Street to die. To die on the old ground, where for twenty-seven years he had waged such a stern fight against tyranny and injustice. But where could a place be found that was more fitting than this for the death of the hero of a hundred fights, the battlefield itself? And there is a satisfaction, a meagre one, 'tis true, in the thought that he died in Fleet Street, where his great conflict was carried on for a period of twenty-seven years.

In the meantime poor Isis, in happy ignorance of all these things, was enjoying herself at the home of Henry Halse, one of the first discoverers of animal magnetism or mesmerism, and she proved a most agreeable subject for his experiments, was frequently put into a mesmeric state, and was very useful in diagnosing cases for Mr. Halse, who was utilising the new science in the cause of health. One morning he had placed her under the influence as usual, but she was so troubled and disturbed, and seemed to be suffering so much mental anxiety that Mr. Halse hastened to release her from the condition. On awakening, her sole thought was of London. "I must go to London at once," she cried, "I am needed in London, there is trouble there, I must go at once." Her friends tried to calm her, and said they would send to London and find out anything that might be taking place there; all to no purpose, they could not stay her for a moment. Her preparations were made in a very short time, and the first conveyance taken that could be had.

226

Arrived in London, she went straight to No. 1, Bouverie Street, to learn if there was anything wrong at Enfield, only to find the whole household there, Enfield a thing of the past, and her beloved husband lying on what was to prove his death bed. She was in time only to be recognised and to assist in nursing him. The shock must have been terrible to her, from happiness to misery in a day. A few days of hope, of fearing, of watching with ceaseless anxiety, and all was over. As it neared the end Carlile roused himself from apparent unconsciousness, and with almost a superhuman effort said, with the greatest difficulty to those around him, "I am the same man I have always been, I have gone neither to the right nor to the left. My aim has been to accomplish one great purpose." This expression was uttered by a powerful effort of nature, and was the last that ever issued from his lips.

CHAPTER VII.

THE LAST DAYS OF ISIS

After the death of Carlile, and as soon as Isis had recovered somewhat from the shock, she went to visit awhile with the Ebworth ladies, taking her two daughters with her, a home being found for the little boy Julian at Harmony Hall, Robert Owen's school. Carlile having died intestate, his eldest son, Richard, succeeded to the business and stock of books, etc., as also a few months afterwards to the annuity, while Isis had only the furniture and personal property. She was thus left totally unprovided for. The sum of £200 a year which had been promised to her by the hitherto generous friends, and upon which Carlile relied, was not forthcoming, and Isis was left perfectly helpless, with three children under ten years of age to be fed, clothed and educated. In a few weeks she was given charge of the sewing room of the "Concordium", as Alcott House was named, where she for some months supported herself and her little daughters, Hypatia and Theophila; but the health of the former giving way she was removed to Charing Cross Hospital. Isis did not remain very many months at Alcott House, but having a small legacy left her by an aunt she removed to London, and taking a large house she furnished apartments. In this way and with the help of some generous friends she managed to keep her little family together. She devoted herself to their care and education, and being an expert needlewoman she always kept them and herself well and comfortably dressed. Being still young and very attractive she had many admirers and would-be lovers, and, as might be expected, many offers of marriage. Such offers had no attraction for her, but rather troubled her than anything else. Her children had some amusing stories to tell of baffled lovers and rejected proposals. Her beauty became rather an annoyance than a pleasure to her, because of the notice and attention it caused her. She seldom went out, and when she did she was always thickly veiled; yet her form and carriage drew the same attention.

Isis struggled along for six or seven years, devoting herself to the care and education of her children, turning every stone to advance them in their studies; in this she was ably assisted by one or two faithful friends. A literary and scientific institute was established at the back of the Warner Street Temperance Hall. A fine lecture room was built and classes of all kinds inaugurated, a debating society formed, and quite a respectable library got together. This promised well at first, and probably would have been successful in other hands, that is, the hands of some experienced business man or woman; but as the manager of the details of such an establishment, Isis was out of place, and acknowledged it. She could grace a rostrum, but failed completely as a "server of coffee". To this place came many respectable young men, and quite a good membership rolled up, and it was in every respect a fitting and a proper place for the youth of both sexes, as educational and moral pursuits (with the relaxation of singing and dancing) only were countenanced.

Among the young men who were attracted by the lectures and debates to this institution was Charles Bradlaugh. He was known as the "Boy Preacher". He was a tall, well-developed youth, and was understood to be studying for the ministry, though he was at that time in the office of Green, Son and Jones, coal dealers, in London. It was understood that he was devoting his leisure hours to the necessary preparatory reading before going to a college or school to complete the course. It so happened that the subject for discussion on one particular week was the then comparatively new one of "Is there a God". There were several names enrolled on the books as taking part in this discussion, both for and against, and some were practised debaters. With something of the spirit of the old chivalric knights, Bradlaugh enrolled himself in the lists to fight for the affirmative side of the question. Not doubting for a moment but that he would be victorious, unluckily for him he had read only his own side of the question, and found himself *hors de combat* at the close of the first night. His opponent, who had been over the ground many times before, knew all the arguments that were likely to be advanced on either side, and thus had a great advantage over young Bradlaugh, who, though clever and intrepid, was very vulnerable to his older and more experienced adversary. The debate lasted three nights. The first night he, Bradlaugh, was thrown; the second night he was vanquished, and the third night he confessed himself completely conquered and threw up his case. But mark the consequence! One morning Julian Carlile, going on the street quite early, met Charles Bradlaugh, who told him that on going home the night before he found the door locked against him. His father speaking to him from a window, bade him never to enter his house again, and denied to his son even a change of linen. He had walked the street all night. On hearing this story from the lips of her son, Isis immediately sent for him, and after a long conference it was decided that he should make his home at the Institution, 1, Warner Place, Hackney Road, sharing the room of Julian, which they did for some time as though they were brothers; and indeed they looked considerably alike, both being of large build, fair complexioned, though Charles was considerably older. But in a few days or weeks he lost his position with the firm, his father withdrawing his security and telling the firm that his son had fallen into bad company. Nor did it rest there; the young man secured more than one position, only to lose it through the misrepresentation of this unnatural father. We know that this has been denied, but it is nevertheless strictly true, and the whole circumstance is as vivid in the mind of the writer (who was then a good-sized girl), as if it were a tale of yesterday; besides there are others living who can corroborate this statement. Bradlaugh then made himself as useful as possible in the Institution as librarian, lecturer, etc., and was to Isis as another son. It was very pleasant to hear him say a few years before his death that he owed all he was or became to her, for had she not counselled him and advised and guided him at that most trying period of his life as she did, he would have been desperate and probably done some rash thing which would have wrecked his life. It was soon after this that the health of Isis began to fail, and though change of scene and circumstances was tried, and some eminent physicians consulted, she was seen to be gradually but steadily losing ground. She had left the Institution by this time and had taken apartments in a very quiet place where there was a nice garden, and where she could have a room on the ground floor, which afforded easy access to the garden, and also a fine view of it from the bed upon which she was beginning to rest longer and longer each succeeding day. Doctors came and looked at her and shook their heads, and spoke outside of the room of her mind and heart, and that it was not a sickness of the body; no-medicine could reach the case. One more sympathetic than the rest suggested her native air, whereupon a kind friend wrote to the mother of Isis, telling what the doctor had said, and asking if they would receive her and let her come to them for a little while; and this was the answer—"As she has made her bed so she must lie". This was the last stroke. In a few days she passed away quietly in her sleep without suffering, indeed she had suffered very little pain during the whole of her illness, just a gradual wasting away of the body. No death could be more peaceful—

"We thought her dying when she slept And sleeping when she died".

The only witness to her passing away was the same little girl of whom the reader has read, now grown larger, but still only a girl.

CHAPTER VIII.

MEMORIES

With the writer, as far as life has yet lasted, have lingered some precious memories. The memories of her birthplace made sweet and hallowed by the remembrance of one who was all tenderness and gentleness, and who spent much time with her, working and walking in the pretty garden, and occasionally in the orchard beyond the garden. Sometimes as we walked by the house the old-fashioned latticed window would be thrown open, and a beautiful face, adorned with long ringlets, would smile down upon us; and she remembers what a pretty frame for this beautiful picture the vines, the jessamine and honeysuckles made. There was, too, a pretty lawn, in the centre of which grew a tree with wide-spreading branches, where seats and a table were always ready to receive gathered flowers and weary little girls, who here loved to climb upon father's knee and fall happily asleep. But oh, the mystery of it. How strange it was that wherever she might fall asleep she always awakened in the same place. This took her a long time to understand. She was quite a bit old before she understood how she always awoke in her own bed. But the garden, what a subject of wonder it was with its old-fashioned flowers, chief among which were its wonderful moss roses which grew to such perfection there, and the mignonette so fragrantly sweet; nor can the writer see these roses or inhale the fragrance of mignonette to this day without being instantly transported back to dear old Enfield Highway of half a century and more ago. This little girl was fortunate—or was it unfortunate?—in having so much of the time of this tender and loving father. She learned long afterwards that it was because of his failing health he had to live in the garden in summer and in his room in the winter, because he could breathe nowhere else; and thus the two least competent ones were relegated to the garden and inactivity, the last baby in the family and its failing head. A few yards down the old highway was an inn with a large space in front where coaches stopped and from whence they started. To this place came travelling shows of all kinds, acrobats, and lovely ladies who rode the most beautiful horses, and who wore most gorgeous gold and silver gowns, and once there came a big van, which bore a learned pig, and a lady who dressed herself in snakes—that is, she wore them in lieu of necklace, bracelets, girdles, sashes, etc. But that awful pig was the cause of much suffering both mentally and physically to this little girl, though it proved to be a very small addition to the small stock of memories that alone were all that were left to her for many years of a beloved parent. But this pig, a pig indeed who could tell all our secrets and one that could answer questions, as this little girl found out to her great consternation, for on this wonderful pig being asked by his master which was the little girl in that company who stole the sugar out of her mother's sugar-pot? this dreadfully wise pig went round the whole company and finally stopped right in front of this little girl, who in the terror of a guilty conscience rushed out of the covered van, tumbled down the steps, and flew home to tell her mother and confess all. But, alas! in her great hurry to reach the house, she fell on the gravelled walk and grazed both hands and knees. She remembers, too, with what tender pity her father hastened towards her, and picking her up, carried her crying to the house, and how gently and patiently he bathed the wounds, and smoothed the grazed skin and bound up the limbs, and nursed her in his arms, while she told the dreadful tale of that pig, and bade her be comforted, and actually laughed about that stolen sugar and kissed her more than ever. She remembered, too, one Sunday when company was expected to dinner, she, with her sister, had been prettily dressed in white Swiss muslin and pretty blue sashes, and the brother in complete Scotch kilt suit, and they being sent out to walk in the garden while their mother also made her toilet. The brother, fired with a love of martial glory, and desiring to improve their dresses with a more warlike appearance, secured from some unknown source a sooty pot, and dipping his fingers first in water, and then rubbing them on the sooty bottom of the saucepan, artistically covered those pure white dresses with innumerable black spots, having done which he hung the pot around his neck for a drum, with a string, and having found two sticks, he beat a tattoo on this unique musical instrument, and we sisters fell in line and marched round the garden, till nearing the house, our father saw us, whereupon he laughed immoderately, and calling up to our mother to look out of the back chamber window, awaited results. They came quickly; with a scream and an exclamation she flew down the stairs, and would have inflicted condign punishment had not father met her at the door, and folding her in his arms, he carried her back to her room and kissed her into good humor again, nor would he allow her to change our clothes until she had promised him neither to scold or whip us, and she kept her word. But the story was too good to keep, and we heard both the guests and our parents laughing heartily at the performance. At another time, when some gentlemen came to dinner to discuss theology and various subjects, it was on Sunday, and as usual in English families the children were brought in with the fruit and nuts at dessert. While the conversation was going on we children were munching nuts, when our father made use of a quotation from the New Testament in which the words "sounding brass and tinkling cymbals" occur. It seems our father got the spirit but not the exact wording of the verse, and the little daughter of gravel-walk notoriety ventured to correct the father's rendering of the verse, when he asked her to give the whole verse, which she did; he then asked her "if she knew any more?" She answered she knew the whole chapter, and repeated it in full, at which peal after peal of laughter rang out at the father's surprise; one of the gentlemen saying something about "out of the mouths of babes and sucklings cometh wisdom, etc." The little girl had been attending an infant school, and had been learning a verse a day, as it happened, of this very chapter. To this school, one day, came a most lovely vision (in this little girl's eyes), a tall beautiful woman in a green silk dress, with lovely curls hanging down her lovely face. Her entrance in the school created a great sensation, and the little girl remembered how the old lady who kept the school curtsied to the beautiful visitor, who, after speaking a few moments with the old dame, left the school leading the little girl by the hand; and how proud the child was to be brought home by this beautiful woman rather than by the maid who usually came for her. In the memory of this little girl too there was a wonderful orchard at the end of the back garden, which seemed to her small feet endless. There were big clappers of wood which were used to frighten the birds away from the fruit. The orchard was literally the place of forbidden fruit to the little folks, who were not allowed there save in company of older people. One afternoon we were all taken to the inn to see the London coach come in on which a large dining-table was which had been sent down from London by our father, and lo and behold, when the table was cleared of its wrappings, what should be with it but a large plum-cake for us children, which father had intended for a surprise. And it was a surprise, indeed. Mother's ejaculation of "Dear, dear, what a man!" brought tears of joy to all our eyes. This little girl never could understand some things, and one was that when we were all out with our nurse that strangers would stop us and ask whose children we were, and after expressing their admiration of the beauty of her sister and brother, would pat her head and only say "She is a nice little thing ". But one memorable day we moved, and all our belongings were in the front garden; the little girl was much surprised to find herself cheek by jowl with a nice old man in marble, who had always lived away up above her reach; but now she could pat him and smooth him over with her hand, and make out some of the letters on the pedestal, which was engraved on all sides. The name she knew, for it was the name of her half-brother, and read Thomas Paine.

These memories and just a few more such were all she was ever to have personally of a loving and devoted father. There is a remembrance of standing before a large house and seeing men unload a lot of furniture, and then the cry coming from someone that "Julian is lost!" and after that all is confusion and worry, but he is found again after awhile. But next day we hear that our father is sick, and we feel that we are for two or three days being kept out of the way, till one night we are awakened for the first time in our lives, and someone carried the little girl to a large room where there were several people, strangers, and where she was held over the bed to kiss what was said to be her father, though she knew it could not be her father, for he always kissed back, and this person did not. Later there was a funeral in the house, and someone lifted this little girl up to see all the people that were walking in the road following a hearse and carriages; and we had no good father any more, only a sad and ever-weeping mother. A very little while and then we go to a very nice house for a few days,* and then to a place called Ham Common, a sort of vegetarian school where everyone works, and the children go to school, and where there is no sugar, no salt, nothing but bread with raisins in it, and fruit and uncooked vegetables, no milk, eggs, or meat. Our brother goes to a different place where he has been before, a place called "Harmony Hall", which was founded and under the direction of Robert

Owen. This was well enough, but in a very short time our sister Hypatia, who had a very delicate constitution, had to be taken away to Charing Cross Hospital, there to be nursed and built up with the most generous diet known to the skilful physicians, in order to save her life. And there she remained for a long period. It was not long before mother and the little girl left Ham Common and went right to a home of our own, where soon we were gathered together and began to be happy again, but never so happy as we had been at Enfield; no, never again so happy after we had lost that dear father.

CHAPTER IX.

SOME WHO HELPED IN THE GOOD WORK

Francis Place.

This gentleman was often spoken of by his friends as a second Benjamin Franklin. With an intellect of the highest order he combined extraordinary business ability, and rose to an enviable position solely by the combination of these rarely united qualities. He built for himself a snug fortune, and had at his house a large and commodious library filled with well-selected works of every description suitable for reference and study.

To this library came many of the members of the House of Commons, and the room being quiet and commodious and always at their service, it grew to be a favorite place for committee meetings, more especially for secret councils. In this way and through his intimacy with so many of the members of the House, he came to know of all the secret projects which were afoot. He was frequently solicited for his advice or opinion, and stood very high in the estimation of most of the public men. He had often been urged to accept office, but preferred not to do so. In this position he was able to be of great service to Carlile, whom he greatly admired, and he kept Carlile informed of all the plots that were hatching for his destruction.

Place kept up a correspondence with Carlile, and may be said to have been his tutor in many things during the long years of his imprisonment. He loaned or otherwise procured many valuable works, and argued and discussed with him all their points of difference, his interest in his pupil never flagging for the best part of their lives. There is no doubt that Place saved Carlile's life more than once by warning him in time, and rendered him invaluable service in more directions than that. Not holding any office or being pledged to any secrecy, he was free to do so without violating any confidence. He certainly was a most valuable friend and coadjutor. It is pleasant to read over their letters and see their regard for each other showing through their pleasant banter. Here is an extract from one of the earlier letters written to Carlile in Dorchester:—

"Excuse me suggesting to you how necessary it is to keep by you an emetic; get about four ounces of antimony wine, and should you be attacked by sickness or pain in the region of the stomach or any uncommon symptoms after eating, be sure to take a tablespoonful of the wine frequently, until the vomiting clears the stomach of its contents. State prisoners frequently expire of anomalous disorders. You should very carefully examine everything before you eat. Be sure to take nothing that has a harsh or astringent taste or that edges your teeth. You ought to have such tests by you as would enable you to analyse your water, milk, or other fluids. Although you and I discard anything but natural agency, yet some supernatural power for all that might drop something into your food. What was the death of Napoleon? What become of Peter Annett, can you tell me? What was the disease of Queen Caroline? Act with suspicion and you will act with caution. The Christians become daily more exasperated against you as you foil one after another.

"The efficiency of your view affords a beautiful reflection. It is far more mighty than the sceptre or the crozier. The pen is levelling both with the dust. Really you have gained a proud triumph! The Christian ruffians, by resorting to force, have acknowledged their defeat, they have in fact confessed that they can no longer fight you with the pen, they have resorted to brute force—the horse and the steam engine. In the empire of reason you reign; you may be said now to have conquered 20,000 regular tithe eaters, all the ultra-quacks, and all the silly people they have succeeded in poisoning with their prejudice and superstition, which may be rated at some millions. Congratulate yourself upon your efforts, and be proud of your individual and single-handed success. Millions of unborn men will repeat your name, and as the age of ignorance is dispelled, you will be still more applauded. From your correspondent,

"Regulator" (Francis Place.)

Julian Hibbert. "*Now bow the head and betid the knee.*" This most remarkable man, so good, so generous, and so noble, was so universally beloved and appreciated by those who knew him, that it became customary among his friends when about to mention him in their letters to each other, to use the above words in reverential recognition of his great goodness and manifold virtues. Yet he was a man of the most retiring disposition and disliked notoriety of any description. His lovely character and sweet disposition were clearly displayed in his beautiful features. His remarkable intellect, combined with his great benevolence and modest sweet demeanor, lent to his presence that quality which might be imagined of Deity itself. Fortunately for himself and others he was possessed of an ample fortune, which enabled him to live in a way that sheltered him from the storms as well as the battles of life. Thus he was able to devote his life to study, to writing, and to acts of benevolence. His health was of the frailest, it could not endure the least strain. The ordinary friction and annoyances of everyday life were torture to him. In his immediate circle all must be peace and goodwill. He separated himself from his family at an early age, and never spoke of them or of his birth to anyone as far as known. His family affairs were a secret to his most intimate friends. There was no doubt that he came of some fine family, but of that or of any other part of his past, or youth, he never spoke. At his death he laid the embargo of silence on all his friends as to himself, and begged them as they loved him to burn all his letters and to cease to speak of him. This was done, unfortunately for posterity, too faithfully by his friends, yet much against their own feelings. It prevents the biographer from giving as full a record of his beautiful life as would make it as perfect an example for all succeeding generations as could be desired.

Notwithstanding this over-weening sensitiveness in private matters, he wielded one of the boldest pens, and encouraged others to greater and more free expression of their opinions than they otherwise would have dared to declare. This very quality in Carlile was what first attracted Julian Hibbert to him, and a friendship was formed between them founded on the mutual appreciation of each other's talents and virtues, which continued uninterruptedly till Julian Hibbert's death in 1834.

Their acquaintance began during the imprisonment in Dorchester. As soon as the public subscription was started, or very soon after, there were some very handsome sums subscribed by one signing himself "An Enemy to Persecution". The frequency and amounts of these contributions aroused the curiosity as well as the gratitude of Carlile, and he begged for the honor of an introduction. This started a correspondence. Julian Hibbert contributed many articles to the *Republican*, and later publications of Carlile's, and rendered him great aid in all of his undertakings. All the advantages of his superior education, rare library and great wealth were at Carlile's service. Not less advantageous and benificial was his brotherly love and companionship; for, indeed, they were akin in their virtues. Both were gentle, loving and patient in their private lives. Both were bold to recklessness in the defiance, publicly, of wrong. Julian Hibbert delivered many lectures at the Rotunda while Richard Carlile and Robert Taylor were in prison, and wrote much during his short life.

He compiled a chronological table of the principal freethinkers of the last three centuries, a galaxy of names that adds lustre to the pages of literature, science, poetry and reformed religion. These tables show considerable research. He was also a poet of no mean order, and Carlile published many pieces of his.

The following short specimen does equal credit to his heart as to his talent.

To which the following was added by Carlile:—

"Julian Hibbert to ye Invincible Richard Carlile.

"Health and tranquillity!

"Thanks for your kind note. I am surprised to hear that you are already free. I thought that the Whigs would have detained you another half year for your rejection of a mere formality. However, as it is, you (and Admiral Napier) have dared more than you ought, and have been gloriously successful—though rashly.

"I hope that now you will turn over a new leaf, i.e., that you will cease to insult the Unions, and to applaud the Duke of Wellington. Leave to the *Times* newspaper the inglorious task of trampling on the low and exalting the powerful. You are at present the most unpopular man in existence.

But you are in the prime of life and full of vigor. You may, therefore, if you choose, as easily write yourself up, as during the last few years you have been writing yourself down. If you want any more of this disagreeable advice, you will call on me whenever you may happen to pass this way. I am most generally here between four and five p.m., but sometimes I am so ill that I do not come to London for a week at a time. Farewell, and try to be more a friend to committees which are the essence of republicanism.

"30 West Norton Street,

"Friday, 9th August, 4 p.m."

The munificence of Julian Hibbert to Carlile as the advocate of Freethought, etc., excelled that of anyone else, though there were many instances of bountiful generosity which might be related. In the ten years or so of their personal acquaintance, Mr. Hibbert gave to Carlile for the cause sums amounting to £7,000 (nearly $35,000). On visiting Carlile in prison one day, the conversation turned upon the fact (which had just been published) of a political leader having been presented with a cheque for £1,000 by his supporters, Mr. Hibbert, saying that it ought not to be said that the advocates of Freethought were less generous to their exponent, sat down and wrote a cheque for the same amount, which he handed to Carlile. This most generous man and most dearly beloved friend died at the age of thirty-four, after a very short illness. His death was supposed to have been caused by a ruffianly verbal attack made upon him by Charles Phillips, a magistrate, who was presiding at a trial to which Mr. Hibbert had been subpoenaed, and was in consequence of Mr. Hibbert's avowal of being an Atheist, when called on to swear upon the Bible. Phillips was known as one of the most ruffianly and ungentlemanly of presiding magistrates, and many stories are extant of his abusive manners. Julian Hibbert, though a giant mentally, was of a peculiarly delicate constitution, and the attack really killed him. He lived but a very few days afterwards. Carlile grieved long and deeply for this dear and sympathetic friend who had stood by him through all his sufferings and weary imprisonments, and in a burst of grief and sorrow at the news of his sudden death, bewailed him as the great, the god-like Julian Hibbert.

Lines written on the death of Julian Hibbert.

Joseph Harris.

The Joseph Harris mentioned in several of the letters of Isis and of Carlile was one of the volunteer shopmen who received a sentence of six months' imprisonment; he again served them when prosecution had well-nigh ceased, but was fined and locked up for one night during the Church tithes trouble. Harris was, like all the other young men who volunteered, an exceedingly intelligent, upright and moral man, and he endeared himself to Carlile and Isis by his upright conduct and exemplary manners. He was of a studious habit, and Isis took great pleasure in assisting him with his studies; he became to her as a brother in the confidence she reposed in him, and he in turn gave to her and all of the name of Carlile his best friendship and assistance in time of need. It was to Joseph Harris Isis turned in her widowhood for advice and sympathy, and received such as a loving brother might give to a sister.

Some time after Carlile's death Harris entered into the London Post Office service as a letter-carrier, and by dint of pure merit rose step by step till he came to-occupy the position of paymaster—a most responsible post—which he held for several years.

Later on he went to America and was elected to the State Senate of Wisconsin in 1863; he had been a newspaper man before that time, publishing a paper called the *Advocate*. The life work of Mr. Harris was the promoting and carrying through of the Sturgeon Bay Canal, and is best known in this connection. To this work he devoted many years of his life, and almost every dollar he had. He was librarian to the United States Senate for eight years, and was special agent for the Impeachment Committee that was organised against Andrew Johnson, President of the United States. Later in his life he was private secretary to Senator Sawyer of Wisconsin. In all these offices he conducted himself as a strictly moral and upright citizen. In every sense a worthy specimen of the sort of young men who earned the name of being pupils and followers of Carlile. This testimony to his noble and superior qualities is given by one who has his history almost from birth.

Gratitude and respect for Joseph Harris is compulsory, for he was indeed the widow and orphan's friend. As he helped Isis and her fatherless children, so he helped the widow and nine orphans of Carlile's eldest son Richard, when he died on shipboard, or rather in hospital, on his return to America after visiting London in 1855.

Mrs. Sarah C. Chichester and Mrs. Welch.

The "West Country friends" to whom Carlile so frequently alluded to in his letters to Turton, sometimes calling them "My Gloucestershire friends", the "Ebworth ladies", and "My lady friends", were two very highly connected ladies, sisters, and both widowed. They were Mrs. Sarah C. Chichester and Mrs. Welch, grandnieces of the Archbishop of York. They were great admirers of Carlile and his principles, and sent him large sums of money to assist him in his various enterprises. They first commenced a correspondence with him under the assumed name of "Clay", but afterwards revealed their identity and invited him to their home, where he spent several happy weeks on different occasions. Isis was, too, a favorite friend and guest, and for some years a constant correspondent. These generous friends always urged Carlile on in his public work, assuring him that they would provide for his wife and family, should he be unable to leave them a support, and an allowance of £200 a year was agreed upon, but for some reason or other this money never reached Isis, possibly through the dishonesty of their chosen agent. These were the ladies who furnished the money to start Bronson Alcotts Concordium at Ham Common, near Richmond, and they sunk large sums of money in that venture, which did not prove a success. Many letters are extant to show how close was the friendship existing between these ladies and Carlile and Isis. Mrs. Welch also made some provision for Carlile's three children in her will, but this provision, like the £200 a year, did not mature. It goes to prove, however, that Carlile's friends were among the best people in the country. These ladies were advanced thinkers, always ready, too, to accept any new thought or help on any new project, and were humanitarians in the largest sense of the word.

I extract the following from Carlile's letters to Turton:—

"June 22nd, 1837.

"Some unknown lady has sent me £30 from Gloucestershire in sympathy for my loss in the *Phoenix*."

"September 20th, 1837.

"Did I tell you that my West of England friends had sent me another handsome remittance before I left, and still promise future good? Mrs. Carlile has been put in fine spirits and is delighted at this."

"Manchester, September 30th, 1857.

"My new friends remitted me £35 for my present excursion."

"December 8th, 1837.

"My friends are very lavish in their gifts of useful books and in supplying me with money. Their remittances already amount to £200. Mrs. Carlile and I are to visit these ladies before I return to Lancashire."

"I have a commission for you; my valuable friends in Gloucestershire write me thus...." [This was a commission to purchase and distribute £10 worth of the pamphlets of one S. Roberts, who wrote and worked in behalf of the poor and ill-used chimney sweeps.]

"London, May 4th, 1838.

"I came on to Cheltenham to visit my new and great and good friends, with whom I spent a most happy week."

"May 15th, 1838.

"I spent eight days with my new and good friends in Gloucestershire, where I was superlatively happy."

Mrs. Susannah Wright.

The only woman outside of the Carlile family to suffer imprisonment in the cause of a Free Press was Mrs. Susannah Wright. This plucky little woman took charge of the shop in Fleet Street, after the Carlile family had all been put in prison; and taking her turn at martyrdom, was indicted and sentenced. She, with her six months' old baby, was treated with great severity and harshness at first, as if she were a felon. She spiritedly resisted the treatment, and was removed afterwards to Cold Bath Fields Prison. There she was treated with more humanity, but being a very delicate woman, she came near dying in consequence of the treatment she had received at Newgate. One month of her term of imprisonment was remitted as well as her fine of £100. Carlile always regarded Mrs. Wright as a model for women to copy, and paid her the highest tribute for her enthusiasm, perseverance, coolness, and dauntlessness. To him individually she was the source of the highest gratification, and he took every opportunity of lauding the work she had done. Immediately on her liberation she paid a visit to Dorchester Gaol, and received hearty thanks and congratulations from Carlile. She soon afterwards removed to Norwich, where, with Carlile's assistance, she opened a little shop for the sale of liberal works. Here she at first met with much opposition, but by dint of her own courage and intrepidity on becoming better known her persecutions ceased, and she was left to follow her vocation in peace. She bears in history the distinctive honor of being the only woman (other than Jane and Mary Anne Carlile) who suffered imprisonment for their services in the battle for a Free Press.

In a letter to Holmes, on Mrs. Wright, Carlile writes:—

"September 21st, 1825.

"I did not write last week for I had Mrs. Wright with me, in whom, after all the slanders that have passed, I can find no fault You will see that I have called her the Pink of us all. She is quite ready to go to the shop again if prosecutions are renewed. Her sufferings as to health have been dreadful since she left the prison, indeed, through all the winter, no one thought of her living, which accounts for nothing having been heard of her. Like you, she is one-eyed, and, as at your visit, I sent her with a letter to Lawrence to see if her sight be recoverable."

In another letter to W. V. Holmes, Carlile says:—"I by no means coincide with what you say of Mrs. Wright, there is scarcely another woman in England who would have done for me what that woman has done, and from my knowledge of her in 1817-18 and 1819, I know that a love of principle has been her ruling motive."

George Jacob Holyoake.

It was the last year of Carlile's life that Mr. Holyoake was tried and imprisoned for Atheism, and it was almost the last public action of Carlile's life to aid and encourage the young warrior in this, his first real battle with the enemies of free thought and free speech. Carlile sat by Holyoake's side during his excellent defence, which lasted nine hours. Holyoake being a delicate man would probably have been exhausted had not Carlile kept him refreshed with raspberry vinegar, etc. Carlile did everything in his power to get the conditions of Mr. Holyoake's imprisonment modified, but with small success. Mr. Holyoake was happily the last man to be imprisoned for so-called "Atheism".

Herewith is appended some correspondence showing the impression Holyoake made upon Carlile, and also some letters which passed between the two men:—

"Richard Carlile to Thomas Turton.

"I wished you present, yesterday, in the Court of Gloucester, to have heard the truly grand display of character, talent, and integrity, made by George Jacob Holyoake.

"I honor your discrimination in seizing upon his great worth and exception to the common run of Radicals and Socialists. He spoke nine hours admirably. I made sure of his acquittal while his defence was in progress, but the judge was an alarmed bigot, and pleaded against him unmercifully without allusion to his noble defence.

"The stupid jury said guilty, after five minutes putting their heads together. He is to have six months' imprisonment.

"In your name, and as a present from you, I shall go to the gaol this morning and present Holyoake a pair of your razors. It is the only thing I have with me here to offer him. I was proud of him, and of myself too, to think I had brought forth such a state of mind. Holyoake was heard by a court fall of ladies, and had they been his jury, he would have been acquitted.

"The more I see and hear of Holyoake the more I like him.

"You would not have grudged the cost (of travel) to have seen Holyoake on Monday. It was a truly beautiful scene to see this young Jesus before the Jews and Pontius Pilate."

Carlile often wished that Holyoake had been his son, and Holyoake as often wished, too, that he had been. Mr. Holyoake expressed this wish quite recently in a letter to the writer. This friendship mutually existing between Carlile and Holyoake is as gratifying and sweet in its remembrance as is the odor of the rose after the vase is shattered, and their freely spoken appreciation of each other speaks well for both:—

"There was praise of the good from the lips of the just."

"July, 1842.

"R. Carlile, Esq., Enfield.

"My Dear Sir,—I have to acknowledge the receipt of your letter of July 11th. Am sincerely obliged by your kind offer of further advice as far as you can assist me. I am lost in London, as you will guess, and scarcely know where I am, or I should have replied to yours before. From your letter to Mr. Ryall, I find that my kind friend Mr. Turton, of Sheffield, has done me the honor to mention me in his letters to him. Mr. Turton is a gentleman whom I highly respect.

"I feel not a little encouraged by the courtesy with which you offer your assistance, and, indeed, have rendered it, as on Sunday last.... I have written to Cheltenham for a *Free Press*, containing your letter on my case, and will forward it the moment received.

"Yours very truly and respectfully,

"G. J. HOLYOAKE."

"London, July 24th, 1842.

"My Dear Sir,—Thank you for your advice. Shall be, I believe, in Cheltenham, before I go to Gloucester. Will write you before that. I elicited some warm cheers for you this morning at the Rotunda.

"Yours truly and respectfully,

"G. J. Holyoake."

"Birmingham, July 30th, 1842.

"R. Carlile, Esq., Cheltenham.

"My Dear Sir,—I am much obliged for your frank and candid advice. It is the most welcome, because you leave me free to reject where I may not approve without fear of offending you. You say, 'I have always thought for myself; do you so'. How many talk of free thought without even extending that privilege, as you do, to others. I am satisfied of your good intention in writing to ————. I object to no proceeding your kindness and experience may suggest so far as you alone take part in it. I thank you for expressly saying that I did not sanction any overtures. I cannot do so. I have no faith in Christians. My experience is limited, I grant, but as far as it goes I feel that any concession on my part would only increase their malignity. Men who have begun with the ferocity they have begun with me will never end by doing me justice.

"Your opinion as to the public, princes, women, and myself, I entirely accord with, and I scarcely know which to admire more, the correctness of the sentiment, or the beautiful manner in which it is expressed. I know the public, etc., is fickle, and have sought a higher reward, the *consciousness of rectitude*; this is not all-enduring, and when it fails I have done. Your estimate of ———— curiously coincides with many I have heard; his objection to discuss theology is puerile indeed. It is, as you say, to object to discussion of the cause of the evils he professes to eradicate.

"Yours obligedly,

"G. J. HOLYOAKE."

"County Gaol, Gloucester, August 18th, 1842.

"R. Carlile, Esq., Cheltenham.

"My Dear Sir,—I was much obliged by your kind letter, and although I must regard your remarks rather as those of a friend than of a critic, yet am I much gratified that my exertions should have met your approval. Your good opinion will compensate me for the unpleasantness of my condition. I shall take care of my health as far as is possible. I learn from Seymour that you have sent him a communication for the *Oracle* [Holyoake's paper]. Your name will do the cause infinite service independently of what you will write. "With many thanks, etc., etc.,

"G. J. HOLYOAKE."

"Gloucester Gaol, October 22nd, 1842.

"My Dear Sir,—I am certainly gratified that you should have taken the trouble to write me so long a letter. The sovereign you so kindly caused to be remitted, duly came to hand by seven o'clock on Monday morning, and at the same time and hour my eldest little girl died, so that it arrived opportunely to assist in defraying the expenses of the melancholy obsequies of the grave.

"You say the word Christian originally meant wisdom and goodness. What it originally meant you can better say than I can; certainly it means nothing of the kind now, therefore I have acquired a distaste for the title. I do not cavalierly adopt that of 'Atheist', names little entice me, and in this

254

case, you will archly rejoin, 'there are no principles to allure.' What you say about the prices of lectures, working-out reforms by poor men's instrumentality, etc., interests me very much, and will occupy my consideration. Your remarks concerning scarcity of subscribers for my support little surprises me. I did not expect what I have received. Enquiring into that subject prior to my imprisonment, or rather to my incurring it, did not present itself. It shows little knowledge of the world, and perhaps insufficient attention to the wants of those depending upon me. Busy with what I conceived to be an important principle, other things had few attractions. Shall I find at last that principles are to be talked of and the world to be lived in?... Should be gratified if you would present my regards to Mrs. Carlile [Isis].

"Yours truly,

"G. J. HOLYOAKE."

APPENDICES

APPENDIX I.

TRIAL OF MR. CARLILE

FOR THE PUBLICATION OF PAINE'S "AGE OF REASON".

The first days' defence was devoted to the reading of the "Age of Reason", the book for which Carlile was prosecuted. He read and commented on it all as he went along, and in this way made the immense concourse of people acquainted with the arguments there used. It is almost unnecessary to say that the sale of the book after the publication of the trial reports was something enormous. Many thousands of Englishmen who never thought on such subjects before dated their awakening of mind from this event. The real "passage of arms" between Carlile and his accusers commenced on the second day.

COURT OF KING'S BENCH, GUILDHALL. From the "British Press", October 14th, 1819.

SECOND DAY.—Wednesday, October 13TH, 1819.

The interest excited by this trial continues unabated. A considerable concourse of people assembled before the great entrance at Guildhall, between eight and nine o'clock. To the gentlemen connected with the public Press every facility was afforded by the secondary, Mr. Collenridge, and by Mr. Temple, the hall-keeper. The former admitted them into the body of the Court at an early hour, where they were accommodated with seats at the table. At a quarter before nine o'clock, the Court was regularly opened; and in a few minutes it was completely filled.

The Counsel for the prosecution, the Attorney and Solicitor General, Mr. Littledale, and Mr. Campbell, took their seats soon after.

At a quarter after nine, Mr. Carlile entered the Courts He was preceded by two friends, who placed on the table an immense pyramid of books, in folio, quarto, octavo, and duodecimo.

At twenty minutes before ten, the jury having arrived, and having answered to their names, the cause of the King v. Carlile was called, the Chief Justice having previously taken his seat.

After a short pause, Mr. Carlile rose, and proceeded with his defence. He said he had endeavored yesterday, by going through the whole of three parts of "The Age of Reason", to show to the jury that it did not contain one immoral sentiment or expression; but that any expressions, which were at all questionable in that work, were quoted from other publications. He endeavored, satisfactorily, he hoped, to prove that Paine's object was to rescue the character of the Almighty from the account which was given of him in those books called "The Bible". He (Mr. Carlile) was anxious as far as possible to make the writings of Paine justify the composition, and the doctrines laid down by him in "The Age of Reason ". In order to do this, he would read a discourse pronounced by Mr. Paine before the Society of Theophilanthropists, at Paris. That discourse contained a complete refutation of the statement that Paine was an Atheist. His character was in fact most remote from Atheism. He had indeed proved that he entertained a more correct idea of the character of the Almighty than was to be found in the Bible. Mr. Carlile then proceeded to read the "Discourse", which is printed along with Paine's "Theological Tracts". [The whole *gist* of this production may be collected from a single paragraph, "The *un verse*", says the author, "is the Bible of a true Theophilanthropist; it is there that he reads of God; it is there that the proofs of his existence are to be sought and to be found. As to written or printed books, by whatever name they are called, they are the work of man's hands, and carry no evidence in themselves that God is the author of any of them. It must be in something that man could not make that we must seek evidence for our belief, and that *something is the universe*—the true Bible—the inimitable word of God." In going over this tract, the whole of which he read, Mr. Carlile made no observation, except in one place, where the text set forth "that persecution had ceased". "Happy", said he, "would it be for me, if persecution had indeed-ceased!" Having concluded the tract, he said this little discourse had been published by some persons, who were so convinced that it was a perfect refutation of Atheism that they sent it into the world with Mr. Paine's name to it. Having gone through so much of "The Age of Reason" as, at present, was necessary for his purpose, he would lay it aside; but he would in a future stage of the trial again to refer to it, for the purpose of supporting certain principles connected with his defence. He would now proceed to examine the book of which Mr. Paine's work was an investigation. But before he went further, he must observe that the Bible was not the only book supposed to be a revelation from God. The Koran, for instance, was supposed, by millions of people, to be of divine origin.

The Attorney-General here interrupted the defendant. He submitted that he could not proceed further with such a line of defence. The expression of the defendant was, that he would go into an examination of the book of which Paine's work was an investigation. He contended that he could not go into such an examination. The question was whether, according to the law of the country, the defendant had been guilty of the offence with which he was charged? It was neither competent for his lordship nor the gentlemen of the jury to go into such an examination as the defendant proposed—an examination of the truth of the Scriptures.

The Chief Justice: You hear the objection taken by the Attorney-General?

Mr. Carlile: Yes, my lord. The Attorney-General states that it is not competent for your lordship or the jury to go into such an examination as I propose; but he has quite forgotten that it is necessary to my defence. I have been brought into this Court to answer charges, and must avail myself of every means of defence. The Attorney-General has stated that I have published a work in which the Scriptures are spoken of as containing obscene stories, voluptuous debaucheries, cruel and tortuous executions, inconsistencies, and contradictions. Now I feel it to be my duty to justify what has been published by appealing to the Bible, which contains them.

The Attorney-General: I did not at all forget that the defendant is very deeply interested in the result of this trial; but this, like all other causes, must be proceeded in according to the rules of law. And, looking to those rules, it is not competent for a defendant, charged with this offence, to go into such an investigation. I beg to call your lordship's attention to the trial of an individual charged with a similar offence—I mean Williams. When he was brought up to the

259

Court of King's Bench to receive judgment, Lord Kenyon said, that "having re-considered what had been done during the trial, he took blame to himself for having listened even to the arguments used on that occasion". In that case of the King and Williams, the whole Court expressed their opinion that they could not allow anything to be said against the established religion of the country—the Christian religion. That is the proposition for which I contend. I trust it will receive the sanction of your lordship, and that the defendant will not be suffered to promulgate blasphemous doctrines as part of his defence.

The Chief Justice: The charge against the defendant on this occasion is the publication of a book calumniating and reviling the Holy Scriptures. It is not that, in any book published by him the doctrines of revealed religion were discussed with that respect, temper, and moderation which ought to be applied to the discussion of every subject, human or divine, public or private. It can be no defence of such a charge that the party against whom it is preferred should reiterate, in his address to the jury, the same sort of calumny as that which is contained in the book, for the publication of which he has been called on to answer; and I should very ill discharge my duty, as a Judge or a Christian, if I suffered this Court to be made a theatre for uttering calumny against the religion of the country. Any thing the defendant can advance to the jury, to explain away what is contained in the book, and to show that its tendency is proper, I am most ready to hear. I wish to give to this defendant, as well as to every other person, an opportunity to defend himself fully and fairly, according to the established law of the land. But I am not to suffer the law of the land to be calumniated by such a defence. I cannot permit it.

Mr. Carlile: The only object I have in view is to clear the book, entitled "The Age of Reason", from the charge make against it, and to justify the observations which it contains on the Old and New Testament. I presume that book cannot be founded on any law of this country. Your lordship has spoken of the law of the land as applicable to this case. I should like to have that law pointed out.

The Chief Justice: I state that the Christian religion is a part of the law of the land—and the most important part—because it is that on which all its institutions are founded, and to which they all refer. I speak of the Christian religion generally. There is one particular mode of faith amongst those who follow the Christian religion which constitutes what is called the Established Church; the law of England, however, admits every other class of Christians to adhere to their religious worship, according to their own particular faith, tenets, and creed; but it permits to no man the right to impugn the whole sum and substance of the Christian religion, and to treat the book which contains its doctrines as a mass of lies and falsehoods. I cannot permit such a defence.

Mr. Carlile: I cannot submit to have my course of defence marked out for me.

The Chief Justice: Whether you submit to it or no, I have stated the law, as was my duty; and it is not for a man, accused of having infringed the law, to rise in this place and declare what is or what is not law. I speak in the hearing of gentlemen who have often attended in this Court, and such of them that know me will answer for the truth of what I assert when I say that, though I lay down the law to them, as I conceive it to be, according to my judgment, yet, when a question of fact arises, I leave it in the fullest manner to their consideration. But I never will suffer the Holy Scriptures to be examined in this Court for the purpose of calumniating and reviling them.

Mr. Carlile: I appeal to your lordship, what proof have we that they are *divine?*

The Chief Justice: I will not answer such a question as that. You have not, I say, been brought here to answer for any work containing a fair and dispassionate consideration of the Christian religion; but for a publication reviling and calumniating the Scriptures. And calumnies and revilings, whatever the subject may be, are contrary to the law of the land. Is it to be supposed that the law, which affords protection to every individual, has not the power to protect itself? Is it not to protect those who, from their youth, from want of education or from weakness of mind, are not so deeply confirmed in their religious feelings as they ought to be, from being exposed to all those aberrations which, not the force of reason, but the influence of calumny, may occasion?

Mr. Carlile: I wish to arrive at the same end; but we take different ways of effecting it.

The Chief Justice: The discussion is somewhat early; but I will let you go on, advising you to keep within the bounds I have pointed out. I cannot suffer this book to be defended by reviling the Christian religion.

Mr. Carlile: If these writings are of divine origin, they cannot receive any injury from investigation or from any comment made on them. I will therefore go into a full investigation of this question, and I cannot do that without examining the book itself, which gave rise to this work.

The Chief Justice: We shall see in what mode you conduct your defence.

Mr. Carlile: I have stated to you that there are many books existing on the face of the earth which are, by certain individuals, believed to be the revealed word of God. One of these I now hold in my hand. It is believed in by a greater number of persons than believe in the Bible. I mean the Koran. I will read to you the manner in which it is represented by its author to have been sent down by the Almighty. It is contained in the 14th chapter, which is headed, "Abraham—revealed at Mecca—supposed to be sent to Mahomet ". The book, it may be observed, is filled up with a great portion of the history of those persons whose names are to be found in the Old Testament. [Mr. Carlile read the whole of the chapter, which embraced various topics, but particularly set forth the joys which God would bestow on those who served him, and the vengeance he would shower down on those who disobeyed him.] This, gentlemen, continued Mr. Carlile, is a specimen of what is called revealed religion, and which they say came down from heaven to Mahomet. It is believed by many millions of men, more than compose the body of Christians—and yet, is there anything in it comparable with the idea of the Almighty which is given by Paine? Certainly not. And yet those who believe it dislike the Christians, and treat them with reproach and contumely. Why, therefore, should such books be considered as the will of God? and how can we tell that they are worthy of being so called unless we examine them? I will read no more of the Koran. What I have read is a fair specimen. There are some fine moral lessons in that work, and some beautiful ideas of the Deity, but they are mixed up with trash which spoils the whole. Mr. Paine is not the only man who has investigated the Old and New Testament, and doubted of their validity. I hold in my hand the work of a man who ranks very high in this country—who was Ambassador to the Court of Naples—and is at present a member of the Privy Council. I allude to Sir W. Drummond—who has canvassed the Scriptures very freely. The book, though never published (a few copies only being printed for the author's friends), shows what the opinions of Sir W. Drummond were. [Mr. Carlile proceeded to read extracts from the work, which we are unwilling to publish at any length, in consequence of an observation that subsequently fell from the Attorney-General.] Sir William commences by stating that it would naturally be asked, by those who saw this volume, why he caused a book to be printed which he had not published? The reason was, because he had treated of a work which was said to be sacred—and, to avoid the calumnies and falsities to-which it might give rise, if published, he had confined it to a narrow circle. Indeed he did not wish his opinions-to be handed about amongst *the mob*. After observing that the ancient Jews had their *isoteric* and *exoteric* doctrines, which were signified by types and figures, the meaning of which was not now known, he proceeds to express an opinion that the language of the Old Testament was symbolical, and he censures those descriptions of the Deity in which he was painted with human passions, and those none of the best. Nothing could be more absurd than to describe the Deity as a material being who dwelt in a box of shittim wood in the temple.

The Attorney-General: I object to such observations.

The Chief Justice: They are indeed very offensive. I caution the defendant against taking that course of defence.

Mr. Carlile: If it be in opposition to the sense and feelings of the jury, I only do myself harm. I wish to-show that others wrote on this subject as well as Paine.

The Chief Justice: That is not the question. The question is whether the book published by you is a blasphemous libel.

Mr. Carlile: I know of no law that takes cognisance of blasphemy.

The Chief Justice: There is such a law.

Mr. Carlile: Then I wish your lordship would define it.

The Chief Justice: I have done so, and will not again.

The Attorney-General: The defendant ought to know, or those who advise him ought to have informed him, that he will have an opportunity of appealing to the Court out of which this process proceeds—the Court of Kings Bench—and, if he pleases, to the last resort in the country, the House of Lords. There he may discuss whether the charge be or be not according to law. This is not the place for that discussion. To the charge preferred against him he has pleaded "Not guilty", and the question now is, whether he be or be not guilty.

Mr. Carlile: I must, as it is necessary for my defence, go through these books.

The Chief Justice: You are not now examining any book—you are merely stating the opinion of another person. You cannot justify one libel by proving that another of the same nature had been written.

Mr. Carlile: It is not proved to be a libel, as yet.

The Chief Justice: I will call it by what name I think proper; but leave it ultimately to be decided by the jury.

Mr. Carlile: You may certainly give it what name you please; but I must defend it to the best of my judgment.

The Chief Justice: I wish you to do so; but I cannot allow the calumny of another person to be introduced as a defence for yours.

Mr. Carlile: I am aware that I need look for nothing from your lordship. I stand alone, unsupported, the array is against me. Sir W. Drummond's work is only a repetition of what may be found in the Old and New Testament. He quotes those works and reasons on them, and he has a right to do so.

Mr. Carlile was proceeding with the passage which had just been objected to, when Mr. Gurney requested his lordship's interference.

Mr. Carlile: You have nothing to do in this cause.

Mr. Gurney: I have the honor of assisting the Attorney-General.

The Chief Justice: I have told you, that you cannot justify one calumny by introducing another.

Mr. Carlile: Is it not actually the case, that God is represented in the text as dwelling in a box of shittim wood in the temple?

The Chief Justice: Certainly not, sir.

Mr. Carlile: If my defence be bad, I only injure myself. He then proceeded to read some remarks of Sir W. Drummond, condemning the reason assigned for God's determining not to curse the earth any more, when he was interrupted by

The Attorney-General, who said: I do trust your lordship will interpose. I say, when a defendant is charged with a publication attacking the truths of Christianity, he cannot be allowed to defend himself by making new attacks. No man can be suffered to make this Court the arena where the calumnies from the pen of Paine, or of any other writer, are to be promulgated. The object of the defendant is evident. He wishes that those calumnies should come forth to the public in a shape more disgraceful than they have hitherto appeared; but in the discharge of my public duty I will take care that such publications shall not pass unnoticed or unpunished.

Mr. Gurney: The Court cannot hear the statute law, as well as the common law of the land, treated with contempt. Those who put the law in motion proceeded on the common law; but the statute of William and Mary is still in force.

Mr. Carlile: The Attorney-General has not founded his information on the statute of William and Mary. He wishes for a different punishment than that statute provides.

The Chief Justice: I am free to confess that I am placed in a very delicate situation. I am unwilling to prevent the defendant from going on with what appears to him fit and necessary for his defence; but, as a Judge, I am bound not to admit the law of the land to be insulted in my presence.

Mr. Carlile: I am not aware of having insulted any law.

The Solicitor-General: I wish to state to your lordship what Lord Ellenborough said on Eaton's trial. When the defendant was addressing him, his lordship interrupted him. "You have already," observed his lordship, "begun a passage, of which I caution you. This is not to be an opportunity for you to revile the Christian religion; and if you persist in doing so, I will not only prevent you, but perhaps animadvert on your conduct in committing an offence which was of the most heinous nature in the eyes of the Court." Defendant answered: "I have no intention of offending the Court." Lord Ellenborough observed, "You have got to a passage that is abominable—you must not read it". Now, my lord, the defendant before you says: "I will prove the truth of what Paine asserts, namely that there are obscenities, inconsistences, and contradictions in the Bible." This, I submit, he can only do by pursuing the course which Mr. Eaton was checked in, which cannot be permitted.

The Chief Justice: Let the defendant go on, if he can advance anything relevant and serviceable to his cause.

Mr. Carlile: It would be as well if the Solicitor-General read a little further, that the Court might see the result of that discussion.

The Solicitor-General: Mr. Eaton observed, "I believe what I am come to is inoffensive"; and nothing offensive was afterwards said.

Mr. Carlile: The fact is, Lord Ellenborough grew angry, and called out repeatedly, "Read it all, read it all!"—which was done.

The Chief Justice: The Christian religion shall not be reviled here.

Mr. Carlile: In what I say, I found myself on the late statute.

The Chief Justice: You made some remarks on it yesterday. At first I thought your idea was erroneous; and on looking into the subject, I see that an Act was passed, in the time of King William, for the punishment of those who impugned the doctrine of the Trinity. An Act was recently passed, respecting that particular part of the statute of William, which it repealed; but it leaves untouched all that is contained in that statute and the common law of the land, for the punishment of those who impugn the truth of Christianity in general. The work in question does not impugn the opinion of any particular sect, but impugns the whole of the doctrines contained in the Old and New Testament. It is directed against the tenets of every sect who believe in the Scriptures as the foundation of revealed religion.

Mr. Carlile: I have been told that the Christian religion is the law of the land. Now that religion is founded on the doctrine of the Trinity; and here is a statute dispensing with a belief in the Trinity, and thereby making Deism a part of the law of the land.

Chief Justice: I say it does not, and I will not hear such a defence.

Mr. Carlile; I stand here alone, and I best know what shape my defence ought to take.

The Chief Justice: In your own opinion it may be so; but it is for me to look to the legal course of defence. If you cannot proceed without reviling the Christian religion, you cannot defend yourself.

Mr. Carlile: The law in question allows me to proceed in this course, for it tolerates Deism.

The Attorney-General: One part of the statute of William and Mary is repealed, but the remainder is in force. It is there treated as a great offence for any persons to deny the Christian religion to be true, or the Scriptures, namely the Old and New Testament, to be of divine origin.

Mr. Carlile: I do not know on what the Christian religion is founded, except on the doctrine of the Trinity.

The Chief Justice: If you have any good legal defence, proceed with it.

Mr. Carlile: I do not know that I am wrong. If there be an allegation that I have published a work in which it is stated that there is an obscene story in the Bible, surely you would not prevent me from referring to the Bible to prove the truth of the assertion?

The Chief Justice: I cannot hear this. The Bible is the history of a sinful people, and of the vengeance of God on them.

Mr. Carlile: I do not think the Bible is true, as a history.

[Considerable agitation was created in Court by this declaration. Murmurs of dissatisfaction were heard from every quarter.]

Mr. Carlile was proceeding with another passage from Sir W. Drummond's book, when he was interrupted by The Solicitor-General, who objected that he was going on in the way which had already been deprecated by the Court.

The Chief Justice: I cannot allow it. If I am mistaken there are means of correcting my error; but I think I am not mistaken when I say, that I cannot and ought not sit in my place and suffer any person to revile the Holy Scriptures.

Mr. Carlile: I have no wish to revile, but merely to examine them.

The Chief Justice: Examination does not consist in, and cannot be supported by, bold denials. It is a repetition of the offence.

Mr. Carlile: Can we compel our minds to receive as true what we do not believe because there is a law in support of it?

The Chief Justice: As long as a man keeps his opinion to himself, it is of no consequence to the community, and no human power can take cognizance of it.

Mr. Carlile: Your lordship's observations argue nothing but the absurdity of legislating on matters of opinion. He was proceeding with Sir W. Drummond's work, when The Solicitor-General again interrupted him. The defendant, he said, wanted to prove that other persons had written on the subject as well as Mr. Paine, which he contended formed no point of defence.

The Chief Justice: I cannot allow such a course to be taken.

Mr. Carlile: I have a right to go on with what I think necessary for my defence.

The Chief Justice: You have no right to go on with a defence of a mischievous nature. It would be a high misdemeanor in me to allow it.

271

Mr. Carlile: My wish is to defend my conduct from the imputation of malicious intention. In the course of their practice, these learned gentlemen quote precedents on all occasions; why then should not I quote Sir W. Drummond, a man of great talent and research?

The Chief Justice: His book has nothing to do with the case before the jury.

Mr. Carlile: The authority of Sir W. Drummond is as good as that of Lord Ellenborough.

The Chief Justice: You had better conduct yourself with propriety.

Mr. Carlile: In my mind, the authority of Sir W. Drummond possesses far greater weight.

The Chief Justice: Don't suppose, because great forbearance has been shown, that there may not come a time when forbearance must end.

Mr. Carlile: I don't want forbearance, I only want justice.

The Chief Justice: Justice you shall have, according to law; but to let you proceed contrary to law would not be justice. It is no justification for you to say that others have committed the same offence.

Mr. Carlile: I am not willing to take your lordship's-opinion that it is an offence.

The Chief Justice: I have said, all along, that the character of the publication would be ultimately left to the decision of the jury.

Mr. Carlile was proceeding, but the Solicitor-General again interposed.

The Chief Justice: I say it is no justification; but still I would not prevent the defendant from going on if the quotation be not offensive. I do not know that to be the work of Sir W. Drummond.

Mr. Carlile: It is his, for it has been answered by the Chaplain to the Archbishop of Canterbury. That is the best way to elicit truth. Sir W. Drummond's name is to it.

The Chief Justice: No matter by whom it is written. I cannot stay in this place and hear the doctrines of Christianity impugned.

Mr. Carlile: It is not yet proven that I have committed error.

The Chief Justice: I know that—I have stated so all along; but you must not revile and calumniate the Christian religion.

Mr. Carlile: I do not calumniate. I wish to enter on a fair examination.

The Chief Justice: You are not allowed, neither is any man, to read in this place matter calumniating the Holy Scriptures.

Mr. Carlile: It is not calumniating.

The foreman of the jury now addressed his lordship. He said the gentlemen of the jury thought the defendant could not do himself any service by going on with such a defence

Mr. Carlile: Am I to understand that to be the sentiment of the jury?

Several Jurymen: Certainly.

After a short pause, Mr. Carlile proceeded. He at length came to a passage in which Sir W. Drummond stated that he did not believe God had ever spoken to Moses.

Mr. Gurney submitted that was the denial of the truth and divine origin of part of the Old Testament, and was punishable by the statute law. It could not therefore be tolerated in that Court.

Mr. Carlile: To what are we to appeal, if not to reason?

The Chief Justice: You are charged with publishing a calumny on the Christian religion; show that the book does not contain such calumny. You cannot prove that there is no calumny in it by reading works of a similar nature.

Mr. Carlile: There are passages in the Bible which I view with as much horror as your lordship does this book. I do not believe them—your lordship does, or you profess that you do. Now it is only by reading controversial disputes on the subject of religion that we can know what is right or what is wrong.

The Chief Justice: We are not here trying the verity of passages of Scripture. I cannot put it to the jury to say whether the Holy Scriptures contain the will of God. This cannot be done in a Christian country.

Mr. Carlile: I am obliged to read, in my defence, things that are disgusting to myself, and which I would not read if I were not compelled to do so.

The Chief Justice: You are not compelled. It can do you no service to read passages of a similar tendency with those which you are charged with having published.

Mr. Carlile: As there is no other passage in this book essential to my defence, I shall now go to the Bible. In reading that work, which the information charges me with calumniating, I can only express my own opinion, as a justification of what I have done. If that opinion is not satisfactory to the minds of the jury, still it would afford some ground for believing that I act from conviction.— [Here Mr. Carlile exhibited a large Bible, which was interleaved for the purpose of entering remarks on different passages.]—The Old Testament, like many other books, begins with giving an account of the creation.—[Mr. Carlile here read several verses from the book of Genesis: "In the beginning God created the heaven and the earth," etc.]—Now (continued he) I have to state to you that that part of society who believe in this book differ in their ideas of the account of the creation. Some believe it to be an allegory—others consider it a statement of a real transaction. Some of the greatest fathers of the Christian Church, one of whom was Origen, considered it an allegory. When we see persons, who call themselves Christians, and who rest all their future hopes on this book, differing on such a passage, I think an individual, whose mind is not made up on the subject, is at liberty to enquire into the reasons offered for one party believing it to be an allegory, and the other for taking it literally. Moses is stated to be the author of the book of Genesis, but I think it is proved by Paine that he did not write it. Whether it was written by him or not did not, however, invalidate the work. When you read, "In the *beginning* God created the heaven and the earth," the philosopher naturally asks, what beginning? If it were said, from the beginning of time, then the world had existed through all eternity, for, to deny the eternity of time, is to deny the eternity of God. But this doctrine did not coincide with that of the Old Testament, although it was founded in reason.

Mr. Carlile was then proceeding with an enquiry into the nature and probability of such a revelation as was mentioned in the Old Testament, but was interrupted by

The Attorney-General, who submitted that no such enquiry could be gone into.

The Chief Justice: It is a very difficult thing to stop a person on his defence, at the commencement of every sentence. I would wish to err on the side of forbearance rather than of severity. Of all cases that can be brought into a Court of Justice, this is the most painful to a Judge. It is not connected with the politics or property of the country, but with its religion. The person on the floor says I profess to be a believer in Christianity. I feel myself called on to say, that I am a firm believer in Christianity. It is most painful to me and to the gentlemen of the jury to hear the observations of the defendant, but still it is a nice and difficult point to stop him.

The Attorney-General said an enquiry into revelation could not be allowed.

Mr. Gurney: His lordship has declared it cannot be admitted.

The Chief Justice: I have said over and over again that we are not to enquire into the truth of the Christian religion; but I am unwilling to stop the defendant till his observations become offensive.

Mr. Carlile: The information charges that the book which I have published describes the Old Testament to contain obscene stories and voluptuous debaucheries, and to be a history of wickedness that has served to corrupt and brutalise mankind. Another account charges me with publishing a book in which the Bible is stated to be full of inconsistencies and contradictions. Now, how can I defend myself but by showing the truth of the book I have published? If I do prove its truth, I can plead that I published it with a good intention.

The Chief Justice: You cannot go into the truth of the Christian religion.

Mr. Carlile: It is a most improper question, I admit, to be brought before a Court of Justice.

The Chief Justice: Whatever you can state to the gentlemen of the jury, that is proper and relative to your case, shall be heard.

Mr. Carlile: But I must enquire into the truth of the Old Testament.

The Chief Justice: No, sir. As I have said before, it is the history of a sinful people, and of the divine vengeance. The gentlemen of the jury, I have no doubt, are well acquainted with it.

Mr. Carlile: You have not pointed out the divine origin of the Scriptures. I am not of opinion that it is divine; and I wish to state my reasons for holding that opinion.

The Chief Justice: Behave with decorum, and I will not interrupt you.

Mr. Carlile: I do not wish to offend any person. It is not my intention. But what I conceive to be truth, I will promulgate, be the consequence what it may.

The Chief Justice: I will take care that you shall not promulgate in this place anything that is improper.

Mr. Carlile: Your lordship has of course read the case of Galileo. He made a great discovery in astronomy, and was arraigned for his opinion before the ecclesiastical tribunals of his country. The alternative was allowed him either to die at the stake or to retract his opinions; to save his life he did change his opinions, though he was convinced of their truth. He however endeavored privately to disseminate those opinions, but was discovered, and the religious government of that country condemned him to three years' imprisonment. But, before the expiration of that time, the truth of his opinion, that the earth was not flat, but round, and that the sun did not move round the earth but the earth round the sun, were established and admitted by his persecutors. Who then will venture to stop human improvement? Who will say we have gone far enough? I believe, from conviction, having considered the subject, and got all the information I could connected with it, that the book which is called the revealed will of God, is a blasphemy of that God. [A murmur of indignation pervaded the Court.]

The Chief Justice: This is too much.

Mr. Carlile: I can state reason for my belief. I am supported by Sir W. Drummond, a man of the finest education, and who had made the most extensive enquiries the human mind could reach. I am deeply impressed with the impropriety of bringing such a subject before a Court of Justice, but I must either do that or go to a prison, from which perhaps I will never be liberated. The consequence is dreadful to me. I must either get the Attorney-General to withdraw the case from the Court, or enter on my defence in the way I think most likely to answer my purpose.

The Chief Justice: There is another alternative; to conduct yourself with decency and decorum.

Mr. Carlile: I am insensible of any indecorum.

The Chief Justice: Whether you are insensible, or cannot be made sensible, it is right that I should check you when you misconduct yourself.

Mr. Carlile: There is a statute which supports Deism

The Chief Justice: You may comment on that statute.

Mr. Carlile: There is a statute by which it is enacted that to impugn the doctrine of the Trinity is not an offence. It is the law of the land.

Mr. Gurney: That part of the statute of William and Mary is in force which renders it criminal for any man to deny the Christian religion to be true, or the Scriptures to be of divine origin.

Mr. Carlile: Why did not the Attorney-General found his information on that statute?

The Chief Justice: Because he did not think proper to do so. That statute imposed certain penalties, and he conceived it was better to proceed on the common law. He was justified in doing so. A riot is punishable by common law; but, as in the case of disturbing a congregation, it may be punished under a particular statute, at the option of the complaining party.

Mr. Carlile: Yes, but the riot is defined. The Riot Act states what shall be denominated a riot. This is not the case here. There was an Act in existence which allowed persons to impugn the doctrine of the Trinity, on which the Christian religion is founded; and by so doing, supported Deism, and admitted the nature of that religion to be investigated. I was extremely unwilling to be brought here; for I think a Court of Justice a most improper place for such a subject. If a book be published containing questionable opinions, they ought to be corrected by the intervention of the Press. I am charged, in the information, with having excited "the great displeasure of Almighty God"! Is not this a gross assumption? Is it not blasphemy? We ought to venerate the Deity; and not speak of him as if he were subject to human passions and frailties. I think I have shown that Paine had a more sublime idea of the Almighty than the Koran contained. I will go further, and say that he had a higher notion of the Divinity than is to found in the Old Testament. I have no wish to proceed under continual interruptions; it is, indeed, impossible that I can proceed; but, I am sure, if anything I offer in my defence is not a justification of my conduct, I alone will be the sufferer. If the book I wished to read be the work of the Deity, it cannot be injured or shaken by the observations of any man. It is, in my opinion, not the work of the Deity.

The Chief Justice: You are now offending against a law which has been quoted more than once.

Mr. Carlile: An Act of Parliament cannot restrain opinions.

The Chief Justice: It may restrain the expression of them.

Mr. Carlile: My case is similar to that of Galileo, in whose defence no man stood forward. If Newton had been on the Continent when he made his discoveries, he would have been treated in the same way that Galileo was. The same course was pursued towards all men who wished to remove bigotry and ignorance. Locke, if I recollect rightly, was expelled the University on account of the freedom of his opinions. He did not deny the Christian religion; but he went very near to that point; and it cannot be denied that the 9th and 10th of William and Mary were passed, in a great measure, to check the circulation of his writings and opinions. The Attorney-General appeals to the authority of Locke, and so may I. The great man says, "Reason only can judge of revelation". I could wish, my lord, to understand whether I am to go into that defence which I conceive to be my only defence, or to be put down unheard? I cannot legally be put down. What I have to say in my defence I think the Court is bound to hear.

The Chief Justice: The Court is not bound to hear the Christian religion impugned.

Mr. Carlile: I must say that the Act to which I have alluded, by dispensing with belief in the Trinity, admits the Christian religion to be impugned.

The Chief Justice: It does no such thing.

Mr. Carlile: It tolerates others in doing it. For those who are really attached to the Christian religion must believe Jesus to be a part of the Godhead; which doctrine is now impugned by this Act. The Attorney-General himself has been bred in the Unitarian belief; he has been taught the Unitarian doctrines—doctrines which go to overthrow the divinity of Jesus—and, if you destroy that divinity, Jesus must be a man; there is no-medium. I feel an awful veneration for the Deity. In conversation I never appeal to his name in vain. He resides only in my mind; he is very seldom in my speech. The whole face of the earth is peopled by nations that differ from each other in their opinions of the Deity. In this country there are hundreds of sects of Christians; they are almost innumerable; and they feel the utmost jealousy and indulge in the greatest bickerings towards each other. How then is it possible to arrive at a knowledge of what is right or wrong, unless we judge for ourselves? The difficulty here arises from the impropriety of bringing a question of this kind into a Court of Justice, where it cannot be freely and fairly judged according to the rules of the Court. It would do honor to the Attorney-General if he would withdraw the record, since I cannot offer in my defence what I deem necessary. I am not like a barrister, who acts according to the statement contained in his brief, and has no opinion of his own. I avow that I published certain opinions, and those opinions I am ready to defend. It is well known, and I am sure your lordship cannot contradict me, that there are many passages in the Old Testament which cannot be reconciled with reason, nor with the feelings of delicacy. It is, I fear, a dislike to hear them repeated which induces your lordship to prevent me from proceeding.

The Chief Justice: It is not any such feeling that actuates me; but an awful veneration for the Scriptures. It is not competent for you to defend yourself by impugning the truth of the Christian religion, with which our hopes of eternal happiness are so nearly connected.

Mr. Carlile denied that he had impugned Christianity.

The Chief Justice: I heard you say that belief in the Scriptures was blasphemy to God.

Mr. Gurney: The defendant said, "It is my firm belief that the Bible is not the revealed will of God".

Mr. Carlile repeated that some parts of the Old Testament abounded in morality, while others, he must observe, were revolting to the feelings of any reflecting man, who wished to publish a book of morality, according to the prevailing moral doctrines. If those parts of the Bible to which he alluded were published by themselves, it would subject him or any other individual to a prosecution by the Attorney-General; or, if he did not prosecute, he would be guilty of a dereliction of his duty. He had already stated that the statute tolerated Deism. It did so, because it tolerated Unitarianism. He was a Unitarian, and therefore a Deist—and, being a Deist, he was therefore a Unitarian. The words Trinitarian and Unitarian were opposed to each other, to distinguish the believers in the Trinity from those who did not agree to that doctrine. The Old Testament, it ought to be observed, was never placed by the Jews in the hands of their children; and the clergy of the Romish Church endeavored to keep the Scriptures from the laity by retaining them in an obscure tongue. It was in this country alone that the copies had been greatly multiplied and placed in the hands of all ranks and ages. He now called the attention of the Court to the "History of the English Bible", which, as it was printed for the Religious Tract Society, his lordship might easily conceive contained nothing offensive.

Mr. Carlile then read the small extract entitled "The History of the English Bible", after the concluding words of which, viz.: Thus, after the lapse of almost 100 years from the first appearance of the English printed Scriptures by the labors of Tyndal, we are come to the present authorised version, of which it has been remarked, that "it is the birth-right of our numerous population, and has proved the means of knowledge, holiness, and joy to millions; and we trust it is destined for ages yet to come, to be the glory of the rich, and the inheritance of the poor; the guide to the way-worn pilgrim, and the messenger of peace to many a dying sinner". He said that in the latter day a Mr. Bellamy had started up, who denied the correctness of this version, asserting that in many parts it did not agree with the original Hebrew, proposed writing a new translation, and got some of the Bishops and the Prince Regent to subscribe for copies. Why did not the Attorney-General prosecute Mr. Bellamy for saying, as he in fact had, that the Scriptures (by which must be meant the authorised translation) did not contain the word of God? After some other observations he proceeded. He could not boast of having got a learned education. He ran through a country school in the way most boys do, up to the age of twelve; and whatever learning he had acquired since was in the time he had spared from his employment and the calls of his business; but, notwithstanding, he had perused a variety of commentators on the Bible, and finding them all disagree, that circumstance created doubt in his mind, which ended in the opinions he now held. He had been brought up in the doctrines of the Christian Church, and his mother used to impress them on him with peculiar earnestness. It was from the apprehension of similar doubts in the people generally that the Bishops in former times universally prohibited the reading of the Scriptures. His intention was to go through that part of the Bible examined by Mr. Paine, and it he should establish that they exactly agreed in the representation of them given by Mr. Paine, he was entitled to a verdict of acquittal.

He then, after several remarks on the statutes before referred to, and objections constantly over-ruled, commenced reading and commenting on the first two chapters of Genesis, after which he read a tract from the book on which the information is grounded, entitled "Extract of a Reply to the Bishop of Llandaff".

After the defendant had concluded reading, he said that he had made it clear from Mr. Paine's work, that Mr. Paine had shown that the book of Job was written prior to the book of Genesis. Having read Mr. Paine's letter to Lord Erskine, on the first and third chapters of Genesis, he now proceeded to the fourth. [Here the defendant proceeded to read the fourth chapter of Genesis.] On that part where it is stated that the Lord had set a mark on Cain, the defendant said that the commentators on the Bible were much puzzled as to what this mark was; some said it was the mark on the African; some, the mark on the Ethiopian—but no one, he said, could give a fair account of it. They also said that in the different genealogical accounts in the Bible, in most cases the accounts disagree with each other. After reading that part where the Lord is said to have repented for having created man, he attempted to comment on the passage. He said it made our Savior a mere human being—to repent of an action was unworthy of a God.

The Chief Justice here interrupted the defendant. His lordship said, that sitting there as an English judge he could not allow the defendant to take that course. By the law of the land, no person was allowed to deny the truth of the Christian religion, or to question the-divine authority of the Holy Scriptures.

Mr. Carlile said he was sorry to observe that there was little of Christianity about those who were around him. Mr. Paine himself said that Jesus Christ was an amiable and benevolent man; he endeavored to change the system of religion in his time—he made innovations on the powers of the high priests of the Jews; and what were the consequences? Why, he fell a victim to their rancor and

285

malice. My lord, the priests in this country are not more merciful, it is-from the priests of this country that this persecution against me has originated.

The Chief Justice: It is unnecessary to read those chapters from Genesis, the jury are acquainted with them.

Mr. Carlile: My lord, I read them for the justification of Paine.

The Chief Justice: This surely cannot be a defence.

Mr. Carlile: My object is to show that Paine was justified in what he asserted; my object is to show that Paine was not guilty of a falsehood.

The Chief Justice: I did not restrain you from reading the publication itself; though if what is contained in it were urged by yourself, I certainly would not allow you to proceed.

Mr. Carlile: My lord, in this country it is easy to-excite religious prejudice. Paine said that no man should be condemned for differing with another in opinion. Such conduct is surely not consistent with the spirit of Christianity, nor with any principle of morality or justice.

The Chief Justice: I have already stated, and I now repeat it, that sitting here as an English judge, I cannot allow any man to deny that the Holy Bible is of divine authority.

Mr. Carlile: My lord, the jury are the judges in my case. I see no law that applies to my case—I appeal to the judgment of the jury. My lord, Mr. Kidd, in his defence of Williams, was going into the same line of defence that I now wish to take; he was interrupted by Lord Kenyon. Mr.

Kidd said he stood there the advocate of the prisoner; that in a Court of Justice every man had a right to a defence; that he saw no course of defence but that which he was about to take, and if he were not allowed to pursue that, he might as well abandon the defence altogether. Lord Kenyon desired him to go on.

The Chief Justice: In that very report you will find that Mr. Kidd was about to read certain passages of the Bible, and on an intimation of the Court, he desisted from doing so. I have allowed you in this case much greater latitude than was allowed to Mr. Kidd in that. You may cite passages, but do not read them.

Here the Attorney-General read a passage from the report of the trial of Williams.

Mr. Carlile: My lord, Mr. Paine said that no book was more read and less examined than the Bible. When I am prevented from reading passages from the Bible, is it because the Bible is not fit to be read?

The Chief Justice: Not to be read irreverently—not to be read for the avowed purpose of proving or attempting to prove that the Bible is not of divine origin.

Here the foreman of the jury interfered. He said that the jury did not think it necessary for the defendant to go any farther into the reading of the Bible.

His lordship again said, that as an English judge, independent of every other consideration, he would not suffer the defendant to question the Scriptures.

Mr. Carlile: My lord, the Scriptures are here considered of divine origin. The Mahometans consider the Koran as divine also. The Mahometans would not permit a man, however conscientious, to doubt the dogmas of the Koran.

The Chief Justice: If you in the Mahometan empire committed an offence against the religion of the State, instead of receiving an impartial and patient trial, as you have here, you would be devoted to instant death.

Mr. Carlile: Yes, my lord, and this shows how cool men should be, and how much consideration should be given to matter of opinion.

The Chief Justice: I cannot allow you to violate the laws of the land, and in affecting to defend yourself, to commit a repetition of the offence.

Mr. Carlile: My lord, the entire case is a matter of opinion. I shall now proceed to read some passages from the writings of Doctor Geddes, the translator of the Hebrew Testament. That celebrated man was educated a Catholic priest, and was one of the most learned and able men of his day. Here he read a number of passages from Doctor Geddes, he was proceeding to read further, when The Attorney-General said, that if the defendant were thus allowed to proceed, he saw no termination to the trial; if permitted, the defendant might continue to read every work published on the gospel. What the defendant was reading had no relation whatever to the charge, and he should not be allowed to occupy the time of the Court.

The Chief Justice: The work the defendant is now reading is very different from the publication of Paine. Dr. Geddes observes on the five books of Moses, and expresses his doubts as to some of them.

Mr. Carlile: My lord, Dr. Geddes doubts some parts of the Bible, and Mr. Paine's publication doubted some part of it.

The Chief Justice: No; the publication of Paine does not go to express doubts, but it impugns the Bible; it says that the entire of the Bible is a tissue of falsehood and imposition.

Here the foreman of the jury said that the jury felt great reluctance in interfering with the defendant; but they felt it necessary to say that the course he was taking did not seem to them to bear on his case.

Mr. Carlile: Then I cannot see what will bear on my case; prejudice has been excited against me, and I am to be crushed.

The Chief Justice: If you will be crushed, it must be by the weight of your publication. If you have done something that cannot be defended without impugning the law of England, then you cannot be allowed to go into that kind of defence.

Mr. Carlile: My lord, I don't see that the law is against me.

The Chief Justice: Sir, I have already given my opinion on this point.

Mr. Carlile: My lord, you said that by the recent statute, but one of the provisions of the Act of William and Mary was repealed. I say that the three provisions were repealed.

The Chief Justice: Well, sir, that is your opinion; it is for the jury to say whether they will take the law from you or from me.

Mr. Carlile: My lord, the law is a very dubious thing.

The Chief Justice: Your course is very wrong. If you urge matter irrelevant, it is a loss of time; if you urge what is profane, it is still worse.

Mr. Carlile: My lord, what was written by Mr. Paine was also written by other eminent men, who were not prosecuted.

The Chief Justice: It does not follow that if the offences of those men were not punished, that others are to follow the same course with impunity.

Mr. Carlile: My lord, Mr. Gibbon has attacked the Christian religion in the most insidious manner. I am at liberty to go into its examination.

The Chief Justice: I say you are not; you are not at liberty to do anything to question the divine origin of Christianity.

Mr. Carlile: My lord, I am a man of humble life, and therefore I am prosecuted. Mr. Gibbon, far from being prosecuted, held an office under the Crown. Mr. Hume, who far exceeded Paine in his attacks on religion—Hume, also, was an Atheist—was sent as Secretary to an Embassy to Paris, and had afterwards a pension of £600 a year. He was never prosecuted, and never questioned, but by the people of the country. My lord, if I am in error, let me be convinced by argument; but let me not be thrown into a prison by those who are formed in concert to crush me.

The Chief Justice: If you attribute anything of concert to me, you attribute that which I am altogether free from. I am here discharging my duty as a judge of the land, and the first dictate of that duty is not to allow the character of the Christian religion to be assailed.

Mr. Carlile: My lord, if you deny one part of the Christian religion you destroy the whole. The first principles of the Christian religion is the belief in the divinity of Christ—the Unitarians do not believe so, yet they are protected by the law; they believe that Christ was the messenger of God, and that he performed some miracles—that he raised from the dead. The statute law protects the Unitarians, and will it be said that the same law does not also apply to those who, like the Unitarians, do not believe in the divinity of Christ? I hold up that statute as the shield of my protection—I have stated the law which tolerated the impugning of the Holy Trinity. If the statute was not passed I never would have published those works. The jury must know that public opinion is liable to-change. Since the convictions that took place for publishing "The Age of Reason", I thought I saw the change in public opinion manifested in this Act of the Legislature. "The Age of Reason" inculcates morality; it is as perfect in this respect as any book that ever was published of the same kind. If, however, I am in error, a loathsome prison is not likely to convince me of my error. My lord, one half of the people of this country are Deists— thousands of persons hold the same opinions that I do, but their situations in life will not allow them to express those opinions. I believe in one God, and no more. The same law that protects others should protect me. The law is express, and if I am not to get its protection, it is of no use to the subject. My lord, I have made great arrangements for my trial, but in consequence of the interruptions I have received, my line of defence is broken down. It was my intention to examine thirty or forty witnesses who should express what their belief is. They are of different sects, yet they are all tolerated, because their belief does not militate against the interests of the priests of this country. I also would produce persons to speak as to my moral conduct— persons who have known me since I was thirteen years of age, and who could swear that I have ever conducted myself as a peaceable and industrious citizen, and as a moral member of society. I do not wish to occupy unnecessarily the public time, but there have been cases of much less importance—the case of Sacheverell, who was tried for holding the doctrine of passive obedience—a doctrine which is now publicly preached from the pulpits of this metropolis, and is hailed by the present system of government; his case took up ten days. Trials for high treason, founded on the most frivolous charges, which were attempted to be worked up to high treason, and which were not of half so much importance as the question between me and the Attorney-General, took up many days. The Attorney-General, in this question, has left his case to be made out by the Court; he has failed to make it out himself. But I will not take the law from the Court; the jury are my judges; I will not take the dictum of his lordship. I cannot sit down without going further into my defence, unless it is positively decided that I shall not proceed.

The Chief Justice: You must not deny the truth of the Christian religion, nor are you to go into irrelevant matter; if I am wrong you can appeal to the Court of King's Bench.

Mr. Carlile: By what means can I appeal to the Court of King's Bench when I am confined within the walls of a prison?

The Chief Justice: I know nothing of the walls of a prison. If I am wrong in point of law, you will be entitled to the benefit of my error.

Mr. Carlile: The law tolerates those who deny the Trinity—therefore it tolerates Deists. I have been frequently interrupted by the Attorney-General; it is, I believe, the first time an Attorney-General has at-tempted to dictate to à defendant what line of defence he should pursue—that at

292

least should be left to the Court. My lord, the work of Dr. Geddes is a fair examination of the Hebrew Scriptures.

The Chief Justice: Geddes doubts some points—Paine denies all.

Mr. Carlile: Paine, my lord, I consider one of the finest writers; his "Age of Reason" is one of the most useful and able works that have been published. My lord, I am prepared with matter to show that in all ages great doubts were entertained of the truth of the Christian religion—and that the works of the Fathers were composed of the most idle and ridiculous tales. Most of them professed to work miracles.

The Chief Justice said these works had no bearing on the question.

Mr. Carlile: My lord, I am left then without a defence. There are two books, one is protected by an Act of Parliament, and the other I am not allowed to-support.

The Chief Justice: I cannot let men be acquitted of a charge of violating the law because they are unbelievers.

Mr. Carlile: Everything that is true should be allowed. Another part of my defence is to show the general persecution that has existed since the commencement of Christianity—that same system of persecution is now exerted against me; because I have published certain opinions, I am to be sent to prison without a defence. My lord, for the truth of opinions hundreds have been burnt in Smithfield and thousands on the Continent. The Attorney-General, I am sure, would pursue me to the stake with the same pleasure and avidity that he now pursues me to a prison.

The Chief Justice: You have no right to say that.

Mr. Carlile: My lord, I shall now proceed to a short examination of a statement made by Bishop Burnet. The Bishop says "that damnation is repugnant to the wisdom and mercy of God". He says in his charge to the clergy that they should not give their real opinions to the world. He says, that the idea of hell is as ridiculous as the idea of Transubstantiation. But it should be recollected, however ridiculous it may appear, hundreds have suffered death for maintaining it; and though he treats it as absurd it was a few years before his time the sacred doctrine professed by the Christian world, venerated as ancient, and revered as the essence of the established religion of his country. Here he went into a recital of some observations of distinguished authors, on the dignity of avowing the truth: Tacitus exclaimed, when will the blessed time arrive when men may think without awe and speak without danger. Milton, Bacon and Boyle expressed themselves in the like terms; but the Attorney-General said he would send me to a prison, merely because I would uphold what I think to be true; not that my opinions are different from his; no, I could hold up the hand of fellowship to Sir Robert Gifford, he is a Unitarian, and a Unitarian is a Deist. If I am once found guilty, I know well that no objections will avail me. I shall be placed in the hands of those who are now my prosecutors.

The Chief Justice: I repeat it, if I am wrong in point of law, you will be entitled to rectify that mistake by applying to the Court of King's Bench. I shall, indeed, myself consult the Court on the subject.

Mr. Carlile: My lord, I have no faith in the Court; I hope for no indulgence—my defence rests on matter of opinion, not of law. Where legislatures enact laws against opinion, their acts are a nullity and absurdity. My lord, I have no hope of bringing the jury round to my opinion; but I had a strong hope that if I was allowed to proceed I should show that I had some reasons to doubt, and that I might have doubted without a malicious intention.

The Chief Justice: I have not excluded you from that line of defence. You may, if you can, show that your intentions were innocent; but you cannot, and must not do that by impeaching the Holy Scriptures.

Mr. Carlile: My lord, there are some parts of the Scriptures which Paine has not touched on, or to which he has slightly alluded; for instance, the Songs of Solomon in the Old Testament. These contain the most voluptuous tales—it was my intention to read them—and then I would ask you, gentlemen of the jury, whether you would put into the hands of your children that book in preference to "The Age of Reason"? The Bible contains tales which no young mind can read un-contaminated. "The Age of Reason" rescues the character of the Deity from the degraded situation in which the Bible placed it, and instead of suppressing the works of Paine by prosecutions, a statue should be erected in this hall sacred to his memory—in this hall, and in every public place in this country. My lord, there were fifty Gospels afloat until the councils of Nice and Laodicea collected them, and selected these Gospels out of them which are now professed by Christians. I am not precluded from showing you the authority of these Councils. The early Christians were celebrated for persecuting each other. [Here he referred to "Eusebius's Ecclesiastical History". After reading some passages, the Court asked with what object he proceeded? He replied, he read it to show that the New Testament was no gift of God to man.]

The Chief Justice: In this Court we assume that the Christian religion is true. I am anxious to give every possible latitude of defence, but I cannot permit the introduction of blasphemy; I cannot allow this day's proceedings to form a precedent that might be dangerous in future times.

Mr. Carlile: I wish to show that there are some reasons to doubt.

The Chief Justice: The publication you are now to answer for does not express doubts; but it calumniates and reviles the Christian religion. You cannot justify by denying the truth of the Christian religion.

Mr. Carlile: Your decision, my lord, sets aside the statute.

The Chief Justice: I have given my opinion on the statute. It is useless, and it certainly is not decorous, to contend against that opinion now. If it be a wrong one, you will have an opportunity of rectifying it.

Mr. Carlile: My lord, I feel that I do not stand in a Court of Justice; but that I stand in an Inquisition, where I am prevented from going into my defence.

The Chief Justice: You stand in a Court where the Christian religion must be observed as the law of the land, and where no man is allowed to revile it; you stand in a Court willing and most anxious to give you the full benefit of every fair, legal and decorous defence.

Mr. Carlile: My lord, I am persecuted because these publications are directed against the revenues of the Church. If it were not for this the publication would be safe. How many odious and absurd doctrines have been tolerated, nay, supported in this country? Johanna Southcote had twenty thousand followers in this country— she was encouraged in her impious and indecent conduct— whilst the publisher of "The Age of Reason" is prosecuted, but not allowed to be defended. My lord, I shall now take leave to show you the persecutions which Luther endured. That persecution originated in the same spirit that now assails me. Luther was the son of a Saxon minister; he was sent to a school in Magdeburg, but was afterwards obliged to beg for his bread; he wrote against the authority of the Pope and the practices of the Church of Rome, and he was denounced as a heretic. He was grievously persecuted for maintaining what he considered truth, and if the Court is not prepared to defend that persecution, his lordship cannot defend his own conduct nor the conduct of the Attorney-General as against me. If Luther was exposed to a trial of this kind—if, like me he was prevented from entering into a defence—he would never have been able to carry the Reformation into effect; but happily for him, before the Pope could lay his hands on him, he found a friend in the Elector of Saxony; if it were not for that fortunate circumstance, the pious Christians of those days would have committed him to the flames. The Attorney-General, like the Friar Hiegostratus, who advised the Pope to commit Luther to the flames, now calls for my conviction to send me to a dungeon, to have my family ruined, and to prevent me from ever rising in the world by any effort of care and of industry. Luther was summoned before the Council. He attempted to defend himself on grounds of argument, but he would not be heard, and finding that his person was in danger, he was obliged to fly. He was excommunicated, he was interdicted, he was hunted down like a wild beast, but this he bore for conscience sake. He had the idea of truth, and when the mind of man is impressed with that heavenly sentiment, he will suffer a hero and a martyr to his principles. Though humble my efforts, yet, like the great reformer, I am impressed with the justice and propriety of the course I have taken. It will not be denied, my lord, that sometimes it is necessary to resist power; nay, sometimes to resist law. It is too often the case that the propagators of new doctrines fall victims to their principles. Luther, Calvin and Knox might be said to be the only exceptions. My lord, falsehood will not bear the light of enquiry, but truth is powerful, it is impossible to stop it; it is not perverseness in me to propagate what I conceive to be for the good of man; like Luther, the mind of a sincere believer, whatever his doctrines may be, would rather perish than retract, while unconscious of error. My lord, I cannot but consider that the same persecuting spirit that harassed him is now directed against me; it is true that the Roman Catholic religion in his day had no Attorney-General, but it had its Inquisition, its accusing officers, the ministers of its vengeance, and the creatures of its power.

He then attempted to show that there was no evidence of the miraculous conception of Jesus Christ, insisted on the alleged discrepancy between the Gospels of St. Matthew and St. Luke, and was entering on an argument to prove that the latter Gospel was not written by St. Luke, when he was interrupted by the Attorney-General. He observed on the consequences of the toleration granted to Unitarians by statute 53 Geo. III, whom, he said, he considered as Deists. He had been denied every opportunity of showing, even from Eusebius, that the books of the New Testament were not written by the persons whose names they bore in our version. He had intended to be prepared the next morning with a list of the names of the persons to whom they had been attributed before the Councils of Laodicea and Nice, but in consequence of having been interrupted in his intended line of defence, everything was in confusion and derangement with him. He had an extract to produce from St. Chrysostom, which stated that there was no evidence that the books of the New Testament were the writings of those who are commonly supposed to be their authors. Was it not then severe that he should be punished for his industry in searching out truth, and endeavoring to diffuse it among the public, for he had most studiously examined all the works written as evidences of Christianity, from Eusebius and Origen down to Addison? They had not convinced him. He had been charged with publishing the work for the purpose of brutalising and demoralising his country; but it was not true. He loved his country with ardor, and his object had been to instruct, enlighten and improve it. The system of morals which now obtained in it was founded on error—true morality could not rest on error—and his intentions in printing the works of Mr. Paine had been to dissipate that error, by calling reasonable men to the investigation and trial of it—and it was for this he was to be persecuted, condemned and punished. He was not to be confuted by argument, but crushed and overwhelmed by penalties. It behoved the jury to look well to it whether he deserved to be given up by them for what had originated from nothing but pure motives. If he was in the right, would it not be most unjust? If he was not, would not such means taken to suppress his opinions cause them to spread the wider? Had not persecution always had that effect; and was it for the present enlightened age to be taxed with attempting to put down opinions by torture and imprisonment? He had intended, had he not been interrupted in his defence, to read to-morrow morning extracts from Bolingbroke, Gibbon and Hume, who had evidently held the same principles with Mr. Paine, and who had published their principles in their writings, though these had passed unnoticed and unobserved by any former Attorney-General. The works of Bolingbroke went quite as far as Mr. Paine. Gibbon had adopted a different mode of attack; he meant the same thing as Mr. Paine, but he did not go about it in so honest a way. Paine proceeded fairly and

299

openly—Gibbon insidiously. Hume went farther than either of these, for he even composed a defence of Atheism. Why had all these escaped with impunity, and Paine and he (Mr. Carlile) to be singled out as victims? The tendency of Mr. Paine's system was to enlarge and elevate the mind, by removing the erroneous and false, and inspiring true notions of the Deity; not to sink and degrade it as alleged by the Attorney-General. But whatever might follow his attempt to render them known in this country (for it should be recollected that the two last tracts had not been before published here), something would be suspected from the Attorney-General's preventing him from pursuing the line of defence he had marked out. Why was the information against him founded not on the statutes the 9th and 10th of William III., but on the common law? What was the common law? It was supposed to reside in the breast of the judge. But what one judge in one term, or in one Court, laid down to be common law, another judge in another term pronounced not to be common law; nay, the same judge frequently varied from his own opinion, and over-ruled what he had on former occasions decided to be law. Let a law be given which people could understand.... He had framed a most extensive system of defence; he had been prepared to lay before them passages from the works of the most eminent divines in different ages, enforcing and insisting on the duty of allowing a full freedom of opinion in religious matters; but he found himself precluded from what he had contemplated, which was the only defence in his power. For he maintained, that if a man did any act, and was then precluded from justifying that act, he was precluded from, and deprived of his natural defence. The first reformers of religion were generally and deservedly applauded for their spirit and boldness, yet they might as well have been prosecuted in their day as himself. Luther ventured much farther than he had, for he had no statute law on which to rest a justification of his conduct, as he

(Mr. Carlile) had. It seemed to him that the Legislature, in passing the statute to which he had so frequently referred, had at length seen and acknowledged the propriety of indulging all persons in a free profession and discussion of their tenets in religion. He had heard most intelligent men say it was a toleration of Deism, and in that light, after the most deliberate reflection, he had looked on it. Deism had been much abused; but what was Deism? It was a belief in one God; and it might as well be opposed to polytheism or idolatry, or any of the ancient systems of superstition, as to the doctrine of the Trinity. But the creed of the Trinity was not in any wise essential to morality of life and rectitude of conduct. Greece and Rome boasted of citizens equal, if not superior, in all the virtues which can adorn men, to any ever trained under the Christian code. It was in vain for him to take up any other volume at present. His whole defence rested on one point. From that he had been debarred, and, in consequence, was disabled from proceeding further into his defence that evening. He had an immense number of witnesses to produce, who would say that his moral character, in every particular, had been at all times unimpeachable; also a vast number ta describe the variety of religions, systems and tenets, held even among Christians. Many of them had been subpoenaed, and more would be subpoenaed to-morrow. But he thought it due to him, when the interruptions he had suffered was taken into consideration, that the Court should adjourn till to-morrow morning. His whole line of defence had been thrown into confusion, and he was totally unable to continue it till to-morrow.

The Chief Justice: What then am I to understand?

Mr. Carlile: That in consequence of the interruption I have met with, I am unable to proceed in my defence to-night, and therefore request that the trial may be adjourned till to-morrow morning.

The Chief Justice: For the purpose of examining witnesses only.

Mr. Carlile: My lord, I have not been allowed this day to read any of the books to the jury I had intended, in order to justify what I am charged with as an offence. I should wish to read some of them, as well as to have witnesses examined.

The Chief Justice: It is not competent to me as a judge, sitting here and expounding the law of England, to permit you to read Bolingbroke, or Gibbon, or Hume or any author who denies the Christian religion to be true, or the Holy Scriptures to be of divine authority, neither can any witnesses be examined who may be brought forward to assert either of these things. As to your moral character it is not at present in question.

Mr. Carlile: Certainly, my lord, I conceive it is.

The Chief Justice: You appealed to me; hear me to the end, that you may see why evidence of that nature would be useless and irrelevant. All evidence to character applies itself and corresponds to the charge against the accused. When a man is charged with murder, he brings forward witnesses to prove that he had the reputation of being humane and benevolent, and not one likely to commit such an offence; in the same manner of robbery, or any other charge. Your moral character, at least in the common sense of the word, is not impeached, therefore there would be a waste of time to disprove an accusation not made. You propose to call witnesses, to state the different systems of religious belief among Christians, all that I should reject as being utterly irrelevant to your case. If the book you are charged with publishing attacked the opinions of any particular sect, it might be relevant, but yours is an attack on all the systems of Christianity that ever were known in the world. Perhaps there are some persons here who will speak to your character now.

Mr. Carlile: I am not aware there are, my lord.

The Chief Justice: But there should have been if you wished to produce evidence of that nature.

Mr. Carlile: I had subpoenaed a number of the leaders of different sects to explain their various doctrines, and the grounds on which they held them; and the inference I proposed to make from their testimony was, that the grounds of their different creeds might be examined into.

The Chief Justice: I certainly could not suffer these to be examined into; they would go for nothing, as you are charged with doing that which would subvert all Christian faith, unless they would lead to a denial of the truth of the Christian religion, or of the Divine authority of the Scriptures, which I would not permit.

Mr. Carlile: Certainly I think it would be very useful to me to put some Unitarians in that box, and have them declare their opinion on the Trinity, which ultimately would come to what Mr. Paine has advanced.

The Chief Justice: If so, I would not hear them.

Mr. Carlile: I also intended to read the opinions of several most eminent divines who inculcate perfect freedom of opinion in religion.

The Chief Justice: Well, if you are not prepared with them, it is not my fault.

Mr. Carlile: Certainly not, my lord. It was also my intention to have persons examined who would state the great variance that exists between the original Hebrew and the authorised version of the Bible here—this is of great consequence to me.

The Chief Justice: Neither would I receive any evidence meant to impugn the correctness of our authorised version of the Scriptures.

Mr. Carlile: Mr. Bellamy asserts it contains passages not in the original Hebrew, and which ought to be expunged.

The Chief Justice: The book against which the information is directed is not an attack on detached passages, but on the very substance and essence of the Bible.

Mr. Carlile: Then, my lord, I pray you to adjourn the Court, to give me an opportunity of quoting the opinions of Locke and others on universal toleration.

The Chief Justice: You ought to have been prepared with them now; but at all events it will do you no injury if they are not read. Everyone is agreed on the reasonableness of permitting a freedom of thinking on, and discussing religious subjects, as long as the discussion is conducted in a calm, temperate manner; and if your object is to impress this truth, the quoting these writers is to no purpose, but if you would quote them to disprove Christianity, I would not suffer them to be heard. So take it either way, adjourning the trial would be of no use to you.

Mr. Carlile: Then, my lord, am I to understand that you refuse my request to adjourn the trial?

The Chief Justice: You have not advanced any proper or relevant ground to induce the Court to consent to an adjournment.

Mr. Carlile: My lord, it is of great consequence to me to prove to the world, that though I may be sent to a prison for three or four years, I have acted in all the relations of life as a conscientious moral man. I again entreat, my lord, you will suffer the trial to be adjourned. I have much important matter to introduce to-morrow morning. I have done all that any mortal could do. I have stood the whole of this day without any refreshment but water; in fact, I am so confused, that I scarcely have a recollection of anything.

The Chief Justice repeated that the adjournment would not be to any purpose.

Mr. Carlile: My lord, it is fit I should add a few observations to my defence.

The Chief Justice: Well, then, add them.

Mr. Carlile: My lord, I am really unable. When I came into Court this morning I was hoarse with the exertions of yesterday.

The Chief Justice: If you have unfortunately spent your strength in doing that which was foolish and improper, you have to blame yourself alone. You have placed me in a most painful situation, but I must perform the duty which is incumbent on me.

Mr. Carlile: Do you wish me, my lord, to proceed now?

The Chief Justice: Sir, the jury are considering.

The jury continued conferring with one another for some minutes, without coming to any conclusion.

The Chief Justice: You say now that you wish your trial to be adjourned. If the Court consent to it, it must be on the understanding that the matter you offer in the morning will be by way of mitigation, and that you don't mean to attempt the same line of defence you did to-day, either by endeavoring a justification of the publication, or by reading authors who only repeat what Paine said.

Mr. Carlile: Undoubtedly, my lord, I will not, as I would only injure myself; it would embarrass me by leaving me open to interruptions which would throw me off my guard.

The Foreman of the Jury: It is the wish of the jury, my lord, to allow him till to-morrow, provided he limits his defence.

The Chief Justice: Then with the pledge that you will limit your defence in the manner I pointed out to you, the Court is adjourned till half-past nine o'clock to-morrow morning.

The Court accordingly rose at half-past seven o'clock.

APPENDIX II.

A LETTER TO LORD SIDMOUTH,

Secretary of State for the Home Department,

ON THE CONDUCT OF THE MAGISTERIAL AND
YEOMANRY ASSASSINS OF MANCHESTER,

On the 16th of AUGUST. 1819.

London, August 18th, 1819.

My Lord,

As a spectator of the horrid proceedings of Monday last at
Manchester, I feel it my duty to give the public a narrative
of those proceedings, through the medium of a letter
addressed to you, who ought to be the *conservator of the
public peace*. My motives for doing this are twofold; the
first is to call on you, as Secretary of State for the Home
Department, to cause the Magistrates of Manchester, and
Yeomanry Cavalry acting under their direction, to be
brought to the bar of public justice, for the unprovoked
slaughter of the peaceable and distressed inhabitants of that
place and neighborhood, whilst legally exercising their
rights in public meeting assembled. For, unless the
administrators of affairs in the governmental department of
the country feel it their duty immediately to take this step,
the people have no alternative but to identify the Ministers
in the metropolis, with the magistrates of Manchester, as
having conjointly violated and subverted that known and
admitted law of the country, *which countenances the
meeting of popular assemblies for a discussion of the best
means to obtain a redress of their grievances.*

And secondly, in case of the default of the existing government to give satisfaction to the full extent of their means and power, to the mangled and suffering, and to the friends of the Murdered Inhabitants of

Manchester, the people, not only of Manchester, but of the whole country are in duty bound and by the laws of nature imperatively called upon to provide themselves with arms and hold their public meetings with arms in their hands, to defend themselves against the attacks of similar assassins, acting in the true *Castlereaghan* character.

The safety of the people is not now the supreme law; the security of the corrupt borough-mongers and their dependent can only be perceived to be the object of the existing administration. Where, my Lord Sidmouth, where are now to be found the assassins with their daggers? Let us hear no more of the assassinal intentions of the advocates for reforming your corrupt system of government; you have used every means within your reach to urge the Reformers to the use of the dagger; they have been too prudent, and you, no longer able to resist their reasonable demands by reasonable argument, have thrown off your mask and set the first example of shedding blood. The people have no alternative but immediately to prepare for a retaliation. The noble spirit and attitude displayed by the Reformers of Manchester on Monday, can never be annihilated, and it is within probability, that before this letter goes to the press, it will return to the attack. Whatever means they resort to at such a moment as the present, they will be justified in. The laws having been violated by those who profess to support them, in an unprovoked attack on a peaceable and unoffending people, in public meeting assembled, that people are no longer bound to deny themselves a mode of defence by respecting and adhering to those laws; but if they value liberty or independence they will immediately rid themselves of those who not only have driven them to starvation and desperation, but now goad them to destruction.

I shall now proceed to give your Lordship a narrative of the proceedings of the meeting, which as far as I could collect from my situation I will vouch for its authenticity. About 11 o'clock the people began to assemble around the house of Mr. Johnson, at Smedley Cottage, where Mr. Hunt had taken up his residence; about 12. Mr. Hunt and his friends entered the barouche.

They had not proceeded far when they were met by the Committee of the Female Reform Society, one of whom, an interesting looking woman, bore a standard on which was painted a female holding in her hand a flag surmounted with the cap of liberty, whilst she trod under foot an emblem of corruption, on which was inscribed that word. She was requested to take a seat on the box of the carriage (a most appropriate one), which she boldly and immediately acquiesced in, and continued waving her flag and handkerchief until she reached the hustings, where she took her stand on the right corner in front. The remainder of the committee followed the carriage in procession and mounted the hustings when they reached them. On leaving Smedley Cottage, bodies of men were seen at a distance, marching in regular military order, with music and colors. Different flags were fallen in with on the road, with various mottoes, such as "No Corn Laws," "Liberty or Death," "Taxation without Representation is Tyranny," "We will have Liberty"; the flag used by the friends of Mr. Hunt at the general election for Westminster, and various others, many of which were surmounted with "caps of Liberty". The scene of cheering was never before equalled. Females from the age of twelve to eighty were seen cheering with their caps in their hand, and their hair in consequence dishevelled; the whole scene exceeds the power of description. In passing through the streets to the place of meeting, the crowd became so great, that it was with difficulty the carriage could be moved along. Information was brought to Mr. Hunt that St. Peter's field was already filled, and that no less than 300,000 people were assembled in and about the intended spot of meeting. As the carriage moved along and reached the shops and warehouse of Mr. Johnson of Smedley, three times three were given, also, at the Police Office and at the Exchange. The procession arrived at the place of destination about one o'clock. Mr. Hunt expressed his disapprobation of the hustings, and was fearful that some accident would arise from them. After some hesitation he ascended, and the proposition for his being chairman being moved by Mr. Johnson, it was carried by acclamation. Mr. Hunt began his discourse by thanking them for the favor conferred on him, and made some ironical observations on the conduct of the Magistrates, when a cart, which evidently took its direction from that part of the field where the police and magistrates were assembled in a house, was moved through the middle of the field to the great annoyance and danger of the assembled people, who quietly endeavored to make way for its proceedure. The cart had no sooner made its way through, when the Yeomanry Cavalry made their appearance from the same quarter as the cart had gone out. They galloped furiously round the field, going over every person who could not get out of their way, to the spot where the police were fixed, and after a moment's pause, they received the cheers of the police as a signal for attack. The meeting at the entrance of the cavalry, and from the commencement of business was one of the most calm and orderly that I ever witnessed. Hilarity was seen on the countenances of all, whilst the Female Reformers crowned the assemblage with a grace, and excited a feeling particularly interesting. The Yeomanry Cavalry made their charge with the most infuriate frenzy; they cut down men, women, and children, indiscriminately, and appeared to have commenced a premeditated attack with the most insatiable thirst for blood and destruction. They merit a medallion on one side of which should be inscribed "The Slaughtermen of Manchester", and a reverse, bearing a description of their slaughter of defenceless men, women, and children, unprovoked and unnecessary. As a proof of premeditated murder on the part of the magistrates, every stone was gathered from the ground, on the Friday and Saturday previous to the meeting, by scavengers sent there by the express command of the magistrates, that the populace might be rendered more defenceless.

This is the social order system which we are exhorted, by Royal Proclamations, to rally round and support. These are the modes of reasoning adopted by villainy in power. I can assure you, my Lord, that the only painful feeling I felt was to see so many thousands of resolute and determined friends of freedom, without the means of self-defence. The *Courier* has this evening claimed the gratitude of the Reformers towards the amiable Mr. Nadin, who, it asserts, saved the life of Mr. Hunt from the fury and vengeance of the Yeomanry Butchers. That these Butchers were ready and willing to cut him in pieces, there is no doubt; but in return, let me remind the Editor of the *Courier*, that nothing but the uniform and steady determination of Mr. Hunt to use no other weapons than our oppressive legislators themselves have sanctioned, nor to encourage the use of any other weapons where he has had any influence, could have saved the lives of these Yeomanry and Police, from a people goaded to desperation by a violent and outrageous attack on their lives. The people of Lancashire, Cheshire, and Yorkshire are fully prepared to assert their rights, either by argumentative reasoning or open combat; neither will the desperate schemes of a Castlereagh repeated, foil them.

Mr. Hunt, and the people about him, stood firm, and began to cheer the military on their approach to the ground, until they were within arms length, and cutting their way with their sabres. I appealed to the females on their fear of the approach of the military, and found them the last to display an alarm. The police were as expert in applying their clubs to the heads and shoulders of the people as the cavalry their sabres, and there was no alternative but to run the gauntlet through the one or the other. The brutality of the police, equalled in ferociousness the massacre of the Yeomanry Cavalry. A better character has been given to the regular troops for their endeavors to disperse the people without wounding or otherwise injuring them. The women appear to have been the particular objects of the fury of the Cavalry Assassins. One woman, who was near the spot where I stood, and who held an infant in her arms, was sabred over the head, and her tender offspring drenched in its mother's blood. Another was actually stabbed in the neck with the point of the sabre, which must have been a deliberate attempt on the part of the military assassin. Some were sabred in the breast; so inhuman, indiscriminate, and fiend-like, was the conduct of the Manchester Yeomanry Cavalry. This, my Lord, is but a faint picture of what really occurred. They are facts and particulars that came under my own sight and cognizance; and I have no hesitation in saying, that if the inhabitants of Manchester cannot resent this massacre of their peaceable inhabitants, by retaliating on the Yeomanry Cavalry and police, collectively, they are called on by the laws of nature, by the love of their country, their fire-sides, and families, to retaliate on them individually.

And again, my Lord, if the administration of that Government, of which you are a member, cannot support itself without violating the laws and compact between the police and people, in an unprovoked and unrelenting massacre of the latter, you had far better retire, and not wait to be driven.

It will be in vain, my Lord, to attempt to palliate this circumstance by exaggerated statements and falsehoods; the many thousand witnesses of this tragical event will proclaim it as it happened. Those who have hitherto opposed the demand for Reform, are now heard to condemn this act, and must awake from the delusion that has too long prevailed over them. The present is an important crisis for England. A reform, or despotism must immediately follow. But I, my Lord, who witnessed the attack of the blood-hounds on the inhabitants of Manchester and its vicinity, do feel a confidence, from the calm and resolute conduct of that meeting, that Despotism and not Reform will be crushed. The people were taken by surprise: when the sabres began to fall on them, they were astonished at the uncalled-for and wanton attack. I, who felt confident of the legality of the proceedings of the meeting, did not expect that any authority would, in this country, have been so far abused as to exceed in atrocity the caprice of a Ferdinand of Spain, a Dey of Algiers, or a Grand Seignior of Turkey. When I saw these Yeomanry Cavalry gallop round, and through the meeting, I had no other idea than that the object of the magistrates was to impress the people with an awe, and to endeavor to terrify them, and to prevent the proceedings of the meeting, by exhibiting the military to its view. But they soon found this would not do, as the people, both men and women, kept cheering until they began to feel their sabres.

After these Yeomanry Cavalry (which belonged to Cheshire and Manchester) had performed this grand achievement of attacking by surprise an unarmed assemblage of people, and dispersing them, they were not content, but persisted in riding after, and cutting down, those who were flying from them. One man, who dropped his hat in his flight, stooped to pick it up, and received a sabre wound in the calf of one leg, whilst the other was dreadfully bruised by the horse trampling on it!

I will now, my Lord, quit the dreadful scene of St. Peter's Field, and examine the conduct of the police and Yeomanry Cavalry in and about the streets of Manchester. Intoxicated with the idea of having dispersed so great an assemblage of persons, they began to increase that intoxication by the use of strong liquors, and, taking them in the aggregate, they were evidently in a state of inebriation. A blacksmith who, from his appearance, had just quitted his work, was standing in the course of the afternoon at the corner of a street, in all his working habiliments; a special constable comes up to him and orders him to walk away; the blacksmith seeing no cause for it, refuses; the constable, without ceremony, draws his staff from his pocket, and strikes him over the head. This was intolerable! the blacksmith struck him down with his fist, and a crowd collecting, he received that treatment which he justly merited, in a town where law and justice were dispensed with by those whose duty it is to enforce them for the protection of those who are under their care.

Another instance, equally disgraceful to the instigator, occurred in the neighborhood of New Cross, just before dusk. A young man, who was one of the Yeomanry Cavalry, called on a Mr. Tate, in that neighborhood; and seeing from the window a number of persons collected on that spot, he imprudently, and with an air of derision and defiance, took out of his pocket a flag that had got into his possession in St. Peter's Field, and shook it from the window before the assembled people. This became the signal for attack. The windows of the house were immediately demolished, and the calling of the military to this spot caused the loss of life to 8 or 10 persons, one of whom was a mere passer by, and was shot in the head at a distance of 500 yards from the scene of action; at this spot a woman was also shot dead.

The conduct both of the Yeomanry Cavalry, and police, was of the most ruffian-like kind; the military always preceded the police, which is contrary to the known and established laws of this country. The advocates of a Reform in the Commons' House of Parliament must now consider themselves as placed out of the pale of the law. A war was declared on them by the late Royal Proclamation, which has been enforced by the Magistrates of Manchester, and the Reformers have no alternative but to make it a trial of strength. They had no man to advocate their cause among the existing authorities. There is not a man in the present Borough-mongers' House of Commons that is "bold enough to be honest, or honest enough to be bold". There is not a man that ventures to rise and tell them of what they are composed. We then can have no hope left by an appeal to that House, nor by an exposition of its character and composition; we must, therefore, appeal to those weapons and that strength which nature has left in the hands of the oppressed to resist the oppressor. The Executive has denounced the demand for Reform, and has thrown itself into the arms of the Borough-mongers. The House of Lords has not pronounced its determination collectively, but when we know that the majority of the Commons are produced by its members, we are justified in the inference, that it will combine with the Executive to protect its own offspring.

And now, my Lord, since a partial triumph has been gained over the Reformers by dispersing them, unarmed in a public meeting, let us examine what would have been the consequences if the dispositions of the Reformers had been so very violent as they have been represented to be. In the first place, they would not have stood and cheered the military until their sabres began to fall on them, but would have been silent, and sought immediately for the best means of defence. What if they had fallen back into the streets, and had filled the houses, and there sought weapons for attack and defence, they would have annihilated every aggressor in a few hours, whilst they themselves would have suffered little or no loss. In a house, an unarmed man will find better means for attack and defence than half a dozen armed, in the streets. Let us hear no more charges of violence or disorder, against the advocates of Reform, but be pleased, my Lord, to take them into your custody, and confer them on the magistrates of Manchester and other places.

I shall anxiously wait, my Lord, to see whether in the executive and administration of the present Government there is sufficient respect for the laws and justice, to enforce them against the magistrates of Manchester; or whether the Executive and Administration will make the cause of the magistrates of Manchester their cause; in either case, my Lord, as an individual, living in a country where the laws will not protect the subject, I shall feel it my duty to make the best preparation for the defence of myself, family, and property, against the attack of a magistrate, police officer, or a troop of Yeomanry Cavalry, who begin to show a contempt for those laws which they are commissioned to respect and enforce.

Your Lordship's Fellow-Citizen,

R. CARLILE.

APPENDIX III.

DEDICATION.

To Posterity.

The first publication in which free discussion has existed is not a publication for the present generation, but for posterity. Others must feel the benefit, though the merit of introducing it be ours.

In such history of man as we have, we have no proof that free discussion is older than the present fourteen volumes of the *Republican*. In its fullest extent it had scarcely been contemplated. The question, What is God? was never before broadly asked and answered in print. Idolatry being a habit on which the mind spiritually feeds, but few will thank one for destroying the source of their devotions. "I have lived fifty years with these impressions and never before had them questioned," cries an old man or woman, "and am I now to yield them to the discoveries of a mere boy? They have been my comfort through life, and though I cannot defend, I will not forsake them." This is ever the reasoning of deep-rooted prejudice. The mere antiquity of error is to such minds a proof of its divinity. Younger folks come on, less ignorant from the new motions given to mind, and they easily discard the follies of their parents.

Thus it is that the *Republican*, though admired by many, and useful to many, has not extended its influence throughout the whole community, in consequence of its unparalleled shocks upon old systems and deep-rooted prejudices. The next generation will grow up acquainted with its doctrines, and those doctrines will most certainly be adopted for practice.

There must be a beginning to all systems and all changes in human action, but it does not follow that he who begins will see the end of his work.

Admirable changes have taken place in public opinion upon the subject of religion within the last ten years, but we feel it rather in the cessation of persecution than in any application of the change to the lessening of religious burdens. Such a legislature as that of this country will ever be the last part of a nation to learn a new doctrine, and a nation is not to be instructed as you would instruct an inquisitive individual. Were a statesman in advance of the knowledge of a nation he would find insuperable obstacles in attempting to act up to the extent of his knowledge. Mankind as a body is ungrateful, and will not thank you for benefits conferred nor see your good intentions to serve it, if you step out of the beaten track. The sound reformer has no other encouragement than to bequeath his merited caresses to his senseless memory, or to enjoy them in anticipation. His patrons live not with him, but are to be his posterity, and from those persons with whom he lives he finds more of insults than of gratitude. They see not the end of his reformation; they appreciate not his motives. It is consolatory to be able to say that, while the foregoing is true of mankind as a body, it has, like every general rule, its exception in a part of that body. The life of a reformer would be intolerable if there were not some keen-sighted individuals who can see his ends and appreciate his motives and who are bold enough to encourage him to proceed, and honest and benevolent enough to assist him. His state would indeed be intolerable but for these exceptions, for his proposed changes constitute an arraignment of all existing political and prejudicial powers, and those powers naturally make war upon him while he is weak enough to suffer from their influence. To posterity, then, I dedicate the fourteen volumes of the *Republican*, and to posterity I appeal, to say whether or not I have done my duty as a Reformer. There are thousands living who will say that I have done it. But I aspire to the approbation of mankind as a body, and that I know must be the approbation of a future generation.

RICHARD CARLILE. 62 Fleet Street, December 28th, 1826.

APPENDIX IV.

LIST OF CARLILE'S IMPRISONMENTS.

1817 (August 15th—December 20th).

Eighteen weeks for selling the Parodies (on the Book of Common Prayer). Compter.

1819 (November 16th)—1825 (November 18th).

Three years for selling the Age of Reason and Palmer's Principles of Nature.

Three years more exacted for non-payment of fine of £1,500. Dorchester Gaol.

1831—1833.

Three years for an article in the Prompter at the time of the Agricultural Riots. Compter.

1834.

Four months for resisting Church Assessments.

Compter.

The actual time of imprisonment undergone was nine years, seven months, and one week.